Access
My eLab
leap 2

TO REGISTER

❶ Go to **mybookshelf.pearsonerpi.com**

❷ Follow the instructions. When asked for your access code, please type the code provided underneath the blue sticker.

❸ To access **My eLab** at any time, go to http://mybookshelf.pearsonerpi.com. **Bookmark this page for quicker access.**

Access to My eLab is valid for 12 months from the date of registration.

WARNING! This book CANNOT BE RETURNED if the access code has been uncovered.

Note: Once you have registered, you will need to join your online class. Ask your teacher to provide you with the class ID.

TEACHER Access Code

To obtain an access code for My eLab, please contact your Pearson ELT consultant.

 I 800 263-3678, ext. 2
pearsonerpi.com/help

W139662 (A39663)

3500

leap 2
NEW EDITION

**READING
AND WRITING**

DR. KEN BEATTY

Product Owner
Stephan Leduc

Managing Editor
Sharnee Chait

Copy Editor
Adam Lawrence

Proofreaders
Adam Lawrence
Paula Sarson

Rights and Permissions Coordinator
Aude Maggiori

Text Rights and Permissions
Rachel Irwin

Art Director
Hélène Cousineau

Graphic Design Manager
Estelle Cuillerier

Book and Cover Design
Frédérique Bouvier

Book Layout
Isabel Lafleur

Cover Photos
Shutterstock © mimagephotography
Shutterstock © Rawpixel.com

Dedication

To Alvin Toffler, who wrote, "The illiterate of the twenty-first century will not be those who cannot read and write, but those who cannot learn, unlearn, and relearn."

The publisher wishes to thank the following people for their helpful comments and suggestions:

Janelle Caballero, University of British Columbia
Roisin Dewart, Université du Québec à Montréal
Michelle Duhaney, Seneca College
Izabella Kojic-Sabo, University of Windsor

Special thanks are due to the following instructors from Fraser International College for their extensive feedback:

Jerry Block, Sheena Bhatia, Stephanie Marie Breck, Rosa Maria Funderburk Razo, Winnie Ma, Yvonne Muir, David Puddiford, Jane Rogers, Liz Rogers, Linda Yauk, and Dani Zheleva

INTRODUCTION

Welcome to the new edition of *LEAP 2: Reading and Writing*. Building on the first edition (*LEAP Intermediate*), this book aims to improve your reading and writing skills with Academic Word List (AWL) vocabulary, grammar, Academic Survival Skills, and Warm-Up and Final Assignments that let you apply what you learn in individual and personalized ways.

There are two new features in *LEAP 2: Reading and Writing*. Focus on Critical Thinking helps you reflect on what you read to develop strategies that can be applied to writing. The Pearson Global Scale of English (GSE) structures *LEAP 2*'s learning goals to give you a clearer idea of the language objectives you should aim to meet.

Each chapter in the book focuses on engaging themes drawn from science, technology, engineering, and mathematics (STEM), as well as education and business fields. Each chapter includes three readings related to the chapter theme, often with divergent perspectives. Most of these readings are authentic and give you the chance to apply your critical thinking skills in pre-reading and follow-up tasks. The readings include a variety of genres that you will encounter in your academic studies, including excerpts from textbooks, journal articles, and reports. The writing component involves different types of paragraphs and other forms, including an essay. To help you better understand each format, the Models Chapter provides clear instructions and examples. Beyond the book, My eLab exercises and documents give you the opportunity to reinforce and build on what you learn.

LEAP 2: Reading and Writing will give you the confidence to take the next steps on your path to academic and career success.

ACKNOWLEDGEMENTS

As always, my thanks to Julia Williams who started this series. With patience and good humour, my editor Sharnee Chait has made the writing process more enjoyable; I thank her and the rest of the Pearson team who bring my words to life and put them in the hands of teachers. I also thank my graduate students and colleagues for ongoing discussions that reinforce my belief that student needs are the starting point for everything important in education.

The influence of teachers too numerous to name are found on these pages. Creating *LEAP 2: Reading and Writing* began with exploring teacher and student needs and finding creative solutions to meet the changing demands of academic English. Consultations with teachers internationally helped fuel the ideas for this book. I appreciate the thoughtful contributions of those dedicated professionals who offered feedback through questionnaires and chapter reviews. I particularly thank those teachers who emailed me and whom I met at conferences, lectures, and workshops this past year in Argentina, Canada, Chile, Colombia, Czech Republic, England, Poland, Slovakia, Uruguay, and the US. Every teacher is a hero.

Dr. Ken Beatty, Bowen Island, Canada

HIGHLIGHTS

Gearing Up uses infographics to spark critical thinking, reflection, and discussion about the chapter topic.

Vocabulary Build strengthens comprehension and builds awareness of key vocabulary on the Academic Word List.

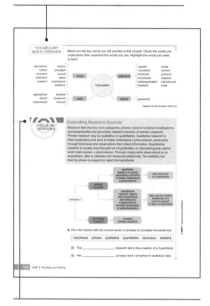

The **overview** outlines the chapter's objectives.

Focus on Reading develops specific strategies you need to fully understand the content and structure of reading texts.

Focus on Critical Thinking helps you learn strategies for thinking critically about what you read and how to apply these strategies to writing tasks.

Each chapter contains three **readings** from a variety of sources, including academic textbooks and journal articles. The readings offer different perspectives on the chapter theme, providing content for writing tasks.

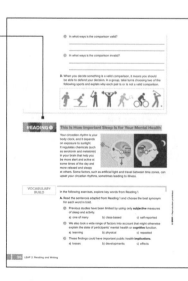

Before, while, and **after reading** activities focus on comprehension and critical thinking.

My eLab provides practice and additional content.

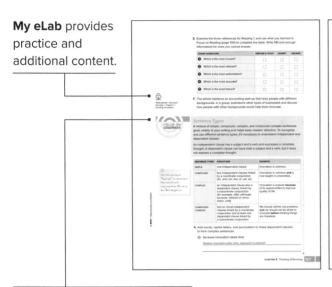

Focus on Writing develops specific skills you need to write effective academic English.

Focus on Grammar reviews important language structures that you can apply when reading and writing academic English.

The Warm-Up Assignment explores a writing task and prepares you for the Final Assignment. Each chapter focuses on a different task.

Academic Survival Skill helps you develop essential skills for academic coursework.

The **Final Assignment** synthesizes the chapter content and theme into an in-depth writing task. Each chapter focuses on a different type of assignment.

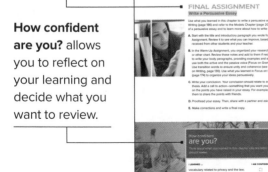

How confident are you? allows you to reflect on your learning and decide what you want to review.

The **Models Chapter** provides instructions and models for the writing tasks in the coursebook.

SCOPE AND SEQUENCE

CHAPTER	READING	CRITICAL THINKING	WRITING

CHAPTER 1
SUCCESS IN BUSINESS
SUBJECT AREAS: business, economics
	• Use skimming and scanning strategies while reading
	  - Learn when to skim and to scan
		• Identify significance in a text
		  - Learn the text features that show significance
			• Write a paragraph
			  - Learn the structure of a paragraph

CHAPTER 2
THE FUTURE OF WORK
SUBJECT AREAS: business, economics
	• Recognize point of view
	  - Ask questions to understand the writer's point of view
		• Identify correlation and causation
		  - Think critically about writers' arguments
			• Explain cause and effect
			  - Learn specific language and structures

CHAPTER 3
FIT FOR LIFE
SUBJECT AREAS: biology, health science
	• Identify main ideas and supporting details
	  - Learn how to recognize main ideas in a text
		• Make valid comparisons
		  - Identify whether comparisons are true and accurate
			• Compare and contrast in a paragraph
			  - Learn two ways to organize a compare and contrast paragraph

CHAPTER 4
A HAPPY LIFE
SUBJECT AREAS: health science, psychology
	• Construct meaning by making inferences
	  - Read for implicit and explicit meaning
		• Examine texts with SQ3R
		  - Learn to survey, question, read actively, recite, and review
			• Write formal and informal definitions
			  - Learn how to explain a term or concept

CHAPTER 5
THINKING DIFFERENTLY
SUBJECT AREAS: innovation, engineering
	• Evaluate research sources
	  - Identify two main categories of research
		• Brainstorm solutions
		  - Follow steps to brainstorm a problem
			• Use register and tone
			  - Consider differences in formal and informal writing

CHAPTER 6
A VIEW OF THE FUTURE
SUBJECT AREAS: artificial intelligence, technology
	• Identify organizational patterns
	  - Learn the kind of information best suited to each pattern
		• Summarize text
		  - Learn how to recognize the important parts of a text
			• Ensure unity and coherence
			  - Learn techniques to write well-structured paragraphs

CHAPTER 7
EDUCATION FOR ALL
SUBJECT AREAS: computer science, education
	• Interpret visual elements
	  - Recognize the kind of data shown in charts and visuals
		• Consider implications and consequences
		  - Imagine positive and negative outcomes
			• Explain processes
			  - Learn the steps to write a process paragraph

CHAPTER 8
RIGHTS AND OBLIGATIONS
SUBJECT AREAS: ethics, technology
	• Distinguish fact from opinion
	  - Learn how to recognize valid opinions
		• Identify persuasive techniques
		  - Learn how to ask rhetorical questions and test a thesis statement
			• Learn how to write a persuasive essay
			  - Examine essay format

VOCABULARY	ACCURACY	ACADEMIC SURVIVAL SKILL	ASSIGNMENTS
• Explore meaning and context • Learn about compound words	• Review simple present and simple past verb tenses - Learn when and how to use the verb forms	• Learn techniques for completing academic assignments successfully	• Write descriptive paragraphs
• Explore meaning and context • Find synonyms	• Use the future tense with *will* and *be going to*	• Take notes - Learn the areas to focus on	• Write a topic sentence • Write a cause and effect paragraph

• Explore meaning and context
• Find synonyms
• Learn about prefixes
	• Review punctuation rules
	  - Learn how to avoid common punctuation errors
		• Learn how to cite and reference sources
		  - Review rules for APA reference format
			• Write compare and contrast paragraphs

• Explore meaning and context • Find word forms	• Review the rules for subject-verb agreement	• Develop vocabulary - Use mind maps and collocations	• Write a short definition • Write a definition paragraph

• Explore meaning and context
• Find word forms
	• Review sentence types
	  - Identify simple, compound, complex, and compound-complex sentences
		• Apply critical thinking techniques
		  - Use techniques to critically evaluate texts
			• Write formal emails

• Explore meaning and context • Find collocations	• Review the correct use of articles	• Avoid plagiarism - Learn to paraphrase and summarize	• Write short and longer summaries

• Explore meaning and context
• Find root words
	• Review pronoun-antecedent agreement
	  - Learn about indefinite pronouns and how to avoid gender-biased writing
		• Work in a group
		  - Learn the steps in a group project
			• Write a process paragraph and give a presentation

• Explore meaning and context	• Use the active and passive voice
	  - Review when to use the passive voice
		• Prepare for an exam
		  - Learn tips to help you succeed
			• Write an introductory paragraph
			• Write a persuasive essay

TABLE OF CONTENTS

CHAPTER 1

Success in Business

Long before graduation, you probably start putting a lot of thought into what you will do for a career. It's logical to assume you would plan one related to your studies. After all, within your field there are likely many jobs to choose from. But fewer and fewer students end up finding employment in their own fields. Instead, many now expect to start their own businesses, that is, become entrepreneurs. Many students have great ideas for new businesses, and only lack money or business skills to put those ideas into action. These challenges are becoming easier to overcome.

What is your ideal business plan?

In this chapter, you will

- learn vocabulary related to crowdfunding and business;
- use skimming and scanning strategies when reading;

- identify significance in a text;
- review simple present and simple past verb tenses;
- learn the structure of a paragraph;

- learn techniques for completing academic assignments successfully;
- write descriptive paragraphs for a crowdfunding project.

GEARING UP

A. Crowdfunding uses social media to support a project by inviting people to donate money to make a new idea or business possible. This graph shows the most popular Kickstarter projects. Look at the graph and then answer the questions.

Kickstarter launched projects

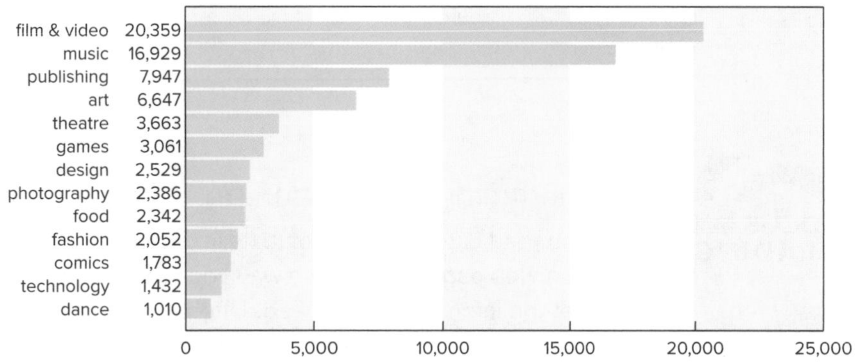

film & video	20,359
music	16,929
publishing	7,947
art	6,647
theatre	3,663
games	3,061
design	2,529
photography	2,386
food	2,342
fashion	2,052
comics	1,783
technology	1,432
dance	1,010

Source: Crisostomo, A. (2012). Kickstarting the crowdfunding trends. *Masters of Media*. Retrieved from http://mastersofmedia.hum.uva.nl/2012/10/05/kickstarting-the-crowdfunding-trends/

1 What are the most popular and least popular types of Kickstarter projects?

_____

2 Pick a project category that interests you. What kind of project would you most likely support with a donation?

_____

3 Why do you think some project types are more popular than others?

_____

_____

4 Crowdfunding projects offer a range of rewards in exchange for support such as T-shirts or tickets to a performance. Pick a category and think of a small reward and a large reward that might be offered.

_____

_____

_____

B. Discuss the questions and your answers, first with a partner, then in a group.

Below are the key words you will practise in this chapter. Check the words you understand, then underline the words you use. Highlight the words you need to learn.

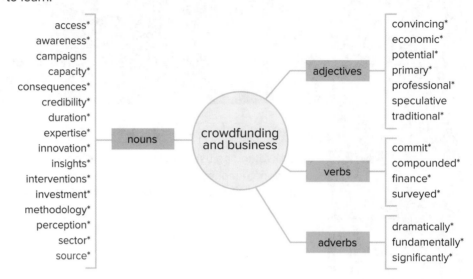

nouns

access*
awareness*
campaigns
capacity*
consequences*
credibility*
duration*
expertise*
innovation*
insights*
interventions*
investment*
methodology*
perception*
sector*
source*

crowdfunding and business

adjectives

convincing*
economic*
potential*
primary*
professional*
speculative
traditional*

verbs

commit*
compounded*
finance*
surveyed*

adverbs

dramatically*
fundamentally*
significantly*

Visit My eLab Documents to review the different parts of speech.

* Appears on the Academic Word List

FOCUS ON READING

Skimming and Scanning

You read different types of texts in different ways. You don't read a bus schedule or a web page in the same way you read a novel. You use different strategies to get the information you need. Often, this is because your time is limited or you simply want to get specific information. Skimming and scanning are two common ways to read different texts.

Skimming gives you a general impression of a text. In a piece of plain text, you may look quickly at the first and last sentences of each paragraph. If there are special features in the text, such as bullet points and quotes, then you may look at these as well. Often the title and subtitles give the main idea, as do photos, diagrams, and charts. Skimming helps you decide if you want to read a text in more detail.

Scanning helps you locate specific details. Use scanning when you have *who, what, when, where, why,* or *how* questions. For example, you might scan an article to find the name of a person or the person's contact information. When you start with a question, look for key words that will lead you to the information you are looking for. Words such as *where* and *when* mean you are looking for a place and a time or date.

A. Consider these types of texts. Which would you skim; which would you scan? Discuss your answers with a partner.

newspapers

flight schedule

dictionary

technical drawings

B. Turn to Reading 1 on page 8. Skim the first sentence of each paragraph and fill in the table below with brief notes about things you understand and things you don't understand.

THINGS I UNDERSTAND	THINGS I DON'T UNDERSTAND

C. Scan this excerpt from Reading 1 and highlight the following information:
- people who use crowdfunding sites;
- crowdfunding sites;
- how much people invest.

> Once limited to artists, musicians, and filmmakers looking to finance their creative projects, crowdfunding has expanded into the world of entrepreneurship. Crowdfunding taps the power of social networking and allows entrepreneurs to post their elevator pitches and proposed investment terms on crowdfunding websites, such as Profounder, Peerbackers, Kickstarter, or Indiegogo, and raise money to fund their ventures from ordinary people who invest as little as $100. Normally, the amount of capital these entrepreneurs seek is small, typically less than $10,000, and the "returns" they offer investors are mere tokens, such as discount coupons and free product samples. However, some entrepreneurs have raised significantly more money with crowdfunding and offer "real" returns.

D. Share your answers to tasks A, B, and C with a partner and discuss any differences.

FOCUS ON CRITICAL THINKING

Identifying Significance

Imagine your home caught fire and you had to choose only three things that you could take with you before leaving. This task relates to identifying significance in a text. You need to be able to distinguish between the most important information in a text versus information that might be interesting but not necessary for comprehension. Like choosing articles in a fire, identifying significance often requires quick thinking and smart decisions.

A. Identifying significance is more than simply identifying the main idea; significance is usually what is important *about* the main idea and other ideas. Look at the following chart. Which text features are likely to show significance when you read? Complete the chart and discuss with a partner.

TEXT FEATURES	SIGNIFICANT	INSIGNIFICANT
❶ adjectives and adverbs	☐	☐
❷ captions	☐	☐
❸ charts, diagrams, graphs, maps	☐	☐
❹ examples	☐	☐
❺ explanations	☐	☐
❻ nouns and verbs	☐	☐
❼ titles and subtitles	☐	☐
❽ topic sentences	☐	☐

B. Read the title and first paragraph of Reading 1. Highlight information that is significant. Then circle words and phrases that you do not understand.

Looking for Money

Angels are a primary source of start-up capital for companies in the start-up stage through the growth stage, and their role in financing small businesses is significant. Research at the University of New Hampshire shows that more than 318,000 angels and angel groups invest $22.5 billion a year in 66,000 small companies, most of them in the start-up phase (Sohl, 2012). In short, angels are one of the largest and most important sources of external equity capital for small businesses. Their investments in young companies nearly match those of professional venture capitalists, providing vital capital to eighteen times as many small companies.

> Don't highlight whole sentences; focus on key words and phrases.

C. In a group, compare what you and your partners have highlighted and circled. Are some of your answers similar? Are some of them different? Write one or two sentences to summarize the paragraph.

_____

_____

_____

_____

READING 1 — Looking for Money

When you start a new business, raising money is one of the greatest challenges. How can you do it? In some cases, you might have worked and saved money, or you might have borrowed from friends and family. Sometimes a bank will give you a loan, but this is seldom enough to start a new business, and you have to look elsewhere. Two popular options are crowdfunding and angel investment. Crowdfunding uses social media to fund your business through the contributions of hundreds or thousands of individuals. Angel investment involves getting money from wealthy individuals or companies who exchange their support for a part of your company.

VOCABULARY BUILD

In the following exercises, explore key words from Reading 1.

A. Fill in the blanks with the correct word or phrase to complete the sentences.

| convincing | economic | primary | ~~professional~~ | significantly |

1. They take their work seriously and are always _____*professional*_____ .

2. Raising money is a _____ greater problem than getting a business idea.

3. Many people doubt what we can do, so our main job is _____ them.

4. The _____ purpose of crowdfunding is to support a new idea.

5. An _____ incentive is one that is based on being paid for something.

B. Choose the word or phrase that best completes each sentence. Key words are in bold.

1. To **finance** a new business involves _____.
   a) borrowing money from the owners
   b) contributing money to get it started
   c) owing money to business clients

2. To find the **source** of a problem, you should start at the _____.
   a) beginning
   b) middle
   c) end

3. When you make an **investment**, _____.
   a) it's like making a free contribution
   b) it's unlikely that it costs you anything
   c) you expect a return on your money

4 An example of a business **sector** is _____.

   a) the restaurant industry

   b) your local restaurant

   c) an idea for a restaurant

5 The **capacity** of a company is _____.

   a) how much it is likely to grow

   b) the time it takes to begin

   c) how much it can handle

Before You Read

A. List two reasons people use social media.

_____

_____

B. Scan the article to find a definition of *angel investor*. Why do you think *angel* is part of the term?

_____

_____

C. Google, Apple, Starbucks, Kinko's, and The Body Shop are all businesses that were partially funded by angel investors. Choose one of these companies and describe what sort of angel investor might have been interested in funding it.

_____

_____

D. Read the text, and then answer the questions that follow.

Looking for Money

Crowdfunding

Once limited to artists, musicians, and filmmakers looking to **finance** their creative projects, crowdfunding has expanded into the world of **entrepreneurship**. Crowdfunding taps the power of social networking and allows entrepreneurs to post their
5 **elevator pitches** and proposed **investment** terms on crowdfunding websites, such as Profounder, Peerbackers, Kickstarter, or Indiegogo, and raise money to fund their ventures from ordinary people who invest as little as $100. Normally, the amount of capital these entrepreneurs seek is small, typically less than $10,000, and the "returns" they offer investors are mere tokens, such as discount coupons and free product
10 samples. However, some entrepreneurs have raised **significantly** more money with crowdfunding and offer "real" returns.

. . .

Crowdfunding sites typically charge a fee of about 4 percent to host a funding request, and many proposals fail to attract enough investors to reach their targets. Currently,
15 a proposal before **Congress** would allow companies to raise up to $2 million in

entrepreneurship (n.): skill of creating and organizing new businesses

elevator pitches (n.): short proposals for new ideas

Congress (n.): law-making body of the USA

equity financing through crowdfunding. The proposal limits investments to $10,000 per year or 10 percent of the investor's annual income, whichever is less (Needleman &
20 Loten, 2011).

Angels

After dipping into their own pockets and **convincing** friends and relatives to invest in their business ventures, many entrepreneurs
25 still find themselves short of the **seed capital** they need. Frequently, the next stop on the road to business financing is private investors. These private investors (angels) are wealthy individuals, often entrepreneurs
30 themselves, who invest their own money in business **start-ups** in exchange for **equity stakes** in the companies. Angel investors have provided much-needed capital to entrepreneurs for many years. In 1938, when World War I flying ace Eddie Rickenbacker needed money to launch Eastern
35 Airlines, millionaire Laurance Rockefeller provided it. Alexander Graham Bell, inventor of the telephone, used angel capital to start Bell Telephone in 1877. More recently, companies such as Google, Apple, Starbucks, Kinko's, and The Body Shop relied on angel financing in their early years to finance growth.

…

40 In many cases, angels invest in businesses for more than purely **economic** reasons—for example, because they have a personal interest or experience in a particular industry—and they are willing to put money into companies in the earliest stages, long before **venture capital firms** and institutional investors jump in. Angel financing, the fastest-growing segment of the small business capital market, is ideal for
45 companies that have outgrown the **capacity** of investments from friends and family but are still too small to attract the interest of venture capital companies. Angel financing is vital to the nation's small business **sector** because it fills this capital gap in which small companies need investments ranging from $100,000 or less to perhaps $5 million or more. For instance, after raising the money from family and friends to
50 launch Amazon.com, Jeff Bezos turned to angels for capital because venture capital firms were not interested in investing in a business start-up. Bezos attracted $1.2 million from a dozen angels before landing $8 million from venture capital firms a year later (Sherrid, 1997).

Angels are a **primary source** of start-up capital for companies in the start-up stage
55 through the growth stage, and their role in financing small businesses is significant. Research at the University of New Hampshire shows that more than 318,000 angels and angel groups invest $22.5 billion a year in 66,000 small companies, most of them in the start-up phase (Sohl, 2012). In short, angels are one of the largest and most important sources of external equity capital for small businesses. Their investments
60 in young companies nearly match those of **professional** venture capitalists, providing vital capital to eighteen times as many small companies.

(602 words)

seed capital (n.): money to start a business

start-ups (n.): new businesses, often original and technological

equity stakes (n.): portions of the company in exchange for an investment

venture capital firms (n.): companies that raise funds to invest in new companies

primary (adj.): main or first

Angel financing

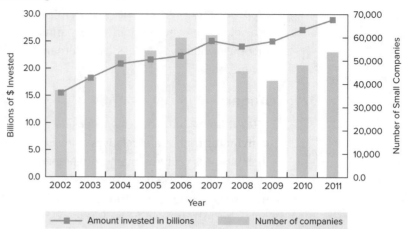

Source: Center for Venture Financing, Whittemore School of Business and Economics, University of New Hampshire
http://www.wsbe.unh.edu/crv-news

References

Needleman, S., & Loten, A. (2011, November 1). When friending becomes a source of start-up funds. *Wall Street Journal,* p. B5.

Sherrid, P. (1997, October 13). Angels of capitalism. *U.S. News & World Report*, 43–45.

Sohl, J. (2012, April 3). *The angel investor market in 2013: The recovery continues.* Durham, NH: Center for Venture Research, University of New Hampshire.

_____

Scarborough, N. M. (2014). *Essentials of entrepreneurship and small business management* (7th ed., pp. 474–476). New York, NY: Pearson.

After You Read

E. Choose the correct phrase to complete each sentence. Try not to look back at the reading. When you have finished, check your answers.

SENTENCES		PHRASES
❶ Crowdfunding was once limited to ...	*d*	a) angel investors.
❷ Profounder, Peerbackers, Kickstarter, and Indiegogo are examples of ...		b) small businesses.
❸ Not finding enough support from crowdfunding makes entrepreneurs seek ...		c) to start his new business.
❹ Crowdfunding websites make a profit by ...		d) creative projects.
❺ Alexander Graham Bell probably didn't have enough money ...		e) venture capital companies.
❻ In terms of growth, The Body Shop probably needed money to ...		f) crowdfunding websites.
❼ Angel investors provide more funding than crowdfunding sites but less than ...		g) open new stores.
❽ Angel investors are extremely important to developing ...		h) charging a fee.

F. Discuss the answers to these inference questions with a partner.

1. Why might a government want to limit the amount that can be raised by crowdfunding for a new company? Why might small business owners and crowdfunding companies not like this decision?

2. Look at the table in Reading 1 and the details for 2007 to 2011. What do you think was happening in terms of angel investment during this time?

G. Return to Focus on Reading, task B, on page 5. Review what you now understand and what you still don't understand. Discuss with your partner.

MyBookshelf > My eLab >
Exercises > Chapter 1 >
Looking for Money

FOCUS ON GRAMMAR

Simple Present and Simple Past Tenses

When you read the text on pages 8–10, you may have noticed examples of the simple present and simple past tenses. Use the simple present tense for

- actions that are happening now: I **write** about crowdfunding;
- repeated actions: I **write** every day;
- facts, opinions, and general truths: I **don't write** for corporations.

SIMPLE PRESENT TENSE	
For the affirmative, add -s to the base form of the verb for the third-person singular.	I **write**. He/She/It **writes**. We/You/They **write**.
Add -es to verbs ending in -sh, -ch, -s, -x, -o.	She **watches** the financial news on television.
For the negative, add do not (don't) or does not (doesn't) before the verb.	I **do not** (don't) **read** the financial news. He **does not** (doesn't) **read** the financial news.
To ask a question, put do or does before the subject.	**Do** you know about crowdfunding? **Does** she know about social networking?
EXCEPTIONS	
VERB *to have*	VERB *to be*
I **have** (I'**ve**)	I **am** (I'**m**)
you **have** (you'**ve**)	you **are** (you'**re**)
he/she/it **has** (he'**s**/she'**s**/it'**s**)	he/she/it **is** (he'**s**/she'**s**/it'**s**)
we/you/they **have** (we'**ve**/you'**ve**/they'**ve**)	we/you/they **are** (we'**re**/you'**re**/they'**re**)

A. Highlight the word in parentheses that is the correct verb form.

1. The company (support / supports) crowdfunding.

2. I (pass / passes) investment ideas to my friends.

3. The start-up (push / pushes) investors to get involved.

4. She (catch / catches) a bus to work each day.

5. We (hit / hits) our funding goal in three weeks.

6. I (toss / tosses) the reports on my desk each afternoon.

Use the simple past tense of regular verbs for actions that began and ended in the past.

SIMPLE PAST TENSE	
For the affirmative form, add -ed to the end of the verb.	She start**ed** TalentEgg four years ago.
For the negative (contracted) form, add *did not* (*didn't*) before the verb.	She **did not** (didn't) start TalentEgg four years ago.
To ask a question, put *did* before the subject.	**Did** she start TalentEgg four years ago?
SPELLING	
For verbs that end in *y*, change the *y* to *i* and add -ed.	(try) He **tried** to find a job after college.
For short verbs that end in a vowel + consonant, double the consonant before adding -ed.	(clap) Everyone **clapped** when her presentation ended.

Many past-tense verbs have *irregular* forms. You have to memorize them.

SIMPLE PAST TENSE OF IRREGULAR VERBS		
AFFIRMATIVE FORM	NEGATIVE (CONTRACTED) FORM	QUESTION FORM
(pay) He **paid** for their services.	(pay) He **did not** (didn't) **pay** for their services.	(pay) **Did** he **pay** for their services?
(give) She **gave** a lot of her time to the project.	(give) She **did not** (didn't) **give** a lot of her time to the project.	(give) **Did** she **give** a lot of her time to the project?
VERB *to be*		
AFFIRMATIVE FORM	NEGATIVE (CONTRACTED) FORM	QUESTION FORM
I/He/She/It **was** late.	I/He/She/It **was not** (wasn't) late.	**Was** I/he/she/it late?
You/We/They **were** late.	You/We/They **were not** (weren't) late.	**Were** you/we/they late?

B. Write each verb in parentheses in the simple past tense.

! Visit My eLab Documents to see the Irregular Verbs List.

1. The climate for youth entrepreneurs (seem) _____*seemed*_____ better than ever.

2. Of the 1000 entrepreneurs (survey) _____, 88 percent believed mentoring programs would boost that support further in the next three years.

3. The online portal (connect) _____ students with jobs, and employers (recruit) _____ off campuses across the country.

4. At each special place he visited, he (collect) _____ a small souvenir.

5. My team are all Gen Y-ers, and we (understand) _____ the market better than anyone else.

MyBookshelf > My eLab > Exercises > Chapter 1 > Grammar Review

© ERPI • Reproduction prohibited

READING ❷ Youth Entrepreneurs

An entrepreneur is someone who starts a business. Often the business is new and risky. The Internet has made it possible for many new entrepreneurs to become successful. In some cases, Internet entrepreneurs create new services that don't require factories or stores. This lowers their costs. The Internet also increases the number of people a new business can reach. But to reach people successfully, entrepreneurs need strong communication skills to sell their ideas. That is, they need to use words to help communicate their ideas and convince people to support them.

VOCABULARY BUILD

In the following exercises, explore key words from Reading 2.

A. Fill in the blanks with the correct words to complete the sentences.

access	credibility	dramatically	methodology	perception

❶ Everyone agreed it was a fact; it wasn't his _____.

❷ No one believed him; he had no _____.

❸ The fireworks slowly stopped; they didn't end _____ at all.

❹ They started the project without any plan; because of that, there was no _____ to the work.

❺ We didn't have passes to get in; there was no public _____.

B. Fill in the blanks with the correct words to complete the paragraph.

expertise	fundamentally	innovation	insights	surveyed

After a decade of _____, the company is staring to introduce new products. The company has dramatically increased its

_____ in computing, and attracted money from venture capitalists. One of the company's _____ was that it needed to better understand its customers. It _____ many young people who use their phones for banking, and found they are _____ different than the older generation. The younger generation prefers the option of never going to a bank.

C. Work with a partner and identify any words you do not know in task B. Practise using these words in sentences.

Before You Read

A. Skim the five numbered points in Reading 2 to get a general idea of what each is about. Then, match these sentences to each point.

_____ People familiar with technology can make money.

_____ More money is available.

_____ It's less expensive to start a business.

_____ It's easier to learn about starting a business.

___1___ New leaders inspire young people.

B. Scan the article to find the sentence on musicians and entrepreneurs. Why does the writer compare these two occupations?

_____

_____

_____

C. The article mentions Gen Y, which stands for *Generation Y* and refers to children born between the 1980s and the early 2000s. They are also called *millennials*. Based on what you know about this generation, do you agree or disagree with these statements?

GEN Y GRADUATES ...	AGREE	UNCERTAIN	DISAGREE
❶ delay getting married or starting a career.	☐	☐	☐
❷ want flexibility on the job.	☐	☐	☐
❸ are less concerned about helping the community.	☐	☐	☐
❹ are more open to new ideas.	☐	☐	☐
❺ want frequent feedback from managers.	☐	☐	☐

D. Discuss your answers with a partner. When you finish, read the text and then answer the questions that follow.

Youth Entrepreneurs

The climate for youth entrepreneurs seems better than ever, particularly in the knowledge sectors where young people have the advantage of low start-up costs and technology know-how. Ajay Agrawal, a professor at University of Toronto's Rotman School of Management, puts this down to five **factors**.

factors (n.): things that influence outcomes

5 1. *Culture:* From Facebook's Mark Zuckerberg to Dropbox's Drew Houston to Tumblr's David Karp, there's a growing parade of leadership examples for young people. Becoming a CEO has become more imaginable.

digital natives (n.): those who have grown up using new technologies

2. *Technology:* The **digital natives** have the **insights** and **expertise** to find profitable niches in the rapidly growing world of mobile, Internet, and social media 10 **innovation**.

3. *Lean **methodology***: Cost barriers to starting up your own business have fallen **dramatically**. With careful planning, it can be done with $10,000 or less rather than $100,000.

4. ***Access** to capital:* Not only are investors more willing to fund twenty-two-year-olds
15   than they were a **decade** ago, but there has been an increase in funds available from **venture capitalists** to the federal and provincial governments.

5. *Infrastructure:* The opportunities for **mentorship**, training, and funding have grown through organizations like the Canadian Youth Business Foundation, Nspire, and The Next 36. Universities are also actively promoting youth entrepreneurship
20   through the University of Waterloo's Conrad Business Entrepreneurship and Technology Centre and Ryerson's Digital Media Zone, as examples.

According to an Ernst & Young survey released late last year, there has been a marked improvement in training, funding, and support for young entrepreneurs in the last five years. Of the 1000 entrepreneurs **surveyed**, 88 percent believed mentoring programs
25 would boost that support further in the next three years.

Rod McNaughton, director of the University of Waterloo's Conrad Centre, says he has noticed a shift in **perception** toward entrepreneurs as well.

Traditionally, even if parents were small business people, they'd encourage their kids to become professionals, he says. "Going home and saying you want to be
30 an entrepreneur was like going home and saying you want to become a musician." But now entrepreneurs are becoming almost a professional class.

The question is whether this entrepreneurial wave is different, he says. He thinks there could be changes in technology and society that are **fundamentally** shifting in favour of smaller, new businesses.

35 So what are the **pros and cons** of being a young CEO?

...

Lauren Friese, Founder of TalentEgg. Age: Twenty-eight

• *Her story:* She started TalentEgg four years ago after seeing how challenging it could be for students to find work after graduation. The online portal connects students
40   with jobs and helps employers recruit off campuses across the country and market themselves toward Gen Y.

venture capitalists (n.): investors in risky businesses

mentorship (n.): advising a less-experienced colleague

pros and cons (n.): advantages and disadvantages

- *Advantages:* Start-ups are a good Gen Y **option**. "It's become more accepted for young people to start their careers in entrepreneurial companies, whether they started them or are working in them." The appeal is being able to [have] more
45 than just a narrow job, to have a say in what goes on and access to leadership.
- Challenges:

Building **credibility**: "When I founded TalentEgg, I was twenty-four, but I looked fifteen then and I look fifteen now. Right away I knew that I wasn't going to go into a meeting and look like the other people selling stuff in my market, so I decided
50 I wasn't going to pretend. I'm a recent graduate, my team are all Gen Y-ers, and we understand the market better than anyone else."

Lack of experience in business: "I worked to turn that to my advantage too … by saying I can approach problems with an open mind."

- *Advice:* "I don't think you could find an entrepreneur out there who could honestly
55 tell you they've never wanted to quit. I think feeling that kind of intense emotion about your business is part of the game." Being an entrepreneur takes hard work, **perseverance** (something that got her through the **recession**), and the ability to step back and reassess what you're doing.

- *Role models:* Her parents, who are both entrepreneurs, and case studies about the
60 many successful entrepreneurs out there.

(668 words)

perseverance (n.): quality of not giving up

recession (n.): temporary economic decline

Hasham, A. (2012, March 2). Youth entrepreneurs: Why launching a business from your childhood bedroom is more possible than ever (and here's proof). *The Star*. Retrieved from www.thestar.com/business/2012/03/02/youth_entrepreneurs_why_launching_a_business_from_your_childhood_bedroom_is_more_possible_than_ever_and_heres_proof.html

After You Read

E. *Who, what, when, where, why,* and *how* questions are often the basis of a news article. Fill in the information about the reading by answering these questions. Write your answers in complete sentences.

QUESTIONS	ANSWERS
❶ WHO is Lauren Friese?	*She is a young entrepreneur who started TalentEgg.*
❷ WHAT does her company do?	
❸ WHEN did she found (start) her company (at what age)?	
❹ WHERE does the company operate?	
❺ WHY did she start TalentEgg?	
❻ HOW does she deal with her lack of experience?	

© ERPI • Reproduction prohibited

16 LEAP 2: Reading and Writing

F. Indicate whether these statements are true or false, according to the text.

STATEMENTS	TRUE	FALSE
❶ More than 80 percent of businesses believed mentoring would increase.	✔	☐
❷ Parents now encourage their children to become entrepreneurs.	☐	☐
❸ Society is now more in favour of larger and older businesses.	☐	☐
❹ TalentEgg was founded to help students find work while they study.	☐	☐
❺ Working for a start-up can provide access to leadership.	☐	☐
❻ Lauren Friese first thought her age would be a disadvantage.	☐	☐
❼ It's almost impossible to find an entrepreneur who has wanted to quit.	☐	☐
❽ Friese's parents and case studies were her role models.	☐	☐
❾ Friese believes that being an entrepreneur is easy; all it takes is a little bit of luck.	☐	☐

MyBookshelf > My eLab >
Exercises > Chapter 1 >
Youth Entrepreneurs

FOCUS ON WRITING

Writing a Paragraph

The paragraph is the basis of many kinds of writing, including essays. A paragraph is a group of connected sentences on the same topic. Paragraphs are structured with a topic sentence, supporting sentences, and a concluding sentence.

A. Read this excerpt from Reading 3 and the explanatory notes to learn how a paragraph is structured.

The **topic sentence** is the first sentence of a paragraph. It lets readers know the main idea, but doesn't give detailed information. It usually includes a topic and controlling idea (underlined). The controlling idea suggests what will follow.

The **concluding sentence** brings the ideas together. It restates the topic sentence in a different way or summarizes supporting sentences or is a transition to a new topic.

> These five points can be seen in a satirical campaign <u>that turned out to be amazingly successful</u>. In 2014, Zack Brown started a campaign to raise a modest $10 to make a bowl of potato salad (Brown, 2014). There was no point in attempting to earn trust; anyone who saw the campaign would have known that it was an attempt at humour. Still, 6911 contributors flocked to the campaign, eventually contributing $55,492 within the one-month duration of the campaign.

Supporting sentences support and expand on the idea or ideas of the topic sentence. They may include facts, examples, and explanations. There are usually three supporting sentences in a paragraph, but this example only has two. A few sentences may help explain a single detail.

B. Read these sentences and then number them in the correct order to form a paragraph with a topic sentence, three supporting sentences, and a concluding sentence.

_____ Again, these were of no direct benefit to investors.

___1___ As for building interest, the potato salad campaigns offered funding targets.

_____ And, for fulfillment, no promises for delivery were made although there was a promise to develop a cookbook.

_____ Such targets would lead to the inclusion of things like better ingredients.

_____ This final target was accomplished two years later (Good, 2016).

C. Use these phrases to write topic sentences.

1 business professionals / three important skills

Most business professionals share three important skills.

_____

2 recipe / success / energy, time, focus

_____

_____

3 many people / not understand / investment

_____

_____

4 new challenges / graduates / become entrepreneurs

_____

_____

5 any business / improved / listening / customers

_____

_____

MyBookshelf > My eLab >
Exercises > Chapter 1 >
Focus on Writing

D. Reread your topic sentences and highlight the controlling idea that suggests what will follow in the paragraph. Hint: it's often the second part of the sentence. In the example, it's "three important skills."

WARM-UP ASSIGNMENT
Write a Descriptive Paragraph

Write a paragraph to describe a project you might finance using crowdfunding. Use the projects in Gearing Up on page 3 to help you think of ideas.

A. Write a topic sentence to introduce the project and include a controlling idea. Then, write three supporting sentences and a concluding sentence. Use this table to outline your ideas.

TOPIC SENTENCE	
SUPPORTING SENTENCE	
SUPPORTING SENTENCE	
SUPPORTING SENTENCE	
CONCLUDING SENTENCE	

Use feedback from your teacher and classmates on this Warm-Up Assignment to improve your writing.

B. Write your paragraph. Refer to the Models Chapter (page 195) to see an example of a descriptive paragraph and to learn more about how to write one.

C. Proofread your paragraph. This means looking carefully to correct any errors and considering ways you can make your message clearer. Use this checklist.

☐ Do you have a topic sentence with a topic and a controlling idea?

☐ Do your supporting sentences flow smoothly from point to point?

☐ Does your concluding sentence bring your ideas together?

☐ Check your verb tenses. Do your subjects and verbs agree?

☐ Check your punctuation.

☐ Have you used the present and past verb tenses correctly?

☐ Read your paragraph out loud. This will allow you to hear errors you might not see.

☐ Put your writing aside for a period of time. When you come back to it, you may spot errors or awkward sentences you missed earlier.

☐ Reread your assignment and compare your paragraph to what you were asked to do. Have you met all the criteria? What could you improve?

D. Make corrections and write a final copy.

Visit My eLab Documents for a writing checklist including tips on proofreading and editing.

Crowdfunding: History and Future

What would make you want to invest in a crowdfunding project? A decade ago, the simple answer was probably that it was a novelty, something fun to do without high expectations. Today, crowdfunding investors have become more selective. One reason for this is that there are now so many projects; Kickstarter has more than 4000 live projects to choose from and more than 150,000 projects have been successfully funded. But many have not, including Kickstarter's first project in 2009—a spray-painted T-shirt. Among these failed projects, some have turned out to be frauds. Innovators who want a successful crowdfunding campaign need to carefully consider the steps necessary to attract investors.

VOCABULARY BUILD

In the following exercises, explore key words from Reading 3.

A. For each of the words in bold, write a definition using the context of the sentence for clues to its meaning. Check your answers with a partner.

❶ New technologies and innovations often have unexpected **consequences**.

_____

❷ Contributors flocked to the campaign, eventually contributing $55,492 within the one-month **duration** of the campaign.

_____

❸ Typically these include funding **traditional** products and events, such as the production of a play.

_____

❹ Crowdfunding will continue to grow, and an **awareness** of the advantages and disadvantages will need to grow as well.

_____

❺ This was **compounded** when the novelty of the potato salad campaign led to widespread media coverage.

_____

B. Synonyms are words that have similar meanings. Highlight the word that has the closest meaning to each word in bold in the sentences adapted from Reading 3.

❶ The Pebble Watch has been one of the most successful Kickstarter **campaigns** ever.

a) investments   b) inventions   c) promotions

❷ There are discounts on the cost of the final product for investors who **commit** to higher levels of support.

a) ignore   b) promise   c) criticize

❸ Crowdfunding can help for individuals, such as a child who needs funding for expensive medical **interventions**.

a) avoidances   b) treatments   c) illegalities

④ A development of crowdfunding is now raising money to support **speculative** projects.

   a) unpredictable   b) preferred   c) easily seen

⑤ Earning the trust of **potential** backers has to do with the need to create a convincing campaign.

   a) impossible   b) unfavourable   c) possible

C. VOCABULARY EXTENSION: *Undertake* is an example of a compound word. A *compound word* is made up of two or more smaller words. Considering the meaning of the individual words makes the compound word easier to understand. Rewrite these compound words, dividing them into the two or three smaller words from which each is made.

① forthcoming   *forth | coming*   ⑥ overlap   _____

② guideline   _____   ⑦ overseas   _____

③ nevertheless _____   ⑧ straightforward _____

④ nonetheless _____   ⑨ undertake   _____

⑤ ongoing   _____   ⑩ widespread   _____

MyBookshelf > My eLab > Exercises > Chapter 1 > Vocabulary Review

D. Discuss the meaning of each word in task C with a partner.

Before You Read

A. Look at the title, first subtitle, and first paragraph of Reading 3. Use what you learned in Focus on Critical Thinking (page 5) to highlight the significant ideas and cross out the details that are of less importance.

B. Write a one- or two-sentence summary of what is significant about the start of Reading 3. Based on your summary in task B, what might the rest of the reading be about? Discuss in a group.

_____

_____

_____

C. Read the text, and then answer the questions that follow.

Crowdfunding: History and Future

What Is Crowdfunding?

New technologies and innovations often have unexpected **consequences**. For example, the Internet was **initially** created to allow scientists to continue to communicate during a nuclear attack. But the Internet led to the development of social media and
5 online payment systems. These two innovations have, in turn, led to the development of crowdfunding: raising money to support a **speculative** project.

Forbes and Schaefer (2017) have identified issues with this and other definitions:

   Crowdfunding has become a loaded term, meaning so much more than just raising money from the public. In fact, it means different things to different people. New
10 and old terms are sometimes being used to describe the same or similar activities. (p. 398)

initially (adv.): at first

Part of the confusion in terms arises from the fact that crowdfunding is used to support such a wide range of goals. Typically, these include funding **traditional** products and events, such as **production** of a play, charity donations for organizations, 15 or help for individuals, such as a child who needs funding for expensive medical **interventions**.

production (n.): putting on an event

Many new technologies seek crowdfunding to get their products into production, and **notable** successes include the Pebble Watch, which has been one of the most successful Kickstarter **campaigns** ever, raising over $20 million. Success in 20 crowdfunding requires careful planning and **execution**.

notable (adj.): worth mentioning

execution (n.): doing

Crowdfunding Success

1 Earning Trust

The question of earning trust of **potential** backers has to do with the need to create a convincing campaign that will both be noticed and will **generate** interest. 25 This is often accomplished in part through an online video that summarizes the benefits of the product or service.

generate (v.): create

2 Choice of Platform

Crowdfunding platforms have proliferated in recent years, creating the challenge of matching a new product, service, or cause to the right platform. Generally, 30 reviewing platforms to find similar projects makes for the best fit.

3 Targets and Deadlines

Many crowdfunding entrepreneurs are unrealistic about their goals. As they face setbacks, such as production delays for a new technology, investors 35 may become impatient and withdraw support. The more realistic the project deadlines, the higher chance that investors will contribute to it and future campaigns.

4 Building Interest

40 Most crowdfunding campaigns feature small and large rewards. For new technologies and other products, these usually include items like custom T-shirts for a minor show of support, and discounts on the cost of the final product for investors who 45 **commit** to higher levels of support. There are also **targeted** funding goals that will release additional benefits, such as the development of a custom case for a camera that is the core focus of the campaign.

targeted (adj.): directed

5 Fulfillment

The term *fulfillment* refers to delivering the products or services in a timely 50 manner. Failure to do so can result in loss of trust and withdrawal of investor funding. Moreover, the crowdfunder's future campaigns can be put at risk as an unsuccessful campaign sows seeds of doubt among future investors.

These five points can be seen in a satirical campaign that turned out to be amazingly successful. In 2014, Zack Brown started a campaign to raise a **modest** $10 to make 55 a bowl of potato salad (Brown, 2014). There was no point in attempting to earn trust;

modest (adj.): to a small degree

anyone who saw the campaign would have known that it was an attempt at humour. Still, 6911 contributors flocked to the campaign, eventually contributing $55,492 within the one-month **duration** of the campaign.

60 The choice of platform, the already successful Kickstarter, meant the campaign had high exposure. This was **compounded** when the novelty of the potato salad campaign led to widespread **media coverage**.

media coverage (n.): news stories

In terms of targets and deadlines, the goals were both extremely manageable and easily met. Investors did not expect any particular returns on their investment other than, perhaps, as a humorous talking point.

65 As for building interest, the potato salad campaigns offered funding targets. Such targets would lead to the inclusion of things like better ingredients. Again, these were of no direct benefit to investors. And, for fulfillment, no promises for delivery were made, although there was a promise to develop a cookbook. This final target was accomplished two years later (Good, 2016).

70 Although there was no requirement for Brown to share the money he attracted, the funds raised by the original potato salad campaign were put to good use, supporting a festival and homeless groups.

In contrast, there are many scam crowdfunding campaigns, where products and services are delayed and never delivered, and personal funding campaigns, such as
75 a GoFundMe campaign by Jennifer Flynn Cataldo, who falsely claimed to have cancer and collected more than $38,000 before being exposed and forced to return the donations.

Crowdfunding will continue to grow, and an **awareness** of the advantages and disadvantages will need to grow as well.

(788 words)

References

Brown, Z. D. (2014, August 2). Potato salad. *Kickstarter*. Retrieved from https://www.kickstarter.com/projects/zackdangerbrown/potato-salad

Forbes, H., & Schaefer, D. (2017). Guidelines for successful crowdfunding. *Procedia CIRP, 60* 398–403. Retrieved from https://www.researchgate.net/publication/316788666_Guidelines_for_Successful_Crowdfunding

Good, O. S. (2016, July 17). The infamous Potato Salad Kickstarter fulfills its final goal with this cookbook. *Polygon*. Retrieved from https://www.polygon.com/2016/7/17/12208840/potato-salad-kickstarter-cookbook-zack-danger-brown

After You Read

D. Match the words or phrases to the correct information from Reading 3.

WORDS/PHRASES		INFORMATION
❶ Internet	_____	a) notable success
❷ a loaded term	_____	b) with small and large rewards
❸ traditional charity	_____	c) makes for the best fit

WORDS/PHRASES		INFORMATION
❹ Pebble Watch	_____	d) potato salad satire campaign
❺ a convincing campaign	_____	e) created to allow scientists to communicate
❻ choice of platform	_____	f) products and services are delayed
❼ targets and deadlines	_____	g) meaning so much more than one thing
❽ building interest	_____	h) a humorous talking point
❾ fulfillment is delivering	_____	i) generates interest
❿ Zack Brown	_____	j) the products or services
⓫ returns on potato salad	_____	k) are often unrealistic
⓬ scam crowdfunding	_____	l) donations for organizations

E. Number the following phrases to create a summary.

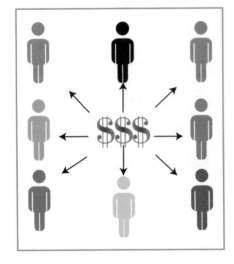

_____ Donating the money to good causes probably increased people's trust in Brown.

_____ Successful campaigns depend on trust, choice of platform, keeping targets and deadlines, the ability to build interest, and timely fulfillment of the product or service.

_____ This is in contrast to scam crowdfunding efforts that take money and give nothing in return.

_____ Zack Brown's campaign succeeded despite ignoring some of these factors.

_____ Crowdfunding was made possible by social media and online payment systems.

F. Write a topic sentence and a concluding sentence to turn the sentences in task E into a complete paragraph.

TOPIC SENTENCE: _____

_____

CONCLUDING SENTENCE: _____

_____

MyBookshelf > My eLab >
Exercises > Chapter 1 >
Crowdfunding: History and Future

Academic
Survival Skill

Completing Academic Assignments

You go to college or university to learn. Assignments and exams are ways to demonstrate both what you have learned and how you think. It's important to be effective and efficient when you work on assignments. You can be effective by asking questions about the assignment and by getting the help you need. You can be efficient by planning your time for research and writing, particularly if you are working with others.

KEY QUESTIONS	WHAT TO DO
What is the assignment?	Read the assignment as soon as you receive it, and make certain you understand each part. Ask your teacher about any missing details or anything you don't understand. Are you expected to write from your own experience, or do you need references from your textbooks, the library, and/or the Internet? How many references?
When is the assignment due?	Check when the assignment is due. Put a note on your calendar so you remember to hand it in.
How much time do you need to do the assignment?	Consider how much time you need to do the assignment. Where will you find the information to complete it? Do you need to spend time online or in a library looking for resources?
When will you do the assignment?	Plan time on your calendar to get the work done. It's usually best to block out more hours than you think you will need. Also, block out a second session to review and revise the assignment. If you have to work with other students, plan your sessions at the start.
What information and/ or tools do you need to do the assignment?	Check to make sure you have everything you need for the assignment before you start. You might need books, tools, or software programs.
Where else can you get help?	Get help from other students. It's a good way to learn how others solve the same assignment problems. Librarians can help you find resources and writing guides.
When you have finished the assignment, how will you check it?	Some teachers provide a checklist with criteria. Make sure your assignment meets the highest standards: check spelling, grammar, citations, and references.

A. The following assignment is not clear. Write three questions you might have for your teacher.

> Write about a successful business. Due next Friday.

1 _____

2 _____

3 _____

B. Discuss your questions with a partner, and rewrite the assignment to make it clear.

_____

_____

FINAL ASSIGNMENT

Write Two Descriptive Paragraphs

Use what you learned in this chapter to write two descriptive paragraphs on your crowdfunding project.

A. Start with the paragraph you wrote for the Warm-Up Assignment. Review the supporting sentences and reconsider your choice of descriptive words (adjectives and adverbs) to make the writing more interesting. Revise and expand it, making improvements based on feedback you received.

B. Write a second paragraph about why you are suitable for undertaking the project. Think about what you have to offer in terms of acquired skills, sports and club participation, part-time jobs, or subjects studied.

C. Use this table to outline your ideas.

TOPIC SENTENCE	
SUPPORTING SENTENCE	
SUPPORTING SENTENCE	
SUPPORTING SENTENCE	
CONCLUDING SENTENCE	

D. Write a draft of your paragraphs. Review the Vocabulary Build sections to see which vocabulary you can include. Review Focus on Grammar (page 11) to make sure you are using the correct verb tenses to describe what you did in the past and what you do now. Refer to the Models Chapter (page 195) to see an example of a descriptive paragraph and to learn more about how to write one.

E. Proofread your draft paragraphs. Use the checklist in the Warm-Up Assignment on page 19.

F. Make corrections and write a final copy.

How confident are you?

Think about what you learned in this chapter. Use the table to decide what you should review.

I LEARNED ...	I AM CONFIDENT	I NEED TO REVIEW
vocabulary related to crowdfunding and business;	☐	☐
skimming and scanning strategies;	☐	☐
to identify significance in a text;	☐	☐
simple present and simple past verb tenses;	☐	☐
the structure of a paragraph;	☐	☐
techniques for completing academic assignments;	☐	☐
how to write descriptive paragraphs.	☐	☐

CHAPTER 2
The Future of Work

Many jobs are changing or disappearing while new ones are being created every day. Certain jobs are being taken over by computers and robots that work more consistently and at a lower cost than humans. You may not be able to compete in some ways, but developing strong critical thinking and effective communication skills will ensure that you are always prepared for new challenges and opportunities.

Which skills are you learning for a career in the twenty-first century?

In this chapter,
you will

- learn vocabulary related to skills and jobs;

- recognize points of view;

- identify correlation and causation;

- explain cause and effect;

- use the future tense with *will* and *be going to*;

- learn how to take notes;

- write a topic sentence and a cause and effect paragraph.

GEARING UP

A. Look at the graph and then answer the questions.

Will a computer or a robot take your job?

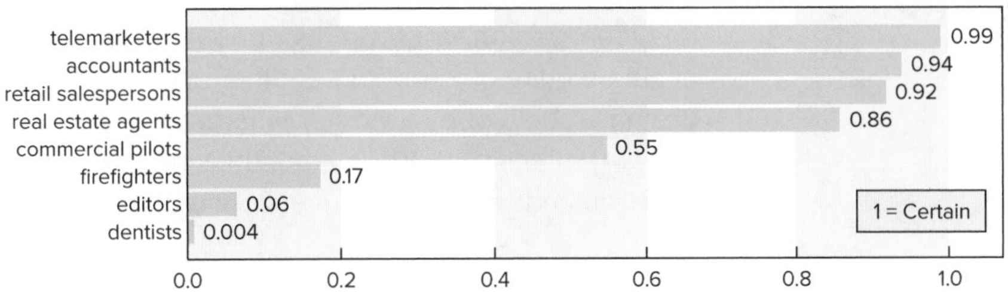

Job	Probability
telemarketers	0.99
accountants	0.94
retail salespersons	0.92
real estate agents	0.86
commercial pilots	0.55
firefighters	0.17
editors	0.06
dentists	0.004

1 = Certain

0.0   0.2   0.4   0.6   0.8   1.0

Source: Frey. C. B., & Osborne, M. A. (2013, September 17). *The future of employment: How susceptible are jobs to computerisation?* Retrieved from https://www.oxfordmartin.ox.ac.uk/downloads/academic/The_Future_of_Employment.pdf

1. Which job is most likely to disappear? Which is least likely to disappear?

   _____

   _____

2. If commercial pilots no longer flew planes, would you feel safe being piloted by a computer? Why or why not?

   _____

   _____

3. In what ways are retail sales staff already being replaced by computers?

   _____

   _____

4. Timed traffic lights have replaced the police officers who once stood in busy intersections directing traffic. Write other examples of the computerization of jobs.

   _____

   _____

B. Discuss the questions and your answers, first with a partner, then in a group.

Below are the key words you will practise in this chapter. Check the words you understand, then underline the words you use. Highlight the words you need to learn.

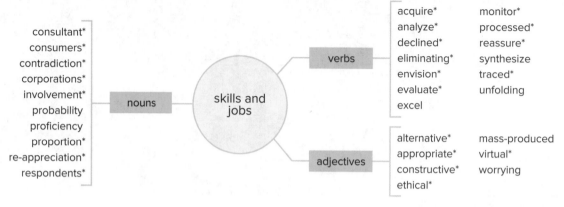

nouns

consultant*
consumers*
contradiction*
corporations*
involvement*
probability
proficiency
proportion*
re-appreciation*
respondents*

skills and jobs

verbs

acquire*   monitor*
analyze*   processed*
declined*   reassure*
eliminating*   synthesize
envision*   traced*
evaluate*   unfolding
excel

adjectives

alternative*   mass-produced
appropriate*   virtual*
constructive*   worrying
ethical*

* Appears on the Academic Word List

FOCUS ON
READING

Recognizing Points of View

When you read, try to understand the writer's point of view, which may favour one idea, person, or group over another. For example, an article about robots might be quite different depending on whether it is written by an engineer who designs robots or by a worker who has lost a job to a robot. You cannot always know a writer's background, but thinking critically about what is written can help you understand the writer's point of view.

Ask these questions:

• Does the writer provide supporting evidence: facts, statistics, or references?

• Does the writer ignore evidence that would support a different point of view?

• Does the writer back general statements with evidence in the form of examples and explanations?

A. Read this excerpt from Reading 1. Think about the underlined numbered sections. What questions might you have about the writer or about what has been written? Discuss with a partner.

> Will Robots Bring about the End of Work? [1]
>
> Hal Varian, chief economist at Google, [2] has a simple way to predict the future. [3] The future is simply what rich people have today. The rich have chauffeurs. In the future, we will have driverless cars that chauffeur us all around. The rich have private bankers. In the future, we will all have robo-bankers. [4]

B. Review the four points from the excerpt and decide which are neutral and which indicate the writer's point of view (POV).

POINTS		NEUTRAL	WRITER'S POV
❶	Is the question neutral, or does it include the writer's point of view?	☐	☐
❷	Do the name and job title provide evidence to whatever is said after?	☐	☐

POINTS		NEUTRAL	WRITER'S POV
❸	Does the language contain the writer's perspective?	☐	☐
❹	Is the concluding sentence logically based on the sentences that came before?	☐	☐

C. Identify the writer's point of view in each excerpt from Reading 1. Explain each one and then discuss them with a partner.

SENTENCES	POINT OF VIEW
❶ "World Bank data has predicted that the proportion of jobs threatened by automation in India is 69 percent, 77 percent in China, and as high as 85 percent in Ethiopia," according to World Bank president Jim Yong Kim in 2016. It really does sound like we might be facing the end of work as we know it.	*The data is factual and from a respected source, but the conclusion seems like a wild exaggeration.*
❷ Many of these fears can be traced back to a 2013 study from the University of Oxford. This made a much-quoted prediction that 47 percent of jobs in the US were under threat of automation in the next two decades. Other more recent and detailed studies have made similar dramatic predictions.	
❸ Even if we have as many as 47 percent of jobs automated, this won't translate into 47 percent unemployment. One reason is that we might just work a shorter week. That was the case in the Industrial Revolution. Before the Industrial Revolution, many worked 60 hours per week. After the Industrial Revolution, work reduced to around 40 hours per week.	

FOCUS ON CRITICAL THINKING

Identifying Correlation and Causation

If a beautiful butterfly landed on your hand at the moment an earthquake occurred, you wouldn't assume that the butterfly caused the earthquake; there was just a *correlation*—two things happening at the same time. But if you went home after the earthquake and found your Wi-Fi not working, you might logically think the earthquake caused it. However, you would still need to investigate to confirm the *causation*; it might be you forgot to pay your bill. When you read, it's important to think critically about writers' arguments to see if they are based on correlation or causation.

A. The sales of Apple iPhones have been increasing over the years, as have the number of people who have died by falling down stairs. In fact, between 2007 and 2010, there was an almost perfect correlation of .994751, or more than 99 percent. Although there appears to be a correlation, do you think that the two factors are related? Why or why not? Discuss with a partner.

Apple iPhone sales correlates with people who died by falling down the stairs

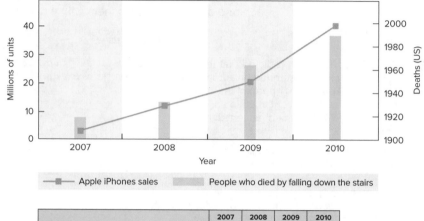

	2007	2008	2009	2010
Apple iPhone sales Millions of units	**1.39**	11.63	20.73	39.99
People who died by falling down the stairs Deaths (US) (CDC)	**1,917**	**1,935**	**1,960**	**1,991**
Correlation: **0.994751**				

Source: Vigen, T. (2018). Apple iPhone sales correlates with people who died by falling down the stairs. *Spurious Correlations*. Retrieved from http://tylervigen.com/view_correlation?id=28669

B. Read the following examples and decide if each is more likely to be an example of correlation or causation.

EXAMPLES		CORRELATION	CAUSATION
❶	low vaccination rates and outbreaks of diseases	☐	☐
❷	increase in bicycle helmets and increase in bicycle accidents	☐	☐
❸	introduction of digital cameras and drop in sales of film-based cameras	☐	☐
❹	shorter work weeks and increase in sales of camping supplies	☐	☐
❺	increase in bridge lengths and increase in car sales	☐	☐

> ❗ A negative correlation is where one factor rises while the other falls.

C. Think of two things that happened in the news; choose one example of causation and one example of correlation. Share your examples a partner.

CAUSATION: _____

CAUSATION: _____

READING ❶ Will Robots Bring about the End of Work?

In business offices, the job of personal secretary was once extremely popular. However, with the arrival of personal computers, many of the secretary's jobs— from typing to filing to scheduling appointments—became easier for others to do on their own. Personal computers were not designed to put secretaries out of work; it just happened. Will robots take away jobs in the same way?

VOCABULARY BUILD

Choose the best definition for each key word in bold.

A. In the following exercises, explore key words from Reading 1.

❶ New jobs will feature tasks where either humans **excel** or where we choose not to use machines.
   a) can spread themselves
   b) are extremely good at

❷ Mass-produced goods tend to lead to a **re-appreciation** of the artisan.
   a) an increase in costs
   b) a renewed interest

❸ I can **reassure** any bicycle repair person that there is zero chance that we will automate even small parts of your job anytime soon.
   a) calm concerns about
   b) reduce impressions of

❹ Many of these fears can be **traced** back to a 2013 study from the University of Oxford.
   a) located in the past
   b) copied in the future

❺ Working hours were reduced during the Industrial Revolution, and the same could happen with the **unfolding** AI Revolution.
   a) messing up
   b) developing

B. Fill in the blanks with the correct words to complete the paragraph.

contradiction	mass-produced	probability	proportion	worrying

The _____ that many jobs will begin to disappear in

coming years is high. But while this may seem _____

to some people, there remains a _____ in the idea that,

with more _____ materials, there continues to be a small

_____ of those same goods made by hand, such as

handmade kitchen knives, despite the easy availability of cheaper

factory-made models.

Before You Read

A. There are many jobs that machines will eventually do. Think of at least one job for each category.

	HUMAN	MACHINE
EXISTING JOBS	❶ jobs today that humans do—but machines will eventually do better	❷ current jobs that humans can't do but machines can
NEW JOBS	❸ jobs that only humans will be able to do—at first	❹ robot jobs in the distant future

❶ _____

❷ _____

❸ _____

❹ _____

B. While you read, highlight indications of the writer's point of view, and check with a partner to see if you agree.

❶ Does the writer provide supporting evidence: facts, statistics, or references?

❷ Does the writer ignore evidence that would support a different point of view?

❸ Does the writer back general statements with evidence in the form of examples and explanations?

Will Robots Bring about the End of Work?

Hal Varian, chief economist at Google, has a simple way to predict the future. The future is simply what rich people have today. The rich have **chauffeurs**. In the future, we will have driverless cars that chauffeur us all around. The rich have private bankers. In the future, we will all have robo-bankers.

5 "World Bank data has predicted that the **proportion** of jobs **threatened** by automation in India is 69 percent, 77 percent in China, and as high as 85 percent in Ethiopia," according to World Bank president Jim Yong Kim in 2016.

It really does sound like we might be facing the end of work as we know it.

10 Many of these fears can be **traced** back to a 2013 study from the University of Oxford. This made a much-quoted prediction that 47 percent of jobs in the US were under threat of automation in the next two decades. Other more recent and detailed studies have made similar dramatic predictions.

15 Now, there's a lot to criticize in the Oxford study. From a technical perspective, some of the report's predictions are clearly wrong. The report gives a 94 percent **probability** that bicycle repair

chauffeurs (n.): personal car drivers

threatened (v.): to suggest one will do something to hurt another person or thing

person will be automated in the next two decades. And, as someone trying to build that future, I can **reassure** any bicycle repair person that there is zero chance that we 20 will automate even small parts of your job anytime soon. The truth of the matter is no one has any real idea of the number of jobs at risk.

Even if we have as many as 47 percent of jobs automated, this won't translate into 47 percent unemployment. One reason is that we might just work a shorter week. That was the case in the **Industrial Revolution**. Before the Industrial Revolution, many 25 worked 60 hours per week. After the Industrial Revolution, work reduced to around 40 hours per week. The same could happen with the **unfolding** AI Revolution.

Another reason that 47 percent automation won't translate into 47 percent unemployment is that all technologies create new jobs as well as destroy them. That's been the case in the past, and we have no reason to suppose that it won't be the case 30 in the future. There is, however, no fundamental law of economics that requires the same number of jobs to be created as destroyed. In the past, more jobs were created than destroyed but it doesn't have to be so in the future.

In the Industrial Revolution, machines took over many of the physical tasks we used to do. But we humans were still left with all the cognitive tasks. This time, as machines 35 start to take on many of the cognitive tasks too, there's the **worrying** question: what is left for us humans?

Some of my colleagues suggest there will be plenty of new jobs like robot repair person. I am entirely unconvinced by such claims. The thousands of people who used to paint and weld in most of our car factories got replaced by only a couple of robot repair 40 people.

No, the new jobs will have to be doing jobs where either humans **excel** or where we choose not to have machines. But here's the **contradiction**. In fifty to a hundred years' time, machines will be super-human. So it's hard to imagine any job where humans will remain better than the machines. This means the only jobs left will be those where 45 we *prefer* humans to do them.

The AI Revolution then will be about rediscovering the things that make us human. Technically, machines will have become amazing artists. They will be able to write music to rival Bach, and paintings to match Picasso. But we'll still prefer works produced by human artists.

50 These works will speak to the human experience. We will appreciate a human artist who speaks about love because we have this in common. No machine will truly experience love like we do.

As well as the artistic, there will be a **re-appreciation** of the artisan. Indeed, we see the beginnings of this already in **hipster culture**. We will appreciate more and more those 55 things made by the *human* hand. **Mass-produced** goods made by machine will become cheap. But items made by hand will be rare and increasingly valuable.   (704 words)

Walsh, T. (2017, October 1). Will robots bring about the end of work? *The Guardian*. Retrieved from https://www.theguardian.com/science/political-science/2017/oct/01/will-robots-bring-about-the-end-of-work

Industrial Revolution (n.): the time (1760–1840) when steam engines fostered new manufacturing processes

hipster culture (n.): a way of life based on following today's latest trends

After You Read

C. Choose the phrase that best completes each sentence.

1 The idea of driverless cars that chauffeur us all around is based in part on _____.

   a) a belief that people won't want to drive cars

   b) the move from riding horses to driving cars

   c) the most expensive cars owned by the wealthy

2 The writer possibly feels that bicycle repair jobs will not be replaced because _____.

   a) bicycle repairs are not worth enough money

   b) in the future, bicycles will never be self-repairing

   c) the number of skills involved are too complex

3 The writer suggests that 47 percent automation won't translate into 47 percent unemployment because _____.

   a) most old jobs won't die

   b) new jobs will be created

   c) people will own the robots

4 It's likely that robots will be smarter than humans in fifty to one hundred years if _____.

   a) we pass laws making that possible

   b) inventors focus more on intelligence

   c) the current rates of development continue

5 When the writer says, "But we'll still prefer works produced by human artists," he _____.

   a) supports his claim with evidence

   b) doesn't support his claim with evidence

   c) needs no evidence for his claim

6 While machine-made objects become cheap, handmade objects become more valuable because _____.

   a) there are fewer people with the skills to produce them

   b) things made in factories are less likely to be local

   c) there are more people with the skills to produce them

D. The writer in Reading 1 makes several predictions. Each one expresses his point of view. Offer an opposite point of view for each one and explain why it may be a valid alternative prediction.

PREDICTIONS	ALTERNATE PREDICTIONS
1 Bicycle repair people will not be replaced.	*Like other appliances, bicycles may become disposable once they break.*
2 We will all have robo-bankers.	
3 The AI revolution could lead to a reduction in hours of work.	

PREDICTIONS	ALTERNATE PREDICTIONS
④ New jobs will not replace all those that are lost.	
⑤ New jobs will include robot repairers.	
⑥ People will still prefer art produced by humans.	
⑦ Items made by hand will be rare and increasingly valuable.	

MyBookshelf > My eLab >
Exercises > Chapter 2 > Will Robots
Bring about the End of Work?

E. Many predictions never come true. For example, in the 1950s, it was common to predict that, by now, everyone would be travelling by flying cars. It didn't happen. Much of this article is the writer's point of view—predictions that are unsupported by facts or statistics. This is often the case when predicting the future. Can statistics about life today be used to predict the future? Why or why not? Discuss in a group.

FOCUS ON WRITING

Explaining Cause and Effect

In Focus on Critical Thinking (page 31), you learned about correlation and causation. When there is causation, a cause is followed by an effect, or multiple effects. Sometimes effects trickle down, such as when a major business opens and other businesses open to support it or simply to feed, house, and entertain the people who work there. Use specific language and structures to explain cause and effect.

A. Read the following words and phrases that show cause and effect. Highlight the ones that show cause.

① as a result

② is due to

③ is responsible for

④ is the effect of

⑤ is the reason for

⑥ leads to

⑦ occurs

⑧ produces

⑨ results from

⑩ results in

B. Imagine you own a factory that introduces robots to replace workers. What are the initial effects? What are the secondary effects caused by each of those initial effects? For example, fired workers leave town, so real estate prices drop.

INITIAL EFFECTS: _____

_____

SECONDARY EFFECTS: _____

_____

C. Read the parts of a cause and effect paragraph, and use what you wrote in task B to write sentences in the second column.

PARAGRAPH SECTIONS	SENTENCES
1 Write a topic sentence that explains how one cause led to three effects.	*Replacing human workers with robots would lead to lower local populations, fewer businesses, and fewer services.*
2 Write a supporting sentence explaining the first effect.	
3 Explain the second effect.	
4 Explain the third effect.	
5 Summarize the causes and effects, and express a point of view.	

MyBookshelf > My eLab > Exercises > Chapter 2 > Focus on Writing

READING ❷   Half of All Jobs Today Will Disappear by 2030

British economist John Maynard Keynes (1883–1946) predicted technology would likely cause widespread unemployment because the labour savings from technology were happening faster than new jobs could be found for workers. His focus wasn't computers, but rather steam and electric engines taking over work that previously required human involvement. Were his predictions realistic?

VOCABULARY BUILD

A. Words with the same meaning are called *synonyms*. Words with the opposite meaning are called *antonyms*. Choose the synonym of each word.

1 consumers	☐ users	☐ producers
2 eliminating	☐ adding	☐ removing
3 monitor	☐ oversee	☐ ignore
4 respondents	☐ interviewers	☐ people who reply
5 virtual	☐ real	☐ simulated

B. Fill in the blanks with the correct words to complete the sentences.

| alternative | appropriate | consultant | corporations | envision |

① It was _____ to thank the other members of the team.

② As a/an _____ , she helps many different companies.

③ Taking a bicycle instead of a car is choosing _____ transportation.

④ A few small businesses grow to become large _____.

⑤ I _____ a future in which everyone has a personal robot.

C. Check your answers with a partner and discuss what each word means. Use a dictionary for help with words that are unfamiliar.

Before You Read

A. In 1900, an American railroad engineer wrote predictions for the year 2000. Have any of these predictions come true? Discuss each one with a partner and then in a group.

PREDICTION 1: Cars will disappear from large cities with all traffic either below or high above the ground, eliminating noise pollution.

PREDICTION 2: Cars will be operated by a half-kilo motor that will be cheaper than a horse and twice as powerful.

PREDICTION 3: Photographs will be telegraphed from any distance and published in newspapers an hour later.

B. Make predictions for these areas for the year 2030.

AREAS	MY PREDICTIONS
TRANSPORTATION	
JOBS	
TECHNOLOGY	
ENTERTAINMENT	

C. While you read, highlight indications of the writer's point of view as outlined in Focus on Reading (page 30).

Half of All Jobs Today Will Disappear by 2030

Building a long-lasting career means at least thinking about what might be ahead in the next ten to twenty years. So what lies ahead? A good question. We checked with the work of **futurists**, career experts, and technologists to see what might happen. Some of what they **envision** is downright scary; some of their predictions might give
5 you hope. But any and all of them should at least get you thinking about what you should do in the near- and mid-term future.

futurists (n.): those who study current trends and innovations and make predictions about the future

1. Half of all jobs today will disappear by 2030.

Futurist Thomas Frey says that the world of work is going to turn upside down as two billion jobs—half of all employment on the planet today—will be gone by 2030.

hinges (v.): depends

decentralized (adj.): control moved away from central authority

ethanol (n.): fuel made from organic material

10 Why: This prediction **hinges** on massive change happening in some major industries. In the power industry alone, moving to renewable energy and **decentralized** power generation will mean many job demands in areas like coal and **ethanol** production, overhead power line maintenance, power plants, and even railroad transportation (to haul the fuel) will drop significantly. Self-driving cars, already a technical reality,
15 could put a lot of taxi, bus, limousine, and delivery drivers out of business. Manufacturing and retail jobs could take big hits as 3D printing eventually lets **consumers** make many products at home without the need to buy from a store.

The opportunities: There will be new areas of hiring. **Corporations** and communities will run their own power facilities and need skilled workers.
20 Replacing the national grid will create jobs in construction and in recycling. Solar, wind, geothermal, and other **alternative** energy systems will need installation crews. People will have to design 3D products, repair printers, and sell the manufacturing "ink" they use.

...

25 ### 2. Robots will become your co-workers and competitors.

Why: If you think of robots as something out of an old science fiction film, it is time to reconsider your views. They already help farmers and could take over fast food jobs. Between 2011 and 2012, employment of robots was up 40 percent worldwide. There are already general purpose robots that cost
30 not much more than a year of minimum wage salary. The move toward robots will only increase as technology pushes productivity by **eliminating** more of those **finicky** and unreliable people who need sleep, time off, and salaries. They're just going to take a lot of different forms, giving them the advantage in many types of work. **Virtual avatars**—faces on screens and voices on speakers—are coming
35 to a point that they can handle many customer service interactions. Medical centres are already testing them to greet physical therapy patients in multiple languages, ask questions about their pain, and teach people **appropriate** exercises, using electronics to **monitor** how well they follow the patterns, according to *Technology Review*. Futurist Mike Walsh says prepare to see avatars at customer service desks in retail, hotels, and
40 banking by 2030.

finicky (adj.): fussy

avatars (n.): figures representing people

The opportunities: As the working world moves toward using robots, virtual avatars, and other devices, someone will have to keep the **tin can clan** doing the right steps. There will be an increase of jobs in design, engineering, and systems management as well as a need for technicians to keep our metallic co-workers up and running.

tin can clan (n.): robots (slang)

45 ...

irony (n.): discrepancy between the expected and actual state of affairs

3. Some Good-Paying Professions Will Be Begging for Job Applicants.

Why: One **irony** of the future is that there will be plenty of good jobs that go begging for applicants because young people often have limited views of what job opportunities to pursue. A recent UK survey of thirteen- to sixteen-year-olds by the non-profit Chartered
50 Institute of Personnel and Development showed that their career aspirations had "nothing in common" with what job markets will want in the future. They will struggle to compete in areas and, by their choices, make getting a job ridiculously harder for many. More than a third of the teenagers interviewed were only interested in one of ten different careers: "teacher, lawyer, accountant, actor, police, IT **consultant**, doctor,
55 sportsperson, army/navy/air force/fire fighter and psychologist." The interests of half of all **respondents** fell into only three of twenty-five different sectors.

The opportunity: When you consider the takeover of new technologies, remember that someone still has to be able to open a lock, fix a leak, and install a new circuit to charge your new high-tech domestic help.

(719 words)

Sherman, E. (2013, September 25). Half of all jobs today will disappear by 2030 and other scary predictions. *AOL Jobs.* Retrieved from http://jobs.aol.com/articles/2013/09/25/predictions-workplace/

After You Read

D. Connect the phrases to summarize the article.

SUMMARY		
1 When you think about a career, …	*e*	a) make many products at home.
2 Futurists and technologists …	_____	b) will be gone by 2030.
3 Frey says that two billion jobs …	_____	c) in multiple languages.
4 Renewable energy and decentralized power generation …	_____	d) and other alternative energy systems.
5 Self-driving cars could mean the end …	_____	e) you should think ahead ten to twenty years.
6 3D printing will let consumers …	_____	f) of job opportunities.
7 People will use solar, wind, geothermal …	_____	g) take over fast food jobs.
8 Robots are more popular now and will help farmers and …	_____	h) will mean more jobs in coal and ethanol production.
9 Virtual avatars will handle many customer service interactions …	_____	i) humans to do them.
10 Jobs in design, engineering, systems management, …	_____	j) will help maintain robots.
11 Young people often have limited views …	_____	k) have mixed ideas about what jobs will be like.
12 Many jobs will still require …	*i*	l) of other forms of driver-based transportation.

E. Skim the article and find examples of jobs that might disappear in the future and possible future job opportunities. Add these jobs to the columns, as well as your own job predictions. Discuss in a group.

JOBS THAT MIGHT DISAPPEAR IN THE FUTURE	POSSIBLE FUTURE JOB OPPORTUNITIES
jobs in coal and ethanol production	*jobs in recycling*

MyBookshelf > My eLab > Exercises > Chapter 2 > Half of All Jobs

F. Review examples of the writer's point of view that you found in the reading and discuss them with a partner.

FOCUS ON GRAMMAR

Future Tense

When you read the text on pages 40–41, you probably noticed examples of the future tense. Use the future tense to write about events that have not yet happened but are expected to occur at a later time.

To form the future tense, use *will* + verb, or *be going to* + verb to express
- actions that will take place in the future: Miranda **will start** university classes in September;
- promises or plans: She **is going to study** robotics;
- predictions: Robots **will take** new forms in the future.

FORMS		
will	**AFFIRMATIVE**	**NEGATIVE (CONTRACTION)**
singular	I / You / He/She/It **will work**.	I / You / He/She/It **will not/won't work**.
plural	We/You/They **will work**.	We/You/They **will not/won't work**.
	QUESTION (Move *will* before the subject.)	
	Will I / you / he/she/it **work**?	**Will** you / we / they **work**?

FORMS		
be going to	**AFFIRMATIVE**	**NEGATIVE (CONTRACTION)**
singular	I **am going to work**.	I **am not going to work**.
	He/She/It **is going to work**.	He/She/It **is not/isn't going to work**.
plural	We/You/They **are going to work**.	We/You/They **are not/aren't going to work**.
	QUESTION (Move *be* before the subject.)	

Am	I	} going to work?	**Are**	you	} going to work?	
Are	you			we		
Is	he/she/it			they		

Adverbs with *will* and *be going to*
Adverbs are words that describe verbs (action words). The adverb in the example sentences below is *eventually*. When you use the future tense with *will*, the adverb comes after *will*. When you use the future tense with *be going to*, the adverb comes between *be* and *going to*.

Robots **will** *eventually* take over all human jobs.
Robots **are** *eventually* **going to** be common in most homes.

A. Rearrange the words to make sentences with *will* or *be going to*.

1. of / career / the / questions / biggest / life / in / one / what / is / you / will / for / a / do

   One of the biggest questions in life is what you will do for a career.

2. of / half / 2030 / all / jobs / will / by / disappear / today

   _____

   _____

3. to / forms / are / robots / take / going / a / of / different / lot / certainly

   _____

   _____

4. cycle / repeating / will / the / keep

   _____

   _____

5. a / your / computer / a / or / robot / job / ? / will / take

   _____

   _____

6. human / are / to / going / affect / robots / the / market / job

   _____

   _____

MyBookshelf > My eLab > Exercises > Chapter 2 > Grammar Review

B. Indicate whether you would use *will*, *be going to*, or either to express each action in the future tense.

ACTIONS	*will*	*be going to*	either
❶ a promise to help someone find work	☐	☐	☐
❷ a question about someone's plan	☐	☐	☐
❸ a prediction about the future of work	☐	☐	☐
❹ talking about what you want to do	☐	☐	☐

WARM-UP ASSIGNMENT
Write a Topic Sentence for a Cause and Effect Paragraph

Reading 1 talks about the threat to jobs from automation. In this assignment, you will consider a job likely to be replaced by automation in the near future and write a topic sentence about it.

A. Choose one job that you consider will be in danger of automation. It may be a career in the discipline you are studying.

A JOB LIKELY TO BE AUTOMATED: _____

B. Use what you learned in Focus on Reading (page 30) to consider a point of view about the automation of that job. For example, you may consider it a positive development because the job is dangerous, or you may consider it negative because it will lose human flexibility.

MY POINT OF VIEW: _____

_____

_____

C. Think of up to ten points about why that job might be replaced by automation. Once you have ideas, choose the three best ones. The best points are those that are distinct and that you can support with examples and explanations.

D. A topic sentence should include a cause, three effects, and your point of view about them. See an example of a topic sentence in Focus on Writing (page 37) and refer to the Models Chapter (page 196) to learn more about how to write one. Write your topic sentence using the information from tasks A, B, and C above. Share it with a partner to get feedback.

TOPIC SENTENCE: _____

_____

_____

E. Keep your notes for the Final Assignment.

Taking Notes

Taking notes is a useful skill to help you remember information that you read, listen to, or think about. Careful note-taking allows you to identify the sources of different ideas. This helps you to avoid plagiarism by mistakenly presenting others' ideas as your own.

When you take notes, focus on four areas:

• main ideas;

• questions raised in the text;

• how the information relates to you or a task you might have;

• what you have to add in terms of questions, comments, and ideas.

Note-taking is also about being efficient. Use symbols to replace words or phrases. Which words or phrases might these symbols replace? In a group, discuss other symbols you could use.

SYMBOLS	MEANING
>	*greater than*
<	
=	
≠	
+	
↑ ↓	

SYMBOLS	MEANING
/	
#	
%	
@	
* [or] !	
?	

READING ③   Old and New Job Skills

It is difficult to know beforehand how inventions might change the future. A painting from 1352 is the first recorded use of someone wearing eyeglasses, although they were probably invented many years earlier. The widespread use of eyeglasses is said to be responsible for the largest one-time intelligence boost in human history by expanding the pool of potentially literate people. In the same way, the computer has probably changed the way you live and work, making knowledge more accessible. But new inventions may lead to a need for different skills and, sometimes, the loss of jobs.

VOCABULARY BUILD

A. Highlight the word in parentheses that best completes each sentence. Key words are in bold.

❶ It's not enough to make the (illegal / legal) choice; you need to make the **ethical** choice.

❷ They took time to **evaluate** the problem, (ignoring / looking at) each fact in turn.

③ She decided to **acquire** more computer skills to make it (harder / easier) to find a job.

④ A **constructive** solution to creating opportunities would be to help people (learn / quit) on their own.

⑤ He was too busy, so he **declined** the offer of (his first / a second) job.

B. Choose the phrase that best completes each sentence. Key words are in bold.

① Industrial robots' **proficiency** refers to _____.
   a) not replacing humans
   b) the different jobs they can do
   c) being limited to on and off

② Our **involvement** in the project means _____.
   a) only you can do the work
   b) we will find others who help
   c) everyone will participate

③ We need to **analyze** the problem _____.
   a) to find the best solution
   b) because it doesn't matter
   c) as a way of guessing

④ To **synthesize** everyone's point of view will require _____.
   a) looking at a lot of data
   b) ignoring any opinions
   c) throwing out their ideas

⑤ Once all the paperwork is **processed**, we will _____.
   a) have to fill out all the forms
   b) be free to start the project
   c) not be able to start the project

C. VOCABULARY EXTENSION: To analyze a problem is to look at its individual parts in detail. Analyzing is one of six ways of learning, from simply remembering to the more complex task of creating. Use the words in parentheses to write definitions for the ways we learn.

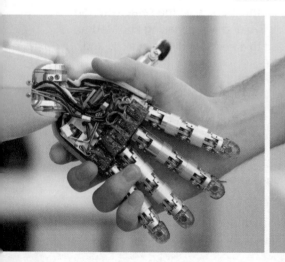

① remember (define, recall, repeat):

_____

_____

② understand (classify, describe, paraphrase):

_____

_____

③ apply (demonstrate, illustrate, operate):

_____

_____

④ analyze (compare, contrast, criticize):

_____

⑤ evaluate (argue, defend, judge):

_____

⑥ create (construct, design, develop):

_____

_____

MyBookshelf > My eLab >
Exercises > Chapter 2 >
Vocabulary Review

Before You Read

A. New technology might make your perfect job disappear. Write six skills you think would be most useful to learn to prepare you for future jobs.

❶ _____

❷ _____

❸ _____

❹ _____

❺ _____

❻ _____

B. While you read, use the symbols you learned in Academic Survival Skill to take notes in the margins on the key points.

Old and New Job Skills

Throughout history, changes in laws, technologies, and demand for products and services have created the need for new job skills. Often, as new skills are required, older skills fall out of favour and are forgotten.

New laws are one reason some jobs appear and disappear. For example, new laws
5 about terrorism have led to growth in the security and law enforcement sectors.[1] On the other hand, once people became aware of the dangers of a building material, such as **asbestos**, its use **declined** and those who **mined** and **processed** it lost their jobs.

Changes in demand sometimes occur when people no longer want or need a product or service. This is particularly the case when new fashions make certain items of
10 clothing more or less popular. For example, hats made from **beaver** fur were popular from the 1700s until around 1830, when silk became the preferred material. The change meant a decline in the employment of those who hunted beavers and prepared their furs. It also meant an increase in employment for those involved in silk production. In modern times, the development of **petroleum**-based fabrics has similarly impacted
15 the importance of traditional wool, leather, and cotton clothing.

asbestos (n.): heat-resistant mineral that can be woven

mined (v.): dug from the earth

beaver (n.): large rodent that lives partly in the water

petroleum (n.): liquid in the earth used to make oil and gasoline

---

1. Staples (2009) says, "Globalization promotes military spending over social spending. Security exceptions in free trade agreements grant governments a free hand in military spending, but place limits on social spending. Thus, governments use military spending to achieve non-defence goals such as job creation, regional development, and subsidization of local corporations through defence contracts" (para. 12).

Today, the biggest impact on job skills is new technologies, particularly computerization. Computerized bank machines have reduced the need for **bank tellers**. Word processing programs have reduced the need for secretaries. Online
20 computer-based bookstores have put many traditional bookstores out of business along with the skilled employees who once worked in them.

You may think that in the future you will have a job that requires computer skills. But it is difficult to predict whether
25 more intel-ligent computers will require less human **involvement**. What is likely is that computers will take over more, reducing or eliminating the need for skilled humans. If so, then how can you prepare yourself for jobs that may not exist today?

bank tellers (n.): customer service employees at a bank

30 The National Council of Teachers of English (NCTE) suggests that twenty-first-century learners need to **acquire** the following six skills to be successful in the workplace.

1. Gain **proficiency** with tools of technology. If you use a computer, are you able to use all the functions of its software? Consider the most common software programs used in your field. Are you competent in using them in practical and creative ways?

35 2. Develop relationships with others and confront and solve problems collaboratively and cross-culturally. Do you have the skills to identify problems in the world around you, particularly in the workplace? Can you use teamwork skills to address these problems in **constructive** ways? Do you have an understanding of other cultures? Can you work with people from other cultures?

40 3. Design and share information for global communities to meet a variety of purposes. Can you create presentations for different audiences? Imagine explaining something you know to a group of friends. Now imagine explaining the same information to a group of people from another culture. Could you do it?

simultaneous (adj.): at the same time

4. Manage, **analyze**, and **synthesize** multiple streams of **simultaneous** information.
45 Can you take information from a variety of sources (e.g., books, social media, websites, conversations) and organize them into simpler ideas?

critique (v.): analyze

5. Create, **critique**, analyze, and **evaluate** multimedia texts. Can you create websites or other multimedia presentations with sound, text, video, and images? Can you look at others' multimedia work and be critical about it?

50 6. Attend to the **ethical** responsibilities required by complex environments. Can you make decisions about ideas of right and wrong in a variety of situations? Consider a difficult choice you might have to make in your life. On what basis would you make your choice?

These skills are the ones that are the most likely to prepare you to work with others
55 in interesting jobs. However, a report prepared for the Association of American Colleges and Universities (Bauerlein, 2010) says that the most important skills are those that would have been familiar to people in the 1700s and earlier. These skills include the ability to effectively communicate orally and in writing. These were the most important skills mentioned by 89 percent of employers. Other important skills
60 were critical thinking and analytical reasoning.

Computers and other technologies will continue to be important in the future, but the abilities to think critically and to communicate effectively might be the most important skills that future employees can learn.

(718 words)

References

Bauerlein, M. (2010, March 9). Employers want 18th-century skills. *The Chronicle of Higher Education*. Retrieved from http://chronicle.com/blogs/brainstorm/employers-want-18th-century-skills/21687

Foster, J. E., & Eccles, W. J. (2013, July 23). Fur trade. *Canadian Encyclopedia*. Retrieved from http://www.thecanadianencyclopedia.ca/en/article/fur-trade/

NCTE. (2013). The NCTE definition of 21st century literacies. *National Council of Teachers of English*. Retrieved from http://www.ncte.org/positions/statements/21stcentdefinition

Staples, S. (2009, May 3). Ten ways globalism promotes militarism. *The Polaris Institute*. Retrieved from http://www.rense.com/general41/prono.htm

After You Read

C. Indicate whether these statements are true or false, according to the text.

STATEMENTS	TRUE	FALSE
❶ Often, as new skills are required, older skills are forgotten.	☐	☐
❷ New laws about terrorism led to a drop in security jobs.	☐	☐
❸ Mining asbestos is an example of a new job opportunity.	☐	☐
❹ Hats made from beaver fur replaced ones made of silk.	☐	☐
❺ Computerization has reduced the need for bank tellers, secretaries, and bookstore employees.	☐	☐
❻ Intelligent computers will require less human involvement.	☐	☐
❼ The ability to effectively communicate orally and in writing remains an important skill.	☐	☐
❽ Critical thinking will no longer be an important skill in the future.	☐	☐

D. Review the six skills proposed by the NCTE. Which skills do you already have? Which do you need to develop? Write the challenges you might face when learning these skills.

SKILLS	HAVE	NEED	CHALLENGES
❶ Gain proficiency with tools of technology.			
❷ Develop relationships with others, and confront and solve problems collaboratively and cross-culturally.			

SKILLS	HAVE	NEED	CHALLENGES
❸ Design and share information for global communities to meet a variety of purposes.			
❹ Manage, analyze, and synthesize multiple streams of simultaneous information.			
❺ Create, critique, analyze, and evaluate multimedia texts.			
❻ Attend to the ethical responsibilities required by complex environments.			

MyBookshelf > My eLab > Exercises > Chapter 2 > Old and New Job Skills

E. Discuss your answers to task D in a group.

FINAL ASSIGNMENT
Write a Cause and Effect Paragraph

In the Warm-Up Assignment (page 44), you wrote a topic sentence on what might cause a particular job to become automated in the future. In this Final Assignment, you will use that topic sentence to write about the cause and effects of automation on the job you selected.

A. Revisit your ideas from the Warm-Up Assignment. Consider examples and explanations of both initial and secondary effects, and indicate your point of view.

B. On a separate page, write your paragraph using the format in Focus on Writing (page 37). Begin by including one or two sentences about the *causes* leading to changes in the job you are discussing, and then write a topic sentence identifying three possible *effects*. Expand these three effects into a sentence each, and then add a concluding sentence that summarizes your point of view, based on what you learned in Focus on Reading (page 30). Refer to the Models chapter (page 197) to see an example of a cause and effect paragraph and to learn more about how to write one.

C. Proofread your work checking to make sure you correctly used the future tense, based on what you learned in Focus on Grammar (page 42). Then, share your work with a partner and ask for feedback.

D. Make corrections and write a final copy.

How confident are you?

Think about what you learned in this chapter. Use the table to decide what you should review.

I LEARNED ...	I AM CONFIDENT	I NEED TO REVIEW
vocabulary related to skills and jobs;	☐	☐
how to recognize points of view;	☐	☐
ways to identify correlation and causation;	☐	☐
how to explain cause and effect;	☐	☐
the future tense with *will* and *be going to*;	☐	☐
how to take notes;	☐	☐
how to write a topic sentence and a cause and effect paragraph.	☐	☐

CHAPTER 3

Fit for Life

You should follow the words of motivational speaker Jim Rohn (1930–2009) to "take care of your body. It's the only place you have to live." But fitness, health, and a proper diet sometimes seem difficult goals. It doesn't help that there are uncertainties surrounding the safety of certain sports and the quality of certain diets. Research on issues like sleep can help to better inform you, but writer bias or corporate influence can make you question the reported results of studies.

When it comes to health and fitness, how do you make decisions about who and what to believe?

In this chapter,
you will

- learn vocabulary related to fitness and health;

- identify main ideas and supporting details;

- explore how to make valid comparisons;

- review punctuation rules;

- compare and contrast texts;

- learn how to cite and reference sources;

- write compare and contrast paragraphs.

GEARING UP

A. Look at the graphic and then answer the questions.

What makes us healthy?

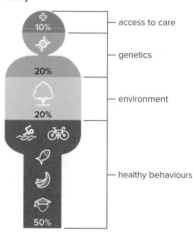

access to care

genetics

environment

healthy behaviours

10%

20%

20%

50%

Source: Bipartisan Information Center. (2014). *Lots to lose: How America's health and obesity crisis threatens our economic future.* Retrieved from https://bipartisanpolicy.org/wp-content/uploads/sites/default/files/5023_BPC_NutritionReport_FNL_Web.pdf

1. Why is genetics different from the other health factors?

   _____

2. Write three examples of healthy behaviour. Consider your own healthy behaviours as well as those you might imagine practising in future.

   _____

   _____

3. Which unhealthy behaviours should you avoid?

   _____

   _____

4. List three environmental factors that can be unhealthy.

   _____

   _____

B. Discuss the questions and your answers, first with a partner, then in a group.

Below are the key words you will practise in this chapter. Check the words you understand, then underline the words you use. Highlight the words you need to learn.

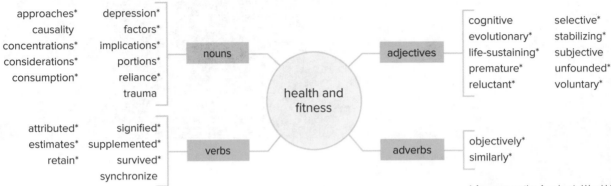

approaches*
causality
concentrations*
considerations*
consumption*

depression*
factors*
implications*
portions*
reliance*
trauma

nouns

health and fitness

adjectives

cognitive
evolutionary*
life-sustaining*
premature*
reluctant*

selective*
stabilizing*
subjective
unfounded*
voluntary*

attributed*
estimates*
retain*

signified*
supplemented*
survived*
synchronize

verbs

adverbs

objectively*
similarly*

* Appears on the Academic Word List

FOCUS ON READING

Identifying Main Ideas and Supporting Details

When you read a text, it helps to identify the main idea as well as the supporting details. The main idea is the argument that the writer puts forward. Supporting details take the form of examples, explanations, and evidence. Being able to identify each element makes it easier for you to evaluate the text and decide whether the argument is convincing.

A. Read this excerpt from Reading 1 and the explanatory notes to learn how the writer states the main idea and then supports it with details.

The first sentence is usually the main idea, but this sentence also sets up a problem that attracts reader interest.

→ If you have ever stepped off a long-haul flight or worked night shifts, you probably noticed changes in your mood, concentration, and general well-being. These changes are ← the result of disturbances to your natural sleep-wake cycle, your "circadian rhythm."

The second sentence is an explanation and defines *circadian rhythm*.

The third sentence gives an explanation of the consequences.

→ And disruptions to this cycle can have worse consequences than just feeling a bit moody or distracted. Our latest research shows that ← it is associated with an increased risk of depression and bipolar disorder.

The last sentence outlines the evidence (*our latest research*) for the main idea and gives extra information.

B. Read the sentences and indicate whether each is a main idea, an example, an explanation, or evidence. In some cases, a sentence may have more than one function.

SENTENCES	MAIN IDEA	EXAMPLE	EXPLANATION	EVIDENCE
❶ Circadian rhythms are variations in biological or behavioural processes that recur on a roughly 24-hour cycle.	☐	☐	☑	☐
❷ We addressed these issues in our study, published in *The Lancet Psychiatry*, by using a large sample (over 91,000 participants, drawn from UK Biobank).	☐	☐	☐	☐

SENTENCES	MAIN IDEA	EXAMPLE	EXPLANATION	EVIDENCE
3 We found that disturbances to circadian rhythms—specifically, increased activity during rest hours and/or inactivity during the day—were associated with a greater risk of mood disorders.	☐	☐	☐	☐
4 It will be important to examine, for example, whether objectively measured circadian disruption can predict new diagnoses or new episodes of mood disorders.	☐	☐	☐	☐
5 We hope that future, long-term studies, following up on the same people in the UK Biobank, will be able to address the issue of cause and effect in more detail.	☐	☐	☐	☐

C. Compare your answers with a partner to see if you agree. Discuss if you do not.

FOCUS ON CRITICAL THINKING

Making Valid Comparisons

You often hear the expression, *You can't compare apples and oranges*. It's meant to explain that two things are too dissimilar to be compared, yet apples and oranges do have some things in common; they are both fruits and both roughly round in shape.

Comparing is an essential critical thinking skill. You look at a new idea and compare it to your prior knowledge and experience to see what fits and what does not. Often, when you read, you will see comparisons in a text and have to consider whether or not the comparisons are valid, that is, whether or not they are true and accurate.

A. In Reading 1, *mental health* is compared to *physical health*. Copy and fill in the Venn diagram, and then discuss your answers with a partner to see if you agree that the comparison is valid or not.

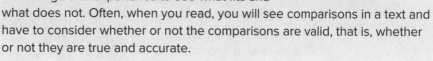

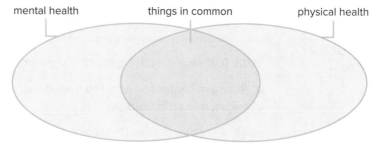

B. Look at your answers to task A. Are the comparisons valid? Why or why not?

C. Read the following sentence from Reading 3 and answer the questions.

Part of the problem is that most people are reluctant to make changes to their diets and instead consider superfoods like magic pills that will undo the effects of the rest of their bad eating habits.

1 What is being compared?

_____

② In what ways is the comparison valid?

_____

_____

③ In what ways is the comparison invalid?

_____

_____

D. When you decide something is a valid comparison, it means you should be able to defend your decision. In a group, take turns choosing two of the following sports and explain why each pair is or is not a valid comparison.

READING ❶ This Is How Important Sleep Is for Your Mental Health

Your *circadian rhythm* is your body clock, and it depends on exposure to sunlight. It regulates chemicals (such as serotonin and melatonin) in your brain that help you be more alert and active at some times of the day and more relaxed and sleepy at others. Some factors, such as artificial light and travel between time zones, can upset your circadian rhythms, sometimes leading to illness.

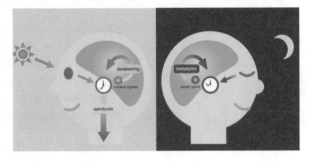

VOCABULARY BUILD

In the following exercises, explore key words from Reading 1.

A. Read the sentences adapted from Reading 1 and choose the best synonym for each word in bold.

① Previous studies have been limited by using only **subjective** measures of sleep and activity.

    a) one of many   b) class-based   c) self-reported

② We also took a wide range of factors into account that might otherwise explain the state of participants' mental health or **cognitive** function.

    a) learning   b) physical   c) repeated

③ These findings could have important public health **implications**.

    a) losses   b) developments   c) effects

④ An increasing **reliance** on artificial light, particularly at night, is associated with disturbed circadian rhythms.

    a) rejection of   b) dependence on   c) purchase of

⑤ People exposed to high amounts of artificial light at night are less able to **synchronize** their rhythms.

    a) differentiate   b) match   c) reform

B. Choose words from the box to complete each of the following sentences.

causality	depression	objectively	stabilizing	trauma

① The difficulties he faced as a child did not lead to any lasting

_____.

② When he was training, his weight went up and down but now it is

_____.

③ In terms of _____, there was a clear relationship between light and mood.

④ Beyond opinions, if you look at the issue _____, the facts emerge.

⑤ People with _____ cannot always identify why they feel bad.

C. The words *objectively* and *subjectively* have opposite meanings. With a partner, explain their meanings and give an example how each might be used in a sentence.

_____

_____

_____

Before You Read

A. Based on the title of this reading and on what you have read so far, can you predict what the reading will be about?

_____

_____

B. Read this excerpt from Reading 1. Then, with a partner, answer the three questions on the next page.

> We have known for a long time that sleep and circadian function are important for physical health, but we are now beginning to recognize their importance for mental health. Part of the work of our research group is to better understand the mechanisms linking circadian disruption and mental ill-health and to use this new knowledge to develop new treatments for conditions such as major depression and bipolar disorder.

1 Is the first sentence a main idea? Why or why not?

_____

_____

2 When the writers say, "Part of the work of our research group," are they providing evidence or an explanation?

_____

_____

3 What "new treatments" might the research group develop?

_____

_____

C. Take notes while you read. Use what you learned in Focus on Reading (page 54) to identify the main idea or main ideas, as well as the supporting ideas.

SUPPORTING IDEA 1:

Earlier studies didn't properly

account for other lifestyle factors.

_____

_____

MAIN IDEA:

A lack of sleep has a negative impact

on your health.

_____

SUPPORTING IDEA 4:

_____

_____

_____

_____

SUPPORTING IDEA 2:

_____

_____

_____

SUPPORTING IDEA 5:

_____

_____

_____

SUPPORTING IDEA 3:

_____

_____

_____

_____

This Is How Important Sleep Is for Your Mental Health

If you have ever stepped off a long-haul flight or worked night shifts, you probably noticed changes in your mood, concentration, and general well-being. These changes are the result of disturbances to your natural sleep-wake cycle, your "circadian rhythm." And **disruptions** to this cycle can have worse consequences than just feeling a bit
5 moody or distracted. Our latest research shows that it is associated with an increased risk of **depression** and **bipolar disorder**.

Circadian rhythms are variations in biological or behavioural processes that recur on a roughly 24-hour cycle. These rhythms occur in body temperature, **hormone** release, and rest-activity patterns, and are thought to be fundamental to our physical and mental
10 health.

disruptions (n.): negative changes

bipolar disorder (n.): a mental condition that leads to extreme shifts in moods

hormone (n.): body chemicals that affect your mood

Previous studies have investigated the relationship between disruptions to circadian rhythms and mental health, but they have been limited by using only **subjective** (self-report) measures of sleep and activity, and have **typically** used very small samples.

15 Also, many of these earlier studies didn't properly account for other lifestyle **factors** that might explain poor mental health, such as childhood **trauma**.

We addressed these issues in our study, published in *The Lancet Psychiatry*, by using a large sample (over 91,000 participants, drawn

20 from UK Biobank) and by **objectively** measuring participants' activity with wrist-worn activity monitors. We also took a wide range of factors into account that might otherwise explain the state of participants' mental health or **cognitive** function.

typically (adv.): in most cases

We found that disturbances to circadian rhythms—specifically, increased activity during

25 rest hours and/or inactivity during the day—were associated with a greater risk of mood disorders (such as depression and bipolar disorder), worse subjective feelings of well-being, and slower reaction times. These changes couldn't be explained by age, sex, smoking status, alcohol **consumption**, average activity levels, education, body mass index, and childhood trauma.

30 Overall, our findings provide strong support for the idea that a disturbed circadian rhythm is associated with poor mental health and well-being. They also suggest that daily activity levels, which can be cheaply and easily measured using a digital activity tracker, could be used to assess people's risk of developing depression or bipolar disorder.

35 Growing, Global Problem

These findings could have important public health **implications**, as increasing **reliance** on artificial light, particularly at night, is associated with disturbed circadian rhythms. This is because people exposed to high amounts of artificial light at night are less able to **synchronize** their rhythms to natural daylight cycles.

40 It is estimated that almost two-thirds of the world's population will live in cities by the year 2030. This means that most people will be subject to conditions that can worsen circadian disruption and, by extension, **vulnerability** to poor mental and physical health.

vulnerability (n.): a weakness for something

What our new study can't tell us is the direction of **causality**. We don't know whether

45 circadian disruption leads to poorer mental health and well-being, whether mood disorders lead to circadian disruption, or whether both are linked to other shared genetic or environmental factors.

We hope that future, long-term studies, following up on the same people in the UK Biobank, will be able to address the issue of cause and effect in more detail. It will be

50 important to examine, for example, whether objectively measured circadian disruption can predict new **diagnoses** or new episodes of mood disorders. It would also be useful to know whether **stabilizing** circadian rhythms in mood disorder patients leads to improved symptoms and well-being.

diagnoses (n.): identifying illnesses

We have known for a long time that sleep and circadian function are important

55 for physical health, but we are now beginning to recognize their importance for mental health. Part of the work of our research group is to better understand the

mechanisms (n.): the processes that make change

mechanisms linking circadian disruption and mental ill-health and to use this new knowledge to develop new treatments for conditions such as major depression and bipolar disorder.

(625 words)

Smith, D., & Lyall, L. (2018, May 17). This is how important sleep is for your mental health. *World Economic Forum*. Retrieved from https://www.weforum.org/agenda/2018/05/disrupted-sleep-wake-cycle-linked-to-mental-health-problems-new-study

After You Read

D. Read the following phrases and complete each one based on what you understand about Reading 1.

1. Taking long-haul flights or working night shifts can _____.

2. Circadian rhythms recur roughly on a _____.

3. Other lifestyle factors that might explain poor mental health include _____.

4. One thing that can disturb your circadian rhythms is _____.

5. Digital activity trackers can be used to assess risks of _____.

6. People exposed to high amounts of artificial light at night are less able to _____.

7. Overall, circadian rhythm disruptions are likely to increase as more people _____.

8. The direction of causality with circadian rhythms and mental health is _____.

9. One area of future study is whether stabilizing circadian rhythms improves _____.

10. Studies of circadian disruption and mental ill-health aim to _____.

E. In Focus on Critical Thinking (page 55), you explored the idea of valid comparisons. Match each of the following points from Reading 1 with its comparison. With a partner, decide if each is a valid comparison, and discuss why or why not.

POINTS		COMPARISONS
❶ depression	_____	a) holding onto a partially torn rope as you swing from mood to mood
❷ bipolar disorder	_____	b) getting lost in time
❸ hormones	_____	c) a broken piece of you that you struggle to fix

POINTS		COMPARISONS
❹ childhood trauma	_____	d) feeling like you're drowning in problems
❺ circadian disruption	_____	e) a magic potion that changes how you feel

F. Has the article made you think about your own circadian rhythms? When the authors mention artificial light, they likely refer to the habit of looking at phone or video screens before bed. Would the article make you think about changing your behaviours? Why or why not?

_____

_____

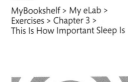

MyBookshelf > My eLab > Exercises > Chapter 3 > This Is How Important Sleep Is

FOCUS ON GRAMMAR

Punctuation

Punctuation helps to clarify your meaning when you write by showing possession, pauses, and emphasis. Punctuation marks go directly after the last letter of a word and are followed by a space. Note that dashes do not have spaces before or after, and apostrophes have a space after if they come at the end of a plural possessive noun.

The **professor's** notebook (one professor's notebook)
The **professors'** notebooks (more than one professor, more than one notebook)
Transportation is changing—particularly in terms of bicycles.

Using Colons and Semicolons

A colon (:) introduces a list of things, an explanation, or a formal quote longer than three lines. A colon in a title indicates that the next words are a subtitle. In book references, a colon separates the place of publication and the name of the publisher.

A semicolon (;) links two complete ideas (independent clauses).

A. Insert the missing colons and semicolons in the following examples.

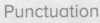

❶ Oscar Wilde tells the story of a man who does not age a painting of him ages instead.

❷ Most of us crave foods that are fatty fries, chips, burgers, cheese, and ice cream.

❸ Taylor, M. R., Simon, E. J., Dickey, J. L., Hogan, K. A., & Reece, J. B. (2018). *Campbell biology Concepts and connections* (9th ed.). Toronto, ON Pearson.

Common Punctuation Errors

It's important to memorize common punctuation rules. Look at your teacher's corrections of your work and see whether any errors are just careless mistakes or examples of not understanding something. There are many things you should not do in terms of punctuation.

• Do not use a comma before *because*.

- Do not use exclamation marks in academic writing. Instead, explain why something is important.
- Do not use the possessive apostrophe with plural years.
- Do not use the possessive apostrophe when you refer to something that belongs to *it*; use *its*. The word *it's* is short for *it is*.
- Do not use contractions (replacing missing letters in a word with an apostrophe) in academic writing; it's not formal enough.

Visit My eLab Documents for additional explanations about punctuation.

MyBookshelf > My eLab > Exercises > Chapter 3 > Grammar Review

B. Correct this paragraph using the punctuation rules above. There is one error in each sentence.

Many university graduates can't find a job locally. A good job is something everyone needs! My mother wanted to work overseas, because she loved to travel. So, during the 1990's, she worked in Africa as a nurse. But she was lonely, and the job soon lost it's appeal for her.

C. While you read, identify examples of different punctuation marks including apostrophes, hyphens, colons, and semicolons.

READING ②   Body Energy: Spending It and Storing It

Calorie with a capital "C" refers to per kilogram; calorie with a lowercase "c" refers to per gram.

The calorie was first identified as a measure of energy in 1819, and ninety-nine years later author Lulu Hunt Peters wrote the first diet book that advocated counting calories in common foods as a way of reducing body weight. Counting calories remains an important part of diets and food labelling, but few people understand exactly what a calorie is and what part it plays in nutrition and fitness.

VOCABULARY BUILD

In the following exercises, explore key words from Reading 2.

A. Fill in the blanks with the correct words to complete the paragraph.

consumption	evolutionary	life-sustaining	selective	~~voluntary~~

There is a debate whether the food choices we make are _____*voluntary*_____ or _____. We all need to do _____ activities like eat and drink. But people tend to be _____ about their food choices as well as how they maintain their fitness. One challenge is the _____ of junk food, as is time spent in front of TVs and computers.

B. Draw an arrow (↓) to indicate where in each sentence the word in parentheses should be placed.

① (estimates) He   usually ↓ the   cost   of   joining   a   fitness   club   before   choosing   one.

2 (portions) The cake was divided into six and shared among the team.

3 (signified) We weren't sure what the language in the letter but it seemed serious.

4 (supplemented) When we were students, each of us our savings with part-time jobs.

5 (survived) Once when we were camping, we barely after a bear destroyed our supplies.

Before You Read

A. Read the first paragraph of the Reading 2. What is the main idea? Discuss it with a partner.

_____

_____

B. Scan the reading to find the word *example*. What example is provided and what does it detail?

_____

_____

C. While you read, take note of the evidence presented to support the writers' main idea.

Body Energy: Spending It and Storing It

continuous (adj.): without interruption

glucose (n.): type of sugar

Your body requires a **continuous** supply of energy just to stay alive—to keep the heart pumping, breathe, and maintain body temperature. Your brain requires a huge amount of energy; its cells burn about 120 grams (g)—about half a cup of **glucose** a day, accounting for about 15 percent of total oxygen **consumption**. Maintaining brain cells
5 and other **life-sustaining** activities uses as much as 75 percent of the energy a person takes in as food during a typical day.

cellular respiration (n.): how your body converts food to energy and waste

Above and beyond the energy you need for body maintenance, **cellular respiration** provides energy for **voluntary** activities. For example, consider the amount of energy it takes to perform some of these activities. The energy units are kilocalories (kcal),
10 the quantity of heat required to raise the temperature of 1 kilogram (kg) of water

by 1° Celsius. (The "Calories" listed on food packages are actually kilocalories, usually **signified** by a capital C.) The values shown do not include the energy the body consumes for its basic life-sustaining activities. Even sleeping or lying quietly requires energy for **metabolism**.

Energy Consumed by Various Activities

ACTIVITY	KCAL CONSUMED PER HOUR BY A **67.5** KG (**150** LB) PERSON*
running (13–14 km/h)	979
dancing (fast)	510
bicycling (16 km/h)	490
swimming (3.2 km/h)	408
walking (6.4 km/h)	341
walking (4.8 km/h)	245
dancing (slow)	204
driving a car	61
sitting (writing)	28

*Not including the kcal needed for body maintenance

15 *Canada's Food Guide* **estimates** that the average adult (ages nineteen to thirty) needs to take in food that provides about 2700 kcal of energy per day for men and about 2100 kcal per day for women. This includes the energy expended in both maintenance and voluntary activity.

…

20 Over-nourishment, consuming more food energy than the body needs for normal metabolism, causes obesity, the excessive accumulation of fat. The World Health Organization now recognizes obesity is a major global health problem. The increased availability of fattening foods and large **portions**, combined with more **sedentary** lifestyles, puts excess weight on bodies. A standard method of determining healthy 25 weight is body mass index (BMI), a ratio of weight to height … A BMI of 25–30 is considered overweight, and above 30 is obese. In Canada, the percentage of obese (very overweight) people has been increasing in recent years, reaching 17.5 percent in 2010. A further 3.1 percent of Canadians are overweight. Weight problems often begin at a young age: about 26 percent of Canadian children and **adolescents** are 30 either overweight or obese.

…

Some of our current struggles with obesity may be a consequence of our **evolutionary** history. Most of us crave foods that are fatty: fries, chips, burgers, cheese, and ice cream. Though fat **hoarding** can be a health **liability** today, it may 35 actually have been advantageous in our evolutionary past. Only in the past few centuries have large numbers of people had access to a reliable supply of high-calorie food. Our **ancestors** on the African **savannah** were hunter-gatherers who

scavenging (v.): searching waste and collecting useful things

famine (n.): time when food is not easily available

gorge (v.): eat greedily

probably **survived** mainly on seeds and other plant products, a diet only occasionally **supplemented** by hunting game or **scavenging** meat from animals killed by other 40 predators. In such a feast and **famine** existence, natural selection may have favoured those individuals with the physiology that induced them to **gorge** on rich, fatty foods on those rare occasions when such treats were available. Individuals with genes promoting the storage of fat during feasts may have been more likely than their thinner peers to survive famines.

45 So perhaps our modern taste for fats and sugars reflect the **selective** advantage it conveyed in our evolutionary history. Although we know it is unhealthy, many of us find it difficult to overcome the ancient survival behaviour of stockpiling for the next famine.

(619 words)

Reece, J. B., Taylor, M. R., Simon, E. J., Dickey, J. L., & Scott, K. G-E. (2015). *Campbell biology: Concepts and connections* (Canadian Edition, pp. 103, 564–565). Toronto: Pearson.

After You Read

D. Comparisons help people to better understand facts and figures. Use the figures in the table in Reading 2 to complete each comparison. For example: running uses 979 calories; bicycling uses 490. The comparison is *almost twice as many*.

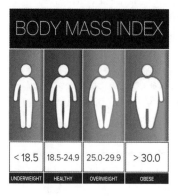

BODY MASS INDEX

< 18.5	18.5-24.9	25.0-29.9	> 30.0
UNDERWEIGHT	HEALTHY	OVERWEIGHT	OBESE

ACTIVITIES		COMPARISONS
❶ Running uses _____ as bicycling.	_____	a) twenty more calories an hour
❷ Running uses _____ as sitting.	_____	b) almost thirty-five times as much energy
❸ Driving a car uses _____ as sitting.	_____	c) almost one hundred calories per hour
❹ Slow dancing uses _____ of swimming.	_____	d) almost twice as many calories
❺ Fast dancing uses _____ than bicycling.	_____	e) half the energy
❻ The difference between fast and slow walking is _____.	_____	f) more than twice as much energy

E. Number these points in the correct order to form a summary of Reading 2.

_____ 33 percent of Canadians and 26 percent of Canadian children and adolescents are overweight or obese

_____ 75 percent of energy used for normal functions

_____ access to a reliable supply of high-calorie food is recent, and many find it difficult to overcome the ancient survival behaviour

___1___ humans require energy for normal functions

_____ adults (aged nineteen to thirty) need 2700 kcal per day for men; 2100 kcal per day for women

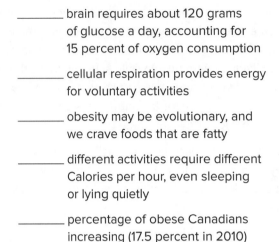

_____ brain requires about 120 grams of glucose a day, accounting for 15 percent of oxygen consumption

_____ cellular respiration provides energy for voluntary activities

_____ obesity may be evolutionary, and we crave foods that are fatty

_____ different activities require different Calories per hour, even sleeping or lying quietly

_____ percentage of obese Canadians increasing (17.5 percent in 2010)

MyBookshelf > My eLab > Exercises > Chapter 3 > Body Energy

MyBookshelf > My eLab > Exercises > Chapter 3 > Body Energy

FOCUS ON WRITING

Comparing and Contrasting in a Paragraph

There are many ways to structure a paragraph. For example, a paragraph can compare two or more things, listing similarities. Or a paragraph can contrast two or more things, explaining their differences. Sometimes a paragraph can do both, compare and contrast.

A. This paragraph from Reading 2 contrasts how we ate in the past with how we eat today. Read the paragraph and then fill in the table with the points of contrast (differences). After, add anything that you think might be compared (similarities).

> Some of our current struggles with obesity may be a consequence of our evolutionary history. Most of us crave foods that are fatty: fries, chips, burgers, cheese, and ice cream. Though fat hoarding can be a health liability today, it may actually have been advantageous in our evolutionary past. Only in the past few centuries have large numbers of people had access to a reliable supply of high-calorie food. Our ancestors on the African savannah were hunter-gatherers who probably survived mainly on seeds and other plant products, a diet only occasionally supplemented by hunting game or scavenging meat from animals killed by other predators.

	IN THE PAST	TODAY
CONTRAST (DIFFERENCES)		
COMPARE (SIMILARITIES)		

B. When you write a compare and contrast paragraph, there are two ways of organizing it. How do these two paragraphs differ in organization? Discuss with a partner.

PARAGRAPH 1

Although modern and prehistoric peoples eat seeds and other plant products, prehistoric people mostly survived on them. Some modern people hunt for food as did prehistoric peoples, but unlike modern people, prehistoric people also scavenged for meat. Fat hoarding is common to both times, but today's reliable supply of high-calorie foods did not exist in prehistoric times.

PARAGRAPH 2

Modern people eat seeds and other plant products. Some modern people hunt for food but generally do not scavenge for meat. Fat hoarding and a reliable supply of high-calorie foods are common today. However, in prehistoric times, people mainly ate seeds and other plant products, hunted extensively and scavenged for meat as well. Prehistoric people hoarded fat to survive because there was no reliable supply of high-calorie foods.

Paragraph 1 uses each point to talk about both modern and prehistoric people; that is called the *point-by-point method*. Paragraph 2 puts ideas about modern people together in one block, then talks about prehistoric people in another block; that is called the *block method*. The words *although*, *however,* and *but* highlight contrasts. Other contrast words include *yet* and *on the other hand*. Comparison words include *similarly, likewise,* and *in the same way*.

C. Your topic sentence for a compare and contrast paragraph should mention both subjects being compared as well as the fact that you are comparing and contrasting some features. Write a compare and contrast topic sentence for one of the above paragraphs.

_____

_____

_____

D. The concluding sentence summarizes the similarities and differences and points out the significance of the comparison or contrast. Which concluding sentence would be the best choice for the two paragraphs?

a) Modern people have little understanding of the diets of prehistoric peoples.

b) Modern and prehistoric diets are mostly similar in terms of foods and ways of cooking.

c) Modern and prehistoric diets are different, and prehistoric diets were probably healthier.

MyBookshelf > My eLab > Exercises > Chapter 3 > Focus on Writing

WARM-UP ASSIGNMENT
Compare and Contrast Two Ways to Keep Fit

Critical thinking includes the ability to consider a topic frommore than one perspective. In this assignment, use what you have learned in Focus on Writing (page 66) to write a paragraph comparing and contrasting two ways to keep fit. You can compare and contrast any two of the following: diets, gym-based exercise routines, or sports.

A. Use a table to sort out the similarities and differences.

WAYS TO KEEP FIT		
COMPARE (SIMILARITIES)		
CONTRAST (DIFFERENCES)		

B. Write a topic sentence that outlines the two things that you are comparing and contrasting. Add information about why the comparison and contrast is important.

C. Write a draft of your paragraph on a separate page. Use either the block method or the point-by-point method. Use compare and contrast words mentioned in Focus on Writing, task B. Refer to the Models Chapter (page 198) to see an example of a compare and contrast paragraph and to learn more about how to write one.

D. Add a concluding sentence that summarizes the similarities and differences and explains the significance. For example: For younger people ... is a better sport than ... because ...

E. Proofread your paragraph. Then, share it with a partner and ask for feedback.

F. Make corrections and write a final copy. You will use this paragraph in the Final Assignment.

> Use feedback from your teacher and classmates on this Warm-Up Assignment to improve your writing.

READING ③   Living Forever, Living Well

In *The Picture of Dorian Gray*, author Oscar Wilde (1854–1900) tells the story of a man who does not age; a painting of him ages instead. Gray is forever young, but his wicked life turns the painting into a horrible image of a man whose years have been wasted. One theme of the book is that living longer is not an advantage if one does not live well. While you cannot expect to find a magic painting to allow you to live forever, you can take steps to ensure that, for the years you do live, you are fit and healthy.

VOCABULARY BUILD

In the following exercises, explore key words from Reading 3.

A. Choose the word or phrase that best completes each sentence. Key words are in bold.

  ①   We started the project too (early / late); it was **premature**.

  ②   Although she (kept / gave away) her car, she decided to **retain** her bicycle.

  ③   Everyone was **reluctant** to begin, so the group (finally / never) started.

  ④   The story was completely **unfounded** because it was based on (gossip / facts).

  ⑤   By **approaches**, he meant the ways that he (involved / avoided) others.

B. Fill in the blanks with the correct words to complete the paragraph.

attributed	concentrations	considerations	factors	similarly

Some approaches to dieting include high _____ of protein.

One of the _____ that influence people's diet choices

is the promise of weight loss that can be _____ solely

to changes in what they eat. _____, some people focus

on only changing their exercise routine, without making changes to

their diets. Among the _____ of how to lose weight

is the choice of the best diet and exercise.

C. VOCABULARY EXTENSION: *Retain* and *reluctant* are examples of words where the root cannot stand on its own without the prefix *re-*, unlike the following words. Define each word and then think about what they all have in common.

  ①   reactivate: _____

  ②   reaffirm: _____

  ③   reappear: _____

  ④   redefine: _____

  ⑤   rediscover: _____

MyBookshelf > My eLab > Exercises > Chapter 3 > Vocabulary Review

Before You Read

A. How well do you live? Contrast healthy and unhealthy factors in terms of your eating and activities.

	HEALTHY FACTORS	UNHEALTHY FACTORS
EATING		
ACTIVITIES		

B. Read this excerpt from Reading 3. Then, work with a partner and rate the importance of the factors that extend a lifespan from 1 (most important) to 7 (least important).

> There is likely a range of considerations that are extending the average lifespan. Britain's Royal Geographical Society suggests the increase can be attributed to a number of factors including "improvements in public health, nutrition, and medicine. Vaccinations and antibiotics greatly reduced deaths in childhood, health and safety in manual workplaces improved, and fewer people smoked."

_____ improvements in public health

_____ improvements in nutrition

_____ improvements in medicine

_____ vaccinations

_____ antibiotics

_____ health and safety in manual workplaces

_____ fewer people smoked

C. While you read, take notes on aspects of each paragraph that are compared or contrasted. For example, the first paragraph contrasts "living forever" with "being old."

Living Forever, Living Well

An old joke observes that everyone wants to live forever, but no one wants to be old. The idea behind the observation is that if you do happen to live for a long time, you want to be fit and in good health.

What is not in question is that people *are* living longer. John Martin Fischer, a University 5 of California Riverside professor, is leading the **Immortality** Project, which is exploring what it would be like to live forever.

immortality (n.): ability to live forever

On the science side, we're living at a time where we've increased our life expectancy dramatically … At the turn of the twentieth century in developed countries the average was about forty-seven years, and at 10 the turn of the twenty-first century it was seventy-six years, and now it's about eighty years. The **trajectory**, he says, is "radically upward" (Moxley, 2014, para. 16).

trajectory (n.): path of an object through the air

There is likely a range of **considerations** that are extending the average lifespan. Britain's Royal Geographical Society (n.d.) suggests the increase can be **attributed** 15 to a number of **factors** including "improvements in public health, nutrition, and medicine. **Vaccinations** and **antibiotics** greatly reduced deaths in childhood, health and safety in manual workplaces improved, and fewer people smoked" (para. 1).

vaccinations (n.): injections to make you immune to a disease

antibiotics (n.): medicines that fight micro-organisms

On the individual level, those who are living longer probably have 20 an awareness of both their diets and their need for fitness. However, many people's eating habits and choice of exercise reject modern insights.

One problem area related to diet has to do with fads that are promoted by food companies and others with little or no scientific 25 support. A recent trend has been to identify certain food items as *superfoods*; among others, the list includes blueberries, chocolate, oily fish, green tea, and wheatgrass. The trouble is that scientific studies, if they are done at all, often focus on **concentrations** that might not be consumed on a daily basis by most people. For example, 30 consuming raw garlic is encouraged because it contains a **nutrient** that is believed to help reduce **cholesterol** and **blood pressure**. However, "you'd have to eat up to twenty-eight cloves a day to match the **doses** used in the lab—something no researcher has yet been brave enough to try" (NHS Choices, 2013, para. 7).

nutrient (n.): chemical or food needed to live and grow

cholesterol (n.): chemical substance found in the blood

blood pressure (n.): force with which the blood travels through the body

doses (n.): quantities of medicine

Part of the problem is that most people are **reluctant** to make changes to their diets 35 and instead consider superfoods like magic pills that will undo the effects of the rest of their bad eating habits. "While the miracle food remains a fantasy, it's pretty well established that obesity and alcohol are the two most common causes of major long-term illness and an increased risk of **premature** death" (NHS Choices, 2013, para. 11).

On the other hand, superstitious criticisms of certain foods, particularly **genetically** 40 **modified organisms** (GMOs), have largely proven to be **unfounded**. One op-ed author writes about the retraction of a biased article published in an important French journal that claimed GMOs caused cancerous tumours.

genetically modified organisms (n.): foods adapted in a lab to improve a quality

Many scientists criticized Seralini's evidence and methods and called for the record to be set straight. One of the major flaws in the study is that Seralini used rats that are highly **susceptible** to tumours, with or without GMOs in their diets, they said. ("Widely Discredited Study," 2013, para. 8)

susceptible (adj.): likely to be influenced or harmed

45

Similarly, in terms of exercise, Palmer (2014) notes that yoga is one of the latest athletic pastimes that is being promoted for health benefits far beyond those common to most forms of exercise.

50 Today, people want to believe that yoga will solve their problems. More than two hundred studies were published about the health benefits of yoga last year. Yoga is supposed to cure everything from low back pain to short **attention span** to several forms of mental illness. (paras. 2–3)

attention span (n.): how long you can focus on something

evidence (n.): factual support

Yoga has some benefits, but many others are exaggerated or completely false. Most 55 of the two hundred studies featured poor methodologies and weak **evidence**.

Despite criticisms of flawed scientific studies of diet and exercise, people seem to only **retain** what they want to hear, particularly if it concerns promises of quick fixes and easy exercise routines. People want to live forever. They do not want to be old. But they will not follow common sense and thoughtful **approaches** that will give them 60 both health and happiness.

(703 words)

References

Moxley, M. (2014, June 23). Living forever, the right way. *Slate*. Retrieved from http://www.slate.com/articles/news_and_politics/uc/2014/06/living_forever_the_right_way.html

NHS Choices. (2013, June 12). *What are super foods?* Retrieved from http://www.nhs.uk/Livewell/superfoods/Pages/what-are-superfoods.aspx

Palmer, B. (2014, March 24). Researchers discredit yoga as medicine. *Herald-Tribune*. Retrieved from health.heraldtribune.com/2014/03/24/researchers-discredit-yoga-medicine/

Royal Geographical Society. (n.d.). *Who wants to live forever? Long life futures*. Retrieved from https://www.rgs.org/schools/teaching-resources/who-wants-to-live-forever/long-life-futures/

Widely discredited study that fuelled fear of genetically modified "Frankenfoods" finally retracted. (2013, November 28). Retrieved from https://nationalpost.com/news/world/widely-discredited-study-that-fuelled-fear-of-genetically-modified-frankenfoods-finally-retracted

After You Read

D. Indicate whether these statements are true or false, according to the text. For those that are false, write the correct answers on a separate page. Check your answers with a partner's.

STATEMENTS	TRUE	FALSE
❶ Overall, life expectancies are decreasing rapidly.	☐	☐
❷ A longer lifespan may be the result of improvements in public health, nutrition, and medicine.	☐	☐
❸ Rejecting modern insights is part of increased health awareness.	☐	☐
❹ Raw garlic has health benefits, but only if you eat twenty-eight cloves a day.	☐	☐
❺ Most people are reluctant to make changes to their diets.	☐	☐
❻ Obesity and alcohol are the two most common causes of major long-term illness.	☐	☐
❼ GMOs have been proven to cause cancerous tumours in mice.	☐	☐
❽ People tend to only retain what they want to hear.	☐	☐

E. Answer these questions. Then, discuss in a group and choose the best answers.

❶ Why do some people avoid vaccinations for themselves and their children?

_____

_____

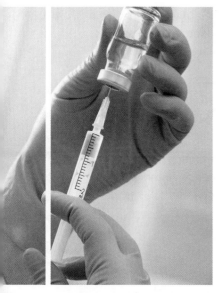

② Why might food companies be among those promoting false or exaggerated food benefit claims?

_____

_____

③ If Seralini made up his evidence of GMOs causing cancer, what might have been his motivation(s)?

_____

_____

④ Why would people ignore health warnings around obesity and alcohol?

_____

_____

⑤ How would your life change if you could live for two hundred years?

_____

_____

MyBookshelf > My eLab > Exercises > Chapter 3 > Living Forever, Living Well

Academic
Survival Skill

Citing Sources and References

Isaac Newton (1643–1727) wrote, "If I have seen farther, it is by standing on the shoulders of giants." He was acknowledging those who went before him. Citing and referencing the work and ideas of others is important in academic writing. When you write, use citations (in the text) and references (at the end of the text) to avoid plagiarism. There are a number of ways to cite and reference sources, and you may have to learn a particular one based on your area of study, but one from the American Psychological Association (APA) is widely used.

APA In-Text Citations

There are slightly different ways to cite text, depending on whether you quote directly, with quotation marks, or you paraphrase, without quotation marks.

Author last name (date) writes, "the quote" (p. 1). Note: If no page number is available, give the paragraph number, e.g., (para. x).

Ghadami (2018) writes, "numerous studies have been conducted to examine the relationship between obstructive sleep apnoea (OSA) and hypertension" (p. 124).

A. Rewrite the following information using APA in-text citation style.

① I read a book by Greg Wells that was written in 2017. It's called _The Ripple Effect_. On page 2, he says, "I was unfit and unhealthy. To anyone on the outside looking at me, I appeared to be successful."

_____

_____

_____

② I read on a website, posted on August 16, 2018, by Sabrina Maddeaux in the *National Post*, that she said, "The explosion of meditation is simple: it works." It was in the fourth paragraph of the website.

_____

_____

APA References

References include details to help you find additional information in books, journals, and websites. Basic information includes the writer or writers' names, the date, titles of sections and books, who published it, and where it was published. Here are some examples:

BOOKS

One author

Author's last name, First Initial(s). (year). *Title of book in italics: And subtitle* [if there is one]. City, province, or state or county [abbreviated]: publisher.

Korn, L. (2018). *The good mood kitchen*. New York: W. W. Norton & Company.

For two authors, use an ampersand (&), comma, in references; no comma between ampersand and second author for in-text citations: Seigel, J., & Bryson, T. P. (2018); (Seigel & Bryson, 2018).

JOURNAL ARTICLES

Authors' last names, First Initial(s). (year). Title of the article [not in italics]. *Name of the Journal, Volume number* [in italics], page numbers.

Cole, E. J. & Barraclough, N. E. (2018, December 1). Timing of mirror system activation when inferring the intentions of others. *Brain Research, 1700,* 109–117.

WEB PAGES

Author's last name, first initial(s). [Organization responsible for the Web page if author is unknown]. (year, Month day [use n.d. if not given]). Title of the article [not in italics]. *Title of the website* [in italics]. Retrieved from [website address]

Wilson, C. (2018, January 19). Hot yoga's high temperature may not have any health benefits. *New Scientist*. Retrieved from https://www.newscientist.com/article/2158929-hot-yogas-high-temperature-may-not-have-any-health-benefits/

B. Rewrite the following information using APA referencing style.

① A book by Oscar Wilde titled *The Picture of Dorian Gray* was published in 1891 in London by Ward Lock & Co.

_____

_____

② A web page article titled "These are the 15 superfoods your kitchen needs this year" was written by Adriana Dickson, and was published on May 11, 2018, on the Popsugar.Fitness website. The address is https://www.popsugar.com/fitness/Best-Superfoods-2018-44256872

_____

_____

_____

Visit My eLab Documents to review APA formats for citing and referencing original content.

FINAL ASSIGNMENT
Write Compare and Contrast Paragraphs

Use what you learned in this chapter to write two (or more) compare and contrast paragraphs with citations and references.

A. Start with your compare and contrast paragraph on two ways to keep fit from the Warm-Up Assignment (page 68). Add to what you wrote; you may include quotes to support your ideas, such as from a journal, a website, or a book. Note: Many journals are available online.

B. For your online search, use key words related to the diets or fitness routines or sports you wrote about, along with compare and contrast words, e.g., "similarities between tennis and ping-pong."

C. If you quote, you need to include citations and references. Refer to Academic Survival Skill to make sure you are using the correct format.

D. Write your compare and contrast paragraph(s). Choose the point-by-point method or the block method. Refer to the Models Chapter (page 198) to see an example of a compare and contrast paragraph and to learn more about how to write one.

E. Proofread your paragraph(s). Pay special attention to punctuation. Then, share with a partner and ask for feedback.

F. Make corrections and write a final copy.

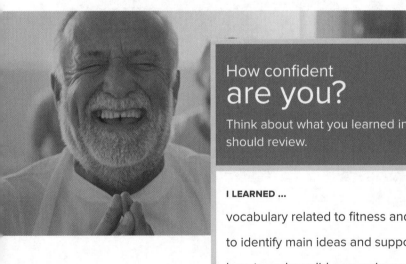

How confident are you?

Think about what you learned in this chapter. Use the table to decide what you should review.

I LEARNED ...	I AM CONFIDENT	I NEED TO REVIEW
vocabulary related to fitness and health;	☐	☐
to identify main ideas and supporting details;	☐	☐
how to make valid comparisons;	☐	☐
punctuation rules;	☐	☐
how to compare and contrast texts;	☐	☐
how to cite and reference sources;	☐	☐
to write compare and contrast paragraphs.	☐	☐

CHAPTER 4
A Happy Life

Although everyone wants to be happy, the concept is difficult to define and different for each person. What is common for almost everyone is the fact that what we *think* will make us happy is often not the case. Lottery winners, for example, are frequently no happier despite their new wealth. Stress can be the enemy of happiness and lead to a situation in which we might feel unable to handle daily problems. Then again, sometimes stress can have positive effects, as when extreme challenges push us to unexpected levels of achievement.

What makes you happy and what causes you stress?

In this chapter,
you will

- learn vocabulary related to happiness and stress;

- construct meaning by making inferences;

- use SQ3R to examine texts;

- review the rules for subject-verb agreement;

- learn how to write formal and informal definitions;

- use mind maps and collocations to develop your vocabulary;

- write short definitions and a definition paragraph.

GEARING UP

A. Look carefully at the pie chart and then answer the questions.

What determines happiness?

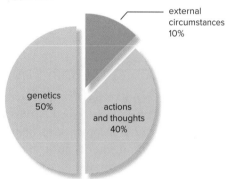

external circumstances 10%

genetics 50%

actions and thoughts 40%

Source: Lyubomirsky, S. (2008). *The how of happiness: A new approach to getting the life you want.* Retrieved from http://connectinghappinessandsuccess.com/overview/happiness-concepts/2-control-your-life/

1 Genetics (inherited characteristics) and other factors can play a role in determining happiness. Describe a family you know where everyone seems happy, or unhappy, and suggest why this might be so.

_____

_____

2 Give three examples of external circumstances that might influence happiness.

_____

_____

3 Give three examples of actions that make you happy.

_____

_____

4 Recalling good memories makes most people happy. Which memories can you recall that make you happy?

_____

_____

B. Discuss the questions and your answers, first with a partner, then in a group.

Below are the key words you will practise in this chapter. Check the words you understand, then underline the words you use. Highlight the words you need to learn.

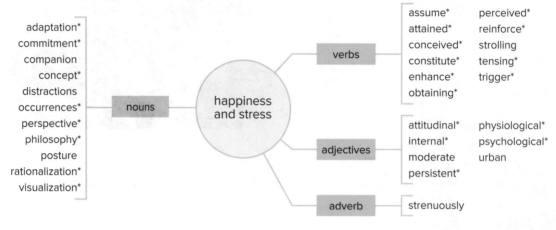

nouns
- adaptation*
- commitment*
- companion
- concept*
- distractions
- occurrences*
- perspective*
- philosophy*
- posture
- rationalization*
- visualization*

happiness and stress

verbs
- assume*
- attained*
- conceived*
- constitute*
- enhance*
- obtaining*
- perceived*
- reinforce*
- strolling
- tensing*
- trigger*

adjectives
- attitudinal*
- internal*
- moderate
- persistent*
- physiological*
- psychological*
- urban

adverb
- strenuously

* Appears on the Academic Word List

FOCUS ON READING

Constructing Meaning by Making Inferences

When you read a word you don't understand, you can infer meaning based on the words that surround it. Constructing meaning from text involves making inferences, or drawing conclusions based on reasoning after considering evidence. When you construct meaning from text, you try to connect prior knowledge and experience with what is in the text to make good guesses.

When you read, you encounter a mix of explicit and implicit details. Explicit details are clearly explained, with no room for doubt or confusion. Implicit details are implied, or suggested, and are not clearly stated.

A. Read this excerpt from Reading 1 and the inferences in blue. Reflect on what you need to understand in order to construct meaning from the text.

The first sentence is an explicit thesis statement; it is clear what the writer is explaining. Supporting details follow.

You can infer from your background knowledge what might be included in *easy to moderate exercise*; this is an implicit detail that you need to figure out.

> Walking can help relieve stress. A study published in the *Annals of Behavioral Medicine* showed that university students who walked and did other <u>easy to moderate exercise</u> regularly had lower stress levels than <u>couch potatoes</u> or those who exercised strenuously. <u>Studies in Japan</u> showed even better effects when walking in a park or forest.

You may not know the name of the journal, but it is an explicit detail.

This phrase is implicit because it is slang, not an exact description. If you don't know the phrase, you must infer what it means.

You can infer that the writer may not have an exact idea of how much research has been done in Japan.

B. Read the sentences. What implicit or explicit meaning can you infer from the underlined sections? Discuss your answers with a partner.

1 Walking gives you time to think, as well as <u>time to get away from stressors</u>.

_____

_____

© **ERPI** • Reproduction prohibited

2 <u>Many people</u> carry stress by tensing their muscles.

_____

_____

3 "All <u>truly great</u> thoughts are conceived while walking," said philosopher Friedrich Nietzsche.

_____

_____

FOCUS ON CRITICAL THINKING

Examining Texts with SQ3R

Experimental psychologist Francis P. Robinson (1906–1983) was working for the military, looking for ways to improve soldiers' learning. He didn't like students' focus on memorization and, in 1946, developed a different approach to get students to *survey*, *question*, *read*, *recite*, and *review new texts*. He called this approach SQ3R. Decades later, it remains an effective way for you to challenge yourself when you read.

!

When you survey a longer text, like a book, estimate how long it will take you to read it.

A. The first step in SQ3R is to *survey*; this means skimming at the text you need to read and quickly trying to understand what it's about. You can do this by checking the title and headings and perhaps reading the topic sentences of some or all of the paragraphs. Survey Reading 1 on page 81 and write a one-sentence summary of what you think it's about. Also reflect on what vocabulary you might need to understand the text.

_____

_____

B. The second step is to *question*. Think of three things you want to learn about this topic, considering why the content is important to you.

QUESTION 1: _____

QUESTION 2: _____

QUESTION 3: _____

C. The third step is to *read* actively. The above questions should help you focus, but you need to take notes as you get new ideas and questions. Think about what you might need to discuss with others. Read the following paragraph from Reading 1 and highlight the parts you need to learn more about.

> **Reconnect with Your Physical Body:** From head to toe, think about how your body is working to carry you along. You may want to practise breathing techniques, and work on your walking form. Feel the sun, breeze, mist, or rain on your skin.

D. The last two steps are *recite* and *review*. To recite, put away your notes and see what you can say about the topic without referring to them. If you're not satisfied that you understand it well enough, go through the first steps again. To review is to change your knowledge into a new form, such as a diagram or flashcards. Close your book and, with a partner, discuss what you know about Reading 1 as well as what you know about SQ3R.

 **READING ①**   **Eleven Ways to Walk Away Stress**

Why walk? Although walking was once the most common way for people to get around, most people today have multiple transportation options, from bicycles and motorcycles to buses and cars. Cars have shaped modern cities, creating vast suburbs of homes that are often far from shops and places of work, making walking impractical. Many people don't necessarily associate walking with improved health and happiness, but the evidence for it is growing.

VOCABULARY BUILD

In the following exercises, explore key words from Reading 1.

A. Match each word to its definition. For words you are not sure of, check the context in the reading for clues. Use a dictionary to check your answers.

WORDS		DEFINITIONS
❶ conceived	_____	a) the position someone holds their body in
❷ internal	_____	b) describing something to do with a city
❸ posture	_____	c) something on the inside
❹ strolling	_____	d) form something, like a plan or idea
❺ urban	_____	e) walking in a relaxed manner

B. Based on the meaning of each word in bold, choose the best phrase to complete each sentence.

   ❶ If you find yourself **tensing** up, _____.

     a) it can feel relaxing

     b) try to tense up further

     c) try stretching to relax

   ❷ Walking **strenuously** may not be relaxing, but _____.

     a) relaxation is often overrated

     b) it can be a good way to get fit

     c) you seldom have a choice

3 Doing things in a **moderate** way means _____.

   a) being open to overdoing it

   b) balancing between extremes

   c) avoiding strong opinions

4 Among the **distractions** many people face is _____.

   a) the rush of city life

   b) country living

   c) long-term sleeping

5 A good definition of a **companion** is _____.

   a) a kind of guard who protects you

   b) someone paid to keep you company

   c) someone you want to spend time with

Before You Read

A. What do you think are the benefits of walking? Discuss with a partner.

_____

B. Read this excerpt from Reading 1. What can you infer from each of the underlined numbered phrases? Inferences might be about the purpose of the text, the assumptions it makes about stress, and the tone of the paragraph. Discuss your answer with your partner.

> **Widen Your Vision:** Stress can give you tunnel vision [1], narrowing your worldview to the immediate problem [2]. Take a walk and observe what is going on around you. What are other people doing? Is a new neighbour moving in? Are co-workers preparing a party? What are they building across the street? Where does this new walking path go? See that there is more to life than your problems [3].

C. The focus of Reading 1 is how to avoid or treat stress. Besides walking, what are three ways to avoid or treat stress?

_____

_____

D. As you read, highlight information that is new and unexpected, and make notes, including questions you might want to discuss with others.

couch potatoes (n.): people who spend too much time watching television

Eleven Ways to Walk Away Stress

Walking can help relieve stress. A study published in the *Annals of Behavioral Medicine* showed that university students who walked and did other easy to **moderate** exercise regularly had lower stress levels than **couch potatoes** or those who exercised **strenuously**. Studies in Japan showed even better effects when walking in a park or
5 forest.

Walking gives you time to think, as well as time to get away from stressors. Getting out of the stressful environment, breathing the air, and feeling your body move is natural stress relief. Other ways walking can relieve stress:

1. **Take a Break:** Put physical and mental distance between you and the stress-causing environment. Get up and take a fifteen-minute walking break.

2. **Loosen Up:** Many people carry stress by **tensing** their muscles. By getting into your correct walking **posture** and form, you unknot those muscles and put them to work. For further relaxation of your shoulder and neck, try the Nordic walking technique with fitness walking poles.

3. **Get Out of Your Head:** Take a break from your **internal** worries. Observe the environment around you; enjoy the trees, flowers, birds, gardens, or sky, or window shop **strolling** past storefronts or in the mall.

4. **Reconnect with Your Physical Body:** From head to toe, think about how your body is working to carry you along. You may want to practise breathing techniques, and work on your walking form. Feel the sun, breeze, mist, or rain on your skin.

convenience food (n.): prepared or fast foods

5. **Burn Calories from Stress Eating:** Many of us turn to comfort food or high-calorie **convenience food** when under stress. Walking is a good way to burn calories without having to change into workout gear. Get up and get moving.

6. **Time to Think:** "All truly great thoughts are **conceived** while walking," said philosopher Friedrich Nietzsche. Take a walk and the blood flow to your brain is increased. It gives you time to consider different aspects of your problems away from the **distractions** of your office or home. Creative ideas and solutions may flow more easily.

7. **Talk and Laugh:** Choose a fun walking **companion** who can distract you from the things causing your stress. Let them entertain you and bring out your happy side. Play on the playgrounds you might pass by. Be silly. Have fun.

8. **Vent:** Choose a walking companion who is willing to listen to what is causing your stress and give you **emotional support** and advice. If you can find a person who is skilled in problem-solving and counselling, this can be productive.

emotional support (n.): help with bad feelings

worldview (n.): perspective on life

9. **Widen Your Vision:** Stress can give you tunnel vision, narrowing your **worldview** to the immediate problem. Take a walk and observe what is going on around you. What are other people doing? Is a new neighbour moving in? Are co-workers preparing a party? What are they building across the street? Where does this new walking path go? See that there is more to life than your problems.

blood pressure (n.): a measure of your circulatory system and heart health

10. **Lower Your Blood Pressure:** Stress can be a factor in high **blood pressure**. Studies have shown that walking can lower your blood pressure and reduce your heart health risk.

11. **Walk in a Park for Increased Stress Relief:** Studies found that walking in a natural environment had greater effects for stress relief than walking in an **urban** setting.

(636 words)

Bumgardner, W. (2018, June 17). 11 ways to walk away stress. *Verywellfit*. Retrieved from https://www.verywellfit.com/walking-for-your-mind-and-spirit-3432871

After You Read

E. Review Reading 1, and use what you learned in Focus on Reading (page 78) to identify inferences for each of the points that the writer makes. After, compare your inferences in a group and choose the best ones.

POINTS	INFERENCES
1 TAKE A BREAK	*The writer assumes most people spend time in stress-causing environments.*
2 LOOSEN UP	
3 GET OUT OF YOUR HEAD	
4 RECONNECT WITH YOUR PHYSICAL BODY	
5 BURN CALORIES FROM STRESS EATING	
6 TIME TO THINK	
7 TALK AND LAUGH	
8 VENT	
9 WIDEN YOUR VISION	
10 LOWER YOUR BLOOD PRESSURE	
11 WALK IN A PARK FOR INCREASED STRESS RELIEF	

F. Complete each sentence with the best choice.

1 The explicit mention of a scientific journal is probably meant to _____.

   a) suggest the other points are scientific

   b) show that the article will be published

   c) indicate that the rest is just opinion

2 An implicit idea in the fifteen-minute walking break is that _____.

   a) you shouldn't overdo your breaks

   b) it can be done before bed

   c) stress can be handled quickly

③ Implicit in the idea of feeling "the sun, breeze, mist, or rain on your skin" is _____.

    a) you should avoid other weather, such as snow

    b) opening a window can relieve stress

    c) experiencing any weather can relieve stress

④ Implicit in the idea that you should burn calories after stress eating is _____.

    a) that stress eating is normal

    b) eating is not something you avoid

    c) that stress eating is necessary

⑤ Implicit in the idea of venting to a companion is the idea that _____.

    a) your boss would make an ideal companion

    b) your problems can be solved with advice

    c) you need to explain that your venting is secret

⑥ The implicit idea behind walking in a natural environment is that _____.

    a) even a hostile desert would work well

    b) you need to be far from other people

    c) the environment is safe and comforting

MyBookshelf > My eLab > Exercises > Chapter 4 > Eleven Ways to Walk Away Stress

G. Work with a partner and use what you learned in Focus in Critical Thinking (page 79) to recite and review what you learned about Reading 1.

FOCUS ON GRAMMAR

Subject-Verb Agreement

In any text, every verb has to agree in number and person with its subject. This means that you need to make sure that the verb form matches the subject you are writing about. In general, if the subject is singular (one person, place, or thing, except for "I" or "you"), the verb must be singular. If the subject is plural (more than one person, place, or thing), the verb must be plural.

Jasper **works** at the university.	Many people **work** at the university.
The university **needs** a new library.	Libraries **need** books.
The government **is** contributing money.	Students **are** contributing books.

RULES	EXAMPLES
SUBJECTS JOINED BY *OR* OR *NOR* When a singular subject is connected to a plural subject by *or*, *nor*, *either*, or *neither*, use the verb form for the subject that is nearest to the verb.	Either Helen or her friends **were** helpful. Neither her friends nor Helen **was** unhappy.
COLLECTIVE NOUNS Collective or group nouns (e.g., team, committee, government) take a singular verb when the subject is the group as a whole and take a plural verb when referring to individual members.	The team (it) **has** won the medal. The team (they) **have** worked hard.
INDEFINITE PRONOUNS Singular verbs agree with indefinite pronouns: *anybody, anyone, anything, each, either, everybody, everyone, everything, much, nobody, no one, nothing, one, somebody, someone,* and *something.* The indefinite pronouns *all, any, half, more, most, none,* and *some* may refer to something singular or plural elsewhere in the sentence.	All visualization techniques **are** helpful. (*Techniques* is plural, so the verb is plural.) All visualization **is** helpful. (*Visualization* is singular, so the verb is singular.)

Highlight the verb in parentheses that best completes each quote.

Use what you learned about subject-verb agreement when you write assignments.

1. "A man should look for what (is / are), and not for what he thinks should be." —Albert Einstein

2. "If you (hasn't / haven't) forgiven yourself something, how can you forgive others?" —Dolores Huerta

3. "Happiness (make / makes) up in height for what it lacks in length." —Robert Frost

4. "He who has health has hope, and he who has hope (has / have) everything." —Arabian proverb

5. "In spite of everything I still (believe / believes) that people are really good at heart." —Anne Frank

6. "Each has his past shut in him like the leaves of a book known to him by heart and his friends can only (read / reads) the title." —Virginia Woolf

7. "Suffering usually relates to wanting things to be different from the way they (is / are)." —Allan Lokos

8. "The ability to be in the present moment (is / are) a major component of mental wellness." —Abraham Maslow

MyBookshelf > My eLab > Exercises > Chapter 4 > Grammar Review

READING 2 Take Control of Stress

When you think about stress, you might think only about its negative effects, but stress can have positive effects as well. Managing the effects of stress in a positive way makes you feel good. But for some people who experience only the negative effects of stress, there can be a loss of alertness and motivation.

VOCABULARY BUILD

In the following exercises, explore key words from Reading 2.

A. Fill in the blanks with the correct words to complete the sentences.

| adaptation | enhance | persistent |
| physiological | | trigger |

1. Failure to succeed on a test could

   _____ unhappiness.

2. Seatbelts were a/an _____ to the design of cars to improve safety.

3. Our class decided to _____ our fitness by riding bicycles to school every day.

4. The difficulty wasn't in his mind but rather

   something that was _____.

5. Her stress didn't just happen once in a while;

   it was a _____ problem.

B. Choose the phrase that best completes each sentence. Key words are in bold.

1 Looking through several **occurrences** of stressful times, she found that _____.

   a) negative stress made her happy

   b) overwork was a common factor

   c) she looked forward to them

2 Looking for another **perspective** on his problem, he _____.

   a) decided to consult a doctor

   b) stopped reading magazines

   c) refused advice from friends

3 The **psychological** problems they encountered were _____.

   a) nothing that they really cared about

   b) encouraged by medical professionals

   c) treated in sessions with a counsellor

4 A period of **visualization** helped the team _____.

   a) imagine how they could solve the problems

   b) see the images that were displayed on TV

   c) forget about everything they were seeing

5 It wasn't obvious at first, but then they **perceived** _____.

   a) almost nothing in particular

   b) what they'd seen all along

   c) a small light in the darkness

C. VOCABULARY EXTENSION: *Physiological* and *psychological* are adjectives that relate to *physiology* (the study of biological processes) and *psychology* (the study of the mind). Write the adjective that relates to the following subjects. Use a dictionary if needed.

THE STUDY OF ...	ADJECTIVES
1 law	*legal*
2 geography	
3 history	

THE STUDY OF ...	ADJECTIVES
4 economics	
5 agriculture	
6 art	

Before You Read

A. Reading 2 suggests a number of ways to manage stress. Rate them in terms of what you think would be the most (1) and least (7) helpful. Discuss your answers with a partner.

_____ learn relaxation techniques   _____ visualization

_____ set realistic goals   _____ maintain a healthy lifestyle

_____ exercise   _____ talk about it

_____ enjoy yourself

B. While you read, use what you learned in Focus on Critical Thinking (page 79) to survey the article, writing questions and notes.

Take Control of Stress

Stress is a fact of life. No matter how much we might long for a stress-free existence, the fact is, stress is actually necessary. It's how we respond to stress that can negatively affect our lives.

Stress is defined as any change that we have to adapt to. This includes difficult life
5 events (bereavement, illness) and positive ones. Getting a new job or going on vacation are certainly **perceived** to be happy **occurrences**, but they, too, are changes, also known as stress, that require some **adaptation**.

Learning to effectively cope with stress can ease our bodies and our minds. Meditation and other
10 relaxation methods, exercise, and **visualization** are all helpful techniques for reducing the negative impact of stress.

Stress can be beneficial—in **moderation**. That's because short episodes of stress **trigger** chemicals
15 that improve memory, increase energy levels, and **enhance** alertness and productivity. But chronic stress has debilitating effects on our overall health. Physically, it can contribute to **migraines**, **ulcers**, muscle tension, and fatigue. Canadian researchers
20 found that chronic stress more than doubled the risk of heart attacks.

moderation (n.): avoidance of excess or extremes

migraines (n.): severe throbbing headaches

ulcers (n.): open sores that will not heal

irritability (n.): state of being upset at things

episode (n.): event occurring as part of a sequence

stressor (n.): something that causes unease

Persistent stress also affects us emotionally and intellectually, and can cause the following:

- decreased concentration and memory
25 - confusion
- loss of sense of humour
- anxiety
- anger
- **irritability**
30 - fear

The link between stress and mental illness has yet to be fully understood, but it is known that stress can negatively affect an **episode** of mental illness.

Managing Stress

First, it's important to recognize the source(s) of your stress. Events such as the death
35 of a loved one, starting a new job, or moving house are certainly stressful.

However, much of our stress comes from within us. How we interpret things—a conversation, a performance review, even a look—determines whether something becomes a **stressor**. Negative self-talk, where we focus on self-criticism and pessimistic over-analysis can turn an innocent remark into a major source of stress.

originates (v.): begins from

40 Understanding where your stress **originates** can help you decide on a course of action. External stressors, like bereavement or career changes, can be managed over time and with the support of family and friends. Internal stressors, caused by our own negative interpretation, require changes in attitude and behaviour.

The goal of managing stress is to cue the "relaxation response." This is the 45 **physiological** and **psychological** calming process our body goes through when we perceive that the danger, or stressful event, has passed.

Here are some tips for triggering the relaxation response:

- Learn relaxation techniques. Practising meditation or breathing awareness every day can relieve chronic stress and **realign** your outlook in a more positive way. 50 Good breathing habits alone can improve both your psychological and physical well-being.

- Set realistic goals. Learning to say no is essential for some people. Assess your schedule and identify tasks or activities that you can or should let go. Don't automatically volunteer to do something until 55 you've considered whether it is **feasible** and healthy for you to do so.

- Exercise. You don't have to train for a marathon, but regular, moderate exercise helps ease tension, improves sleep and self-esteem. Making exercise a habit is key.

- Enjoy yourself. Taking the time for a favourite hobby is a great way 60 of connecting with and nurturing your creative self.

- Visualization. Athletes achieve results by picturing themselves crossing the finish line first. Use the same technique to practise "seeing" yourself succeed in whatever situation is uppermost in your mind.

65 - Maintain a healthy lifestyle. A good diet is often the first thing to go when we're feeling stressed. Making a meal instead of buying one ready-made may seem like a challenge, but it will be probably cheaper and certainly better for you and the simple action of doing something good for yourself can soothe stressful feelings.

70 - Talk about it. Sharing your troubles with a friend may help you to put things in **perspective** and to feel that you're not alone. You may also learn some other ways to manage stress effectively.

(664 words)

Canadian Mental Health Association. (2014). Benefits of good mental health. Retrieved from http://calgary.cmha.ca/mental_health/benefits-of-good-mental-health/#.U_JlbsVdWSo

After You Read

C. Fill in the blanks with words from the reading to complete the sentences.

1 How we respond to stress can _____ affect our lives.

2 Meditation and other _____ methods help reduce stress.

3 Short episodes of stress _____ chemicals that improve memory.

4. Chronic stress has _____ effects on our overall health.

5. Stress can negatively affect a/an _____ of mental illness.

6. How we interpret things determines whether something becomes a/an

   _____.

7. External stressors can be managed with others' _____.

8. Internal stressors require changes in _____ and behaviour.

9. The relaxation response happens after a/an _____ event has passed.

D. Based on your understanding of the text, what can you infer about the writer's attitude? Choose the best answer.

☐ The writer thinks that stress is not a big problem and that people would not have it if they would just learn a few simple stress-management techniques.

☐ Although the writer thinks that there are many causes for stress, the suggestion is that the causes can be treated with one or more techniques.

☐ The writer's view of stress is that it is like a serious disease and that most people probably won't be able to take care of it themselves, even with the suggested techniques.

E. Now that you have read the article, which stress-management techniques would work for you? Which techniques would not work for you? Discuss with your partner.

MyBookshelf > My eLab >
Exercises > Chapter 4 >
Take Control of Stress

FOCUS ON
WRITING

Writing Definitions

Academic writing is often about introducing new ideas. Sometimes you have to explain a term or concept your readers may not be familiar with. In such cases, you can write an informal definition or a formal definition to ensure that your message is clear and that your reader will better understand the term or concept. This is particularly important when a word or phrase has more than one meaning. For example, *edge*, as a noun, can mean "an advantage, a sharp side, or an outside limit." As a verb, *edge* can mean "to move gradually and carefully." If the meaning of the term or concept is not clear through context, then you should define it.

FOR INFORMAL DEFINITIONS, USE ...	EXAMPLE
a synonym, e.g., for the word *danger*	This is the physiological and psychological calming process our body goes through when we perceive that the danger, **or stressful event**, has passed.
one or more examples, in commas or parentheses	This includes difficult life events **(bereavement, illness)** and positive ones.
words and phrases such as *defined as* or *relates to* or *can be explained as*	Stress is **defined as** any change that we have to adapt to.
a second sentence, e.g., when defining the term *relaxation response*	The goal of managing stress is to cue the "relaxation response." **This is the physiological and psychological calming process our body goes through when we perceive that the danger, or stressful event, has passed.**

FOR FORMAL DEFINITIONS, USE ...	EXAMPLE
the term with an explanation of what it is not before explaining what it is	**Stress** is **not always a problem**; it can be **the motivator** that provides a boost of energy.
the term being defined	stress
the part of speech	noun
the class: an explanation of how it fits with similar terms	state of emotional strain
an explanation of what makes the term different from others in its class	that makes one feel overwhelmed

Note: Make sure your class and explanation words are in simple, easy-to-understand English. Don't repeat a form of the term in the explanation (e.g., **Relax**ed means the feeling of **relax**ing).

A. Write informal definitions for the terms in bold. Set the definition off with commas or parentheses as needed.

1 Learning to effectively **cope** (synonym) _____ with stress can ease our bodies and our minds.

2 **Persistent stress** (example) _____ affects us emotionally and intellectually.

3 Physically, stress can contribute to migraines, ulcers, muscle tension,

and **fatigue** (synonym) _____.

B. Write formal definitions for these terms. Include the class and an explanation, and highlight the class in each one. Use a dictionary if necessary.

1 anxiety: _____

_____

2 performance review: _____

_____

3 healthy lifestyle: _____

_____

MyBookshelf > My eLab > Exercises > Chapter 4 > Focus on Writing

WARM-UP ASSIGNMENT
Write Short Definitions

Write a paragraph with three or more strategies that people can use to reduce stress.

A. For each strategy, include brief informal definitions. Use the techniques and example words or phrases in Focus on Writing if you need help. For example:

Most people want to have a good quality of life, **as defined** in part by a healthy diet and enough exercise.

B. Add supporting details in the form of examples and explanations. Each detail may have its own informal definition: A healthy diet **(a balanced mix of vegetables and fruit, milk and alternatives, grains, meat and alternatives)** helps reduce cardiovascular disease, **problems with the heart and blood vessels.**

C. Write your paragraph. Refer to the Models Chapter (page 200) to see an example of a definition and to learn more about how to write one.

D. Share your paragraph with a partner. Use this checklist to assess each other's writing and then revise based on your partner's comments.

My partner did the following:

☐ spelled each word correctly

☐ avoided bland words by choosing more interesting ones

☐ included sentences that flow smoothly from point to point

☐ ensured subjects and verbs agree

☐ used present and past verb tenses correctly

☐ added correct punctuation

☐ understood the assignment and met all the criteria

Use feedback from your teacher and classmates on this Warm-Up Assignment to improve your writing.

READING ③   Defining Happiness

When physicist Stephen Hawking (1942–2018) was twenty-one, he was diagnosed with the disease that left him paralyzed, unable to walk. However, he considered himself happy and felt he was more fortunate than many others. This is in part because he was able to continue his work and write best-selling books. His achievements in mathematics and astronomy have been recognized internationally.

VOCABULARY BUILD

In the following exercises, explore key words from Reading 3.

A. Highlight the word that has the closest meaning to each word in bold.

❶ They wanted her to stay at the company, but she wouldn't make a **commitment**.

   a) break   b) offer   c) promise

❷ To **reinforce** the rule, he made signs and posted them throughout the school.

   a) ignore   b) emphasize   c) weaken

❸ They used a/an **attitudinal** survey to find out what the group preferred.

   a) informal   b) opinion   c) formal

❹ They found a/an **rationalization** for happiness based on five hundred people's best memories.

   a) explanation   b) dismiss   c) encourage

❺ He **assumes** that money can buy happiness.

   a) believes   b) remembers   c) explains

B. Fill in the blanks with the correct words to complete the paragraph.

| attained | concept | constitutes | obtaining | philosophy |

When we do not understand something, we often look at

_____ as a way of exploring a/an _____ like

happiness. We look at people who have _____ happiness as

well as others, whose attempts at _____ happiness have

failed. But we often find that what _____ happiness for one

person many not be the same as for someone else.

Before You Read

A. The approval of others was probably an important part of Stephen Hawking's happiness. Write your definition of happiness.

_____

_____

_____

B. Read this excerpt from Reading 3, which raises and answers a question related to happiness. Based on the excerpt, what can you infer about happiness levels in your country compared to other countries? Discuss with a partner.

> Another question is whether wealthier people are happier than poorer people. Diener (2000) notes that some countries are better able to meet people's basic needs—such as for food, clean water, and health—and this leads to greater happiness. But beyond satisfying basic needs, more wealth does not seem to translate to greater happiness.

C. Reading 3 gives definitions of happiness. While you read, highlight them and use what you learned about SQ3R in Focus on Critical Thinking (page 79) to ask and answer questions as you take notes.

Defining Happiness

When Helen Keller (1880–1968) was nineteen months old, a brief illness made her both deaf and blind. Cut off from the world, she struggled to communicate her most basic needs (Keller, 1905). With such **limitations**, how could Keller ever be expected to find happiness?

5 Because everyone **assumes** happiness is a personal **concept**, making it difficult to define. Many people throughout history have tried. Greek scientist and philosopher Aristotle (384–322 BCE) wrote, "Happiness depends upon ourselves," which is not a definition but an observation that individuals are responsible for their own happiness. Roman statesman and philosopher Lucius Seneca (4 BCE–AD 65) wrote of a particular 10 quality of happiness, saying, "True happiness is to enjoy the present, without **anxious** dependence upon the future." Seneca's interpretation centres on the idea that you are happy when you have **attained** freedom from worry, but it, too, fails to define

MyBookshelf > My eLab > Exercises > Chapter 4 > Vocabulary Review

limitations (n.): lack of abilities

anxious (adj.): uneasy or nervous

happiness. Indian statesman Mahatma Gandhi (1869–1948) came closer with
15 the idea that happiness has a quality of being true to yourself: "Happiness is when what you think, what you say, and what you do are in **harmony**."

Is there a scientific basis for happiness?
20 Researcher Sonja Lyubomirsky (2014) suggests happiness is a matter of perspective: "… truly happy individuals **construe** life events and daily situations in ways that seem to maintain their
25 happiness, while unhappy individuals construe experiences in ways that seem to **reinforce** unhappiness" (para. 2).

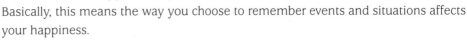
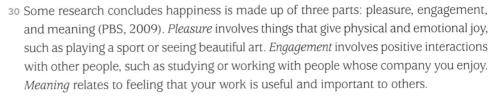

Basically, this means the way you choose to remember events and situations affects your happiness.

30 Some research concludes happiness is made up of three parts: pleasure, engagement, and meaning (PBS, 2009). *Pleasure* involves things that give physical and emotional joy, such as playing a sport or seeing beautiful art. *Engagement* involves positive interactions with other people, such as studying or working with people whose company you enjoy. *Meaning* relates to feeling that your work is useful and important to others.

35 Even with scientific **rationalization**, questions remain. For example, are younger people happier than older people? In fact, the opposite seems to be true. This may be because younger people tend to experience higher levels of negative emotions, such as anxiety and anger. The young also have less control over their lives because they lack both independence and the ability to make many of their own decisions.

40 Another question is whether wealthier people are happier than poorer people. Diener (2000) notes that some countries are better able to meet people's basic needs—such as for food, clean water, and health—and this leads to greater happiness. But beyond satisfying basic personal needs, more wealth does not seem to translate to greater happiness.

45 Perhaps the most important question is whether you can change how happy you are. Studies of identical twins (De Neve, Christakis, Fowler, & Frey, 2012) suggest that genetics forms about half of your happiness level. Beyond this, your quality of life **constitutes** about 10 percent of your happiness. That means about 40 percent of your happiness is determined by your choices and actions.

50 Helen Keller, despite the severe disabilities that left her unable to hear or see, was reportedly an extremely happy person. Why? Lyubomirsky, Sheldon, and Schkade (2005) note that aspects of happiness are partly "… determined by global **attitudinal** or meaning-based factors. Thus, a person who 'suffers for a cause' might still feel very happy because her suffering demonstrates her **commitment** to, and also perhaps
55 moves her closer to **obtaining**, an important life-goal" (p. 25).

From this explanation we can see that one way you can make yourself happier is to set goals. Keller had a definition of happiness in keeping with this idea. She thought most people didn't understand true happiness and contrasted the idea of **self-gratification**

fidelity (n.): faithfulness to someone or something

with **fidelity** to a worthwhile purpose. She felt
60 happiness did not come from simply trying to satisfy your own desires but rather by contributing your time and skills to improve the world in some way (Keller, 1905).

How was Keller's **philosophy** reflected in her own
65 life? When she was seven years old, Keller was fortunate to meet a specially trained teacher, Anne Sullivan (1866–1936), who introduced Keller to the idea of letters spelled out in the palm of her hand. This allowed Keller to better communicate
70 and learn Braille, a **tactile** writing system for the

tactile (adj.): connected with the sense of touch

blind. Despite her limitations, Keller went on to learn to speak and sing, to write twelve books, and to give lectures around the world, inspiring millions of people.

Even if you are unable to achieve a goal that makes the world better in some small way, simply trying will likely give your life meaning and, at the same time, happiness.

(767 words)

References

De Neve, J-E., Christakis, N. A., Fowler, J. H., & Frey, B. S. (2012). *Genes, economics, and happiness* (CESifo Working Paper Series No. 2946). Retrieved from SSRN: http://ssrn.com/abstract=1553633

Diener, E. (2000). Subjective well-being: The science of happiness and a proposal for a national index. *American Psychologist, 55*(1), 34–43.

Keller, H. (1905). *The story of my life.* New York, NY: Doubleday, Page & Company.

Lyubomirsky, S. (2014). *Sonja Lyubomirsky* [personal webpage]. Retrieved from http://sonjalyubomirsky.com/

Lyubomirsky, S., Sheldon, K. M., & Schkade, D. (2005). Pursuing happiness: The architecture of sustainable change. *Review of General Psychology, 9*(2), 111–131.

PBS. (2009). What is happiness? *This Emotional Life, PBS.* Retrieved from http://www.pbs.org/thisemotionallife/topic/happiness/what-happiness

After You Read

D. Number these sentences in the correct order to form a summary of Reading 3.

_____1_____ Helen Keller's deafness and blindness cut her off from the world.

_____ About 40 percent of your happiness is determined by your choices and actions.

_____ Happiness includes elements of depending on yourself, being responsible for your own happiness, and enjoying the present without worry.

_____ Happiness is based on pursuing an important life goal.

_____ Happiness is made up of pleasure, engagement, and meaning.

_____ Lyubomirsky suggests happiness is a matter of perspective based on how you choose to remember events and situations.

_____ Wealthier people are not happier than poorer people who have had their basic needs met.

_____ Mahatma Gandhi thought happiness was when what you think, what you say, and what you do are in harmony.

_____ Younger people are not happier than older people.

_____10_____ Happiness comes from contributing time and skills to improve the world.

MyBookshelf > My eLab >
Exercises > Chapter 4 >
Defining Happiness

E. Based on your understanding of Helen Keller's life and her perspective on happiness, what can you infer about her likely agreement with the other writers? Complete the survey and then discuss in a group.

	COMPLETELY AGREE		NEITHER AGREE NOR DISAGREE		COMPLETELY DISAGREE
❶ Happiness depends upon ourselves.	1	2	3	4	5
❷ True happiness is to enjoy the present, without anxious dependence upon the future.	1	2	3	4	5
❸ Happiness is when what you think, what you say, and what you do are in harmony.	1	2	3	4	5
❹ Truly happy individuals construe life events and daily situations in ways that seem to maintain their happiness.	1	2	3	4	5

Academic
Survival Skill

Developing Vocabulary

You will never finish learning new vocabulary. Even if you could memorize a dictionary, new words are being created every day. What you need is a system for learning words that are useful to you and your studies.

Decide which words are useful. The word *stress* is an important concept in this chapter. Not only is it repeated frequently, but several forms of it are used as in collocations. *Collocations* are pairs or groups of words frequently used together. On the other hand, some words or phrases, such as *necrotizing fasciitis*, appear only once: in Reading 1. Unless you are studying medicine, it may not be a useful word to learn.

Keep a computer file or notebook and develop mind maps to show the relationships of key words, parts of speech, and definitions. Add common collocations. Also include other words and phrases you know. For example, *stressed out*, though not in this chapter, is an example of a phrase you can use to build your mind maps as you encounter new vocabulary.

Review your mind maps frequently and build on them. Display them around your home or desk. You can also write key vocabulary on sticky notes to carry with you as portable flash cards.

Find opportunities to use new words. Include them in your writing, in your conversations, and in your communications, such as in assignments and emails.

Write a definition for each of these terms.

While you read, learn the pronunciation of new words. This helps you recognize and reinforce the words when you hear them.

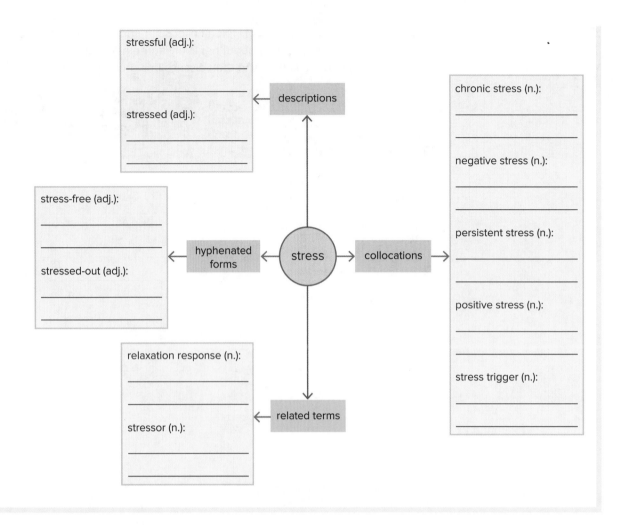

stressful (adj.):

_____

_____

stressed (adj.):

_____

_____

descriptions

chronic stress (n.):

_____

_____

negative stress (n.):

_____

_____

persistent stress (n.):

_____

_____

positive stress (n.):

_____

_____

stress trigger (n.):

_____

_____

stress-free (adj.):

_____

_____

stressed-out (adj.):

_____

_____

hyphenated forms

stress

collocations

relaxation response (n.):

_____

_____

stressor (n.):

_____

_____

related terms

FINAL ASSIGNMENT
Write a Definition Paragraph

Use what you learned in this chapter to write a definition paragraph. A definition paragraph features a topic sentence that is a formal definition. A formal definition includes the term, the class, and a brief explanation. Supporting sentences give examples and explanations.

A. Focus on Grammar (page 84) quotes a number of famous people who write what happiness means to them. Choose one of the quotes for your paragraph.

QUOTE: _____

_____

_____

B. Research the author of your quote to better understand the context of when and why it might have been written.

C. Write your definition of happiness. Explain whether or not the quote you chose supports your definition. Give examples and explanations. Use collocations and vocabulary learned in this chapter.

D. Use this table to organize your ideas.

TOPIC SENTENCE, WITH TERM, CLASS, AND BRIEF EXPLANATION	
SUPPORTING SENTENCE, WITH AN EXAMPLE AND EXPLANATION	
SUPPORTING SENTENCE, WITH AN EXAMPLE AND EXPLANATION	

E. Refer to the Models Chapter (page 201) to see an example of a definition paragraph and to learn more about how to write one.

F. Proofread your paragraph. Check the grammar. Is there subject-verb agreement? Then, share it with a partner and ask for feedback.

G. Make corrections and write a final copy.

How confident
are you?

Think about what you learned in this chapter. Use the table to decide what you should review.

I LEARNED ...	I AM CONFIDENT	I NEED TO REVIEW
vocabulary related to happiness and stress;	☐	☐
to construct meaning through inference;	☐	☐
how to use SQ3R to examine texts;	☐	☐
the rules for subject-verb agreement;	☐	☐
about formal and informal definitions;	☐	☐
how to use mind maps and collocations to develop vocabulary;	☐	☐
how to write short definitions and a definition paragraph.	☐	☐

CHAPTER 5
Thinking Differently

The idiom "march to the beat of a different drummer" is used to describe independent thinking: challenging the normal ways of doing things and looking for new solutions to old problems. This kind of innovative thinking is wrapped up in a willingness to take risks and try something new. Throughout history, some who have thought differently have been celebrated and become wealthy or influential because of their new ideas. However, others have been ignored or punished.

Will you take the risk to think differently and march to the beat of your own drummer?

In this chapter, you will

- learn vocabulary related to innovation;
- evaluate research sources;
- brainstorm solutions;
- review sentence types;
- consider register and tone in formal and informal writing;
- apply critical thinking techniques;
- write formal emails.

GEARING UP

A. Look at the infographic and then answer the questions.

1. Most problems are obvious. Why is it important to define them? Think of an example.

   _____

   _____

2. Why is it better to think of multiple solutions before choosing one?

   _____

   _____

3. What's the difference between choosing a solution and having a plan of action?

   _____

   _____

4. Think of a problem in your life. Would this process work? Why or why not?

   _____

   _____

B. Discuss the questions and your answers, first with a partner, then in a group.

Below are the key words you will practise in this chapter. Check the words you understand, then underline the words you use. Highlight the words you need to learn.

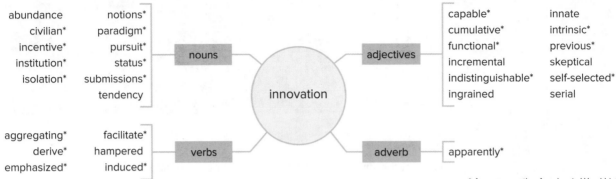

nouns

abundance
civilian*
incentive*
institution*
isolation*

notions*
paradigm*
pursuit*
status*
submissions*
tendency

innovation

adjectives

capable*
cumulative*
functional*
incremental
indistinguishable*
ingrained

innate
intrinsic*
previous*
skeptical
self-selected*
serial

verbs

aggregating*
derive*
emphasized*

facilitate*
hampered
induced*

adverb

apparently*

* Appears on the Academic Word List

FOCUS ON READING

Evaluating Research Sources

Research falls into two main categories: *primary research* (original investigations and experiments) and *secondary research* (reviews of primary research). Primary research may be qualitative or quantitative. Qualitative research is often exploratory and aims to better understand a phenomenon, particularly through interviews and observations that collect information. Quantitative research is usually more focused on a hypothesis—or educated guess—about what might explain a phenomenon. Through measurable observations or an experiment, data is collected and measured statistically. The statistics can then be shown to support or reject the hypothesis.

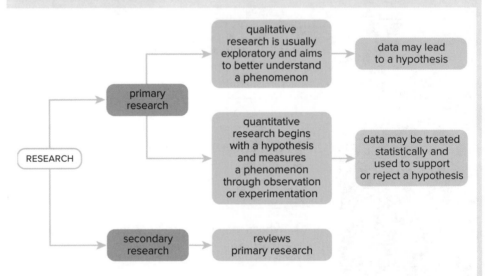

A. Fill in the blanks with the correct words or phrases to complete the sentences.

| hypothesis | primary | qualitative | quantitative | secondary | statistics |

❶ The _____ research led to the creation of a hypothesis.

❷ Her _____ surveys were converted to statistical data.

③ The _____ suggested that the highest paid person's opinion undeservedly influences decisions.

④ Her _____ research reviewed twelve current studies.

⑤ The _____ research resulted in the rejection of the hypothesis.

⑥ Their hypothesis was supported by the _____.

B. The CRAAP Test was developed by Sarah Blakeslee, a librarian at the Meriam Library, California State University, Chico, to help evaluate research sources. Read what each letter stands for and the related questions, and then give an example of a research source you might reject.

CRAAP	QUESTIONS	EXAMPLE OF WHAT TO REJECT
CURRENCY	Is the article reasonably recent?	*Data on university student attitudes published forty years ago.*
RELEVANCY	Does the information match your research needs? Who is the intended audience: academic, professional, or the general public?	
AUTHORITY	Is the information professionally written, edited, and published? Is the author an expert on the topic?	
ACCURACY	Is the information based on facts that can be verified through other sources?	
PURPOSE	What is the purpose of the information? Is it biased in favour of one point of view?	

FOCUS ON CRITICAL THINKING

Brainstorming

A storm is both random and destructive. In similar ways, a *brainstorm* session comes up with new, unexpected ideas and demolishes old ones. Although there are many techniques, brainstorming usually starts by letting group members think of as many ideas as possible, without pausing to criticize each one. Sometimes a wild idea might work best or lead the group's thinking to another better idea.

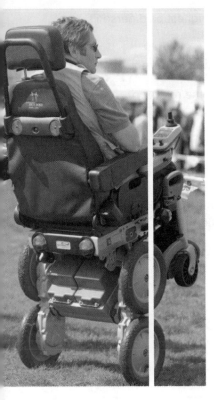

A. Consider this problem: *Although wheelchairs are efficient for flat surfaces, they are impractical in terms of climbing stairs*. Look at the table below. Which are traditional solutions, and which are solutions that are likely to have come from brainstorming? Compare your answers in a group and brainstorm one new idea.

SOLUTIONS		TRADITIONAL	BRAINSTORM
❶	Redesign the wheelchair so that it can climb stairs.	☐	☑
❷	Install small elevators for wheelchair passengers.	☐	☐
❸	Adapt drone technology to add propellers that will fly wheelchairs up a flight of stairs.	☐	☐
❹	Build ramps so wheelchair users can roll up and down them.	☐	☐
❺	Replace the wheels with flexible feet that will climb stairs like a caterpillar.	☐	☐
❻	Ask wheelchair users to use elevators.	☐	☐

B. Work in a small group to brainstorm a problem in your area of study or from among your interests. Follow these steps.

❶ IDENTIFY: Select a problem or issue that does not have an easy solution. For example, it could be a social issue such as homelessness.

❷ CONTRIBUTE: Give group members a chance to think about the problem and think of their own solutions. Give each group member an equal chance to speak without interruption. One way to do this is to ask everyone to write ideas on sticky notes and share them at the same time.

❸ SHARE: Let everyone examine each idea and ask questions to make sure everyone understands each idea; do not criticize.

❹ EVALUATE: Look at each of the solutions and discuss the pros and cons of each one.

 **READING ❶**

Avoiding Innovation

Do you remember slide rules? Probably not. They were invented in 1620, and the last ones were made in the mid-1970s, replaced by pocket calculators.

For a few years, the calculator was an innovation that faced strong opposition. Math teachers comfortable with slide rules argued that students would not have to think to get answers. People will resist a new innovation for a variety of reasons, especially when it threatens their jobs. Fortunately, slide rule companies could not keep things the way they were.

In the following exercises, explore key words from Reading 1.

A. Fill in the blanks with the correct words to complete the sentences.

abundance	hampered	paradigm	previous	tendency

1. A traditional employment _____ is working at the same job for your whole life.

2. The _____ today is for employees to have several jobs to build up experience.

3. The situation is helped by an _____ of employers who are comfortable with short-term contracts.

4. Opportunities to get a new job are no longer _____ by having left a few previous ones.

5. Employers recognize that an applicant's _____ jobs can often provide new insights that will help their companies.

B. Choose the best definition for each word. For words you are not sure of, check the context of the word in Reading 1 for clues. Use a dictionary to check your answers.

1. apparently
   a) in a manner like a mother or father
   b) as far as one knows or can see

2. functional
   a) relating to the way something works
   b) a service provided by a machine

3. incentive
   a) something that motivates or encourages
   b) money lost because of gambling debts

4. institution
   a) a place meant for the confinement of criminal or socially unstable persons
   b) an organization founded for an educational, professional, or social purpose

5. status
   a) an update in the form of an informative message
   b) a social or professional position relative to others

Before You Read

A. Besides having your job threatened, what are three other reasons you might object to a new innovation?

_____

_____

_____

B. Skim the first paragraph of Reading 1 below. The paragraph ends with a question. Without reading the rest of the article, use what you learned in Focus on Critical Thinking (page 101) to brainstorm the question in a group and think of three or more reasons.

_____

_____

C. With a partner, think of an everyday object you both use. What innovation would make it better? Why do you think this innovation has not happened?

_____

_____

Avoiding Innovation

Around 2.6 million years ago, early peoples in the Olduvai Gorge, in what is now Tanzania, began chipping away rocks to make tools and weapons (Leakey, 2009).

Olduvai Gorge

generates (v.): creates

They, and others after them, continued to do so there for 1.1 million years. Although there were small changes, the 5 techniques and the products continued to be much the same. Why did the Olduvai people not innovate?

We live in an age of innovation, where new products and services are created daily. Small innovations drive us to purchase things we do not need. The reason for doing so is 10 often more about **status** than improvements in function, such as new phones that do little more than our **previous** phones.

The Present Is Functional

This provides the first clue as to why the Olduvai people might not have innovated: the stone tools they created were 15 **functional**, and, until the development of metal tools, there was no better alternative for hunting and cutting food. Innovation usually happens because something does not work well enough or **generates** other problems. For example, before cars, horses created enormous amounts of waste on city streets.

side-step (v.): avoid

20 An Abundance of Resources

Related to hunting is another factor that makes people **side-step** innovation: an **abundance** of resources. The Olduvai people lived at a time when the African continent was richly covered with animals and plants for them to eat. However, in places where food has been **scarcer**, hunters needed to develop better tools to find 25 food. In contemporary society, concerns about the car's pollution of the climate are helping to push the development of electric cars.

scarcer (adj.): less available than before

semi-aquatic (adj.): living partly on land and partly in water

HIPPO

acronym (n.): an abbreviation formed from the initial letters of words and pronounced as a word

Another problem for the Olduvai people might have been the existence of their version of HIPPOs—not the **semi-aquatic** animal but the **acronym** version that stands 30 for the "highest paid person's opinion" (DeRose & Tichy, 2013, para. 5). This relates

© **ERPI** • Reproduction prohibited

quash (v.): reject as invalid

elder (n.): a senior person valued for knowledge or wisdom

to the **tendency** of leadership to **quash** the ideas of those who are less powerful or less experienced, even when new ideas are superior. We can imagine an **elder** criticizing the first metal tools and urging everyone to keep making stone ones.

35 Nikola Tesla was confronted with the same problem when he worked with Thomas Edison. Tesla developed the now popular alternating current (AC), while Edison was heavily invested in direct current (DC). Tesla had to leave Edison to make his electrical innovation a reality.

Tradition

sticking to tradition (v.): avoiding new approaches

A variation on the HIPPO is **sticking to tradition**. Even if Olduvai cultures had no 40 clear leaders, the fact that your parents and grandparents chipped stone was a strong argument for you to follow in their footsteps and continue.

bankrupt (n.): a company (or a person) that has lost all its money

The same is seen today in companies that seem unable to change, despite clear signs of rising competition. For example, ten years before it went **bankrupt**, the video rental business Blockbuster turned down an offer to buy Netflix, now among the most 45 successful entertainment companies ever. **Apparently**, Blockbuster executives were too focused on their own model to entertain ideas about the future.

Narrow Job Descriptions

Part of Blockbuster's failure was likely the narrow job definitions of those in the organization. We do not know if the Olduvai people had clear rules about who could 50 or could not chip stone tools and weapons, but looking at other cultures, it seems likely that they did. If so, making some people responsible for some jobs and not others may have **hampered** innovation and discouraged experimentation.

The apprenticeship system, popular for thousands of years and still popular today, involves a novice learning from a master. The system has little **incentive** to fuel 55 innovation as the apprentice is meant to be learning what the master knows, not developing new skills. But today, many innovative companies encourage everyone in the organization to contribute ideas regardless of their position.

An example that goes even farther is the small business accounting start-up, Bench. It has an unusual hiring process that looks beyond traditional accounting students to 60 anyone who might contribute:

> "We're not looking for people who look a certain way or talk a certain way or have a particular background," founder Ian Crosby explains. "We've had philosophy-diploma grads that are way more successful than top-**institution** accounting grads. What we look for a lot more is 65 just attitude and people who are just excited to go build something together." (Wilson, 2018, p. 11)

Maybe that's what changed things for the Olduvai people: a philosopher who came along with a metal tool or perhaps suggested a new **paradigm**: farming instead of hunting.

(742 words)

References

DeRose, C., & Tichy, N. (2013, April 15). What happens when a "HiPPO" runs your company? *Forbes*. Retrieved from https://www.forbes.com/sites/derosetichy/2013/04/15/what-happens-when-a-hippo-runs-your-company/#31b6e10e40cf

Leakey, M. (2009). *Olduvai Gorge*. Cambridge, UK: Cambridge University Press.

Wilson, K. (2018, September 13). Bench on the lookout for talent. *The Georgia Straight, 52*(2644), 11.

After You Read

D. Choose the phrase that best completes each sentence.

1. The reason why many people want new phones is often about _____.
   a) actual needs rather than status
   b) advertising rather than costs
   c) status rather than actual needs

2. Something does not work well enough or creates other problems _____.
   a) is a reason for innovation
   b) makes innovation impossible
   c) can discourage innovation

3. An abundance of resources is likely to make people _____.
   a) ignore opportunities for innovation
   b) use them for innovative practices
   c) embrace opportunities for innovation

4. Car pollution is helping to push the new innovations such as _____.
   a) climate change
   b) greenhouse gas
   c) electric cars

5. The reason that HIPPOs are more likely to have their ideas accepted is that _____.
   a) their ideas are based on years of experience
   b) they have more power in a decision-making process
   c) their value has already been recognized by the company

6. The lesson of Nikola Tesla is that sometimes you have _____.
   a) to forget your own ideas to succeed
   b) to leave your peers to be a success
   c) to fail repeatedly before you can innovate

7. The example of the video rental business Blockbuster shows how _____.
   a) ignoring innovations leads to bad decisions
   b) every business has a natural growth cycle
   c) ignoring bad decisions leads to innovations

8. A way that some organizations discourage innovation is by _____.
   a) allowing too many individuals in a company to share ideas
   b) not sharing new ideas developed outside of a company
   c) only allowing some individuals in a company to share ideas

E. Examine the three references for Reading 1, and use what you learned in Focus on Reading (page 100) to complete the table. Write NEI (not enough information) for ones you cannot answer.

CRAAP QUESTIONS		DEROSE & TICHY	LEAKEY	WILSON
❶	Which is the most current?	☐	☐	☐
❷	Which is the most relevant?	☐	☐	☐
❸	Which is the most authoritative?	☐	☐	☐
❹	Which is the most accurate?	☐	☐	☐
❺	Which is the most biased?	☐	☐	☐

MyBookshelf > My eLab >
Exercises > Chapter 5 >
Avoiding Innovation

F. The article mentions an accounting start-up that hires people with different backgrounds. In a group, brainstorm other types of businesses and discuss how people with other backgrounds would help them innovate.

FOCUS ON GRAMMAR

Sentence Types

A mixture of simple, compound, complex, and compound-complex sentences gives variety to your writing and helps keep readers' attention. To recognize and use different sentence types, it's necessary to understand independent and dependent clauses.

An *independent clause* has a subject and a verb and expresses a complete thought. A *dependent clause* can have both a subject and a verb, but it does not express a complete thought.

SENTENCE TYPES	STRUCTURE	EXAMPLE
SIMPLE	one independent clause	Innovation is common.
COMPOUND	two independent clauses linked by a coordinate conjunction (*for*, *and*, *nor*, *but*, *or*, *yet*, *so*)	Innovation is common **and** is now taught in universities.
COMPLEX	an independent clause plus a dependent clause, linked by a subordinate conjunction (*for example*, *after*, *although*, *because*, *instead of*, *since*, *when*, *until*)	Innovation is popular **because** of its opportunities to improve quality of life.
COMPOUND-COMPLEX	two (or more) independent clauses linked by a coordinate conjunction and at least one dependent clause linked by a subordinate conjunction	We should rethink old problems, **and** we should not be afraid to innovate **before** thinking things are hopeless.

❶ *Use the acronym "fanboys" to remember the coordinate conjunctions: for, and, nor, but, or, yet, so.*

A. Add words, capital letters, and punctuation to these dependent clauses to form complex sentences.

❶ because innovation takes time

Because innovation takes time, teamwork is essential.

_____

2 when a company encourages innovative practices

_____

_____

3 before the popularity of the Internet

_____

_____

4 although some people reject innovations

_____

_____

Use what you learned about sentence types when you write your assignments.

5 since an innovative solution can save money

_____

_____

B. Highlight the word or phrase in parentheses that best completes each sentence.

1 Home refrigerators were only introduced (after / with) they had been used for forty years in industry.

2 Innovations in industry are often adapted for domestic use (when / for example) people see opportunities to make money.

3 We should learn from such examples (although / and) use them as a source of inspiration.

MyBookshelf > My eLab > Exercises > Chapter 5 > Grammar Review

4 Ice boxes were perfectly acceptable (during / until) refrigerators were seen as more convenient.

5 Refrigerator technology may have peaked, (so / when) innovations focus on things like USB-powered fridges and drawer fridges.

READING ❷

The Quirky Secrets of the World's Greatest Innovators

Is there a type of person who becomes an innovator? Do famous innovators have some things in common? These are questions that are increasingly asked as people look to replicate the success of famous innovators. But, in some cases, it might merely be the case of being in the right place at the right time.

In the following exercises, explore key words from Reading 2.

A. Choose the word or phrase that has the closest meaning to each word in bold.

1. **skeptical**   a) certain   b) disbelieving   c) agreeable
2. **facilitate**   a) assist   b) desist   c) consist
3. **serial**   a) granular   b) televised   c) sequential
4. **pursuit**   a) dressed up   b) chase   c) worn-out
5. **aggregating**   a) distributing   b) refreshing   c) combining

B. Choose the phrase that best completes each sentence. Key words are in bold.

1. Although she worked for the military, she was a **civilian**, that is, she _____.
   a) was only involved in combat
   b) was unqualified for her job
   c) did not hold a particular rank

2. It's possible to **derive** many innovative ideas from nature, that is, _____.
   a) be inspired by nature
   b) compete with nature
   c) improve on nature

3. An idea that has been **emphasized** has been _____.
   a) stressed in some way
   b) ignored in some way
   c) given up for good

4. An **incremental** change in a new product is a _____.
   a) big change
   b) profitable change
   c) small change

5. To look at a new idea in **isolation** means to _____.
   a) consider it in context
   b) consider it alone
   c) imagine how it will change

Before You Read

A. Consider the following innovators. What is each one famous for? Compare answers with a partner and look up those you don't know.

1. Marie Curie: _____ *X-ray theories* _____
2. Thomas Edison: _____
3. Albert Einstein: _____
4. Benjamin Franklin: _____
5. Dean Kamen: _____
6. Steve Jobs: _____

Steve Jobs

⑦ Elon Musk: _____

⑧ Nikola Tesla: _____

B. Reading 2 focuses on the qualities of a great innovator. In a group, brainstorm ideas for the qualities that make an innovator great. Which are the most important ones? Why?

C. Lists of the most significant innovations of all time often include the wheel, the nail, the compass, the printing press, and the light bulb. In a small group, have each member choose one of these innovations (or others) and argue why each was the most important innovation.

The Quirky Secrets of the World's Greatest Innovators

Thomas Edison

foibles (n.): minor weaknesses or eccentricities

obsessive (adj.): preoccupied with a particular goal or detail

sacrifice (v.): give up something valuable

unrelenting (adj.): continuously, without stopping

mania (n.): an enthusiastic craze for something

In *Quirky*, NYU Stern professor Melissa Schilling embraces what you might call the "great person" view of innovation. Many recent studies of innovation have focused on the importance of collaboration and social setting, and **emphasized** the ways in which good ideas are
5 typically the product of many minds, rather than one. Schilling looks instead at eight individuals whom she calls "**serial** breakthrough innovators": Benjamin Franklin, Marie Curie, Nikola Tesla, Thomas Edison, Albert Einstein, Dean Kamen, Steve Jobs, and Elon Musk.

The approach Schilling takes with *Quirky* is a variant of the case
10 study method—instead of companies, the cases here are the lives of great inventors. She examines their lives to uncover the common personality traits and **foibles** that helped them see what others did not. Schilling argues that serial breakthrough innovators are different from the rest of us because they're able to come up with ground-
15 breaking innovations over and over again, rather than just once. And their innovations represent dramatic leaps rather than **incremental** improvements.

Great innovators, she argues, tend to be **obsessive** workers who sleep very little and are willing to **sacrifice** almost everything to the **pursuit**
20 of their goals. They're able to do so in part because they have an **unrelenting** drive for achievement and because they **derive** tremendous pleasure from work, which offers them that feeling Mihaly Csikszentmihalyi famously called "flow."

Innovators also have exceptional working memory, and the ability to hold many concepts in their mind at once. This allows them to "search longer paths through
25 the network of associations in their mind," increasing the chances they'll make interesting and unexpected connections between ideas. Schilling also suggests that there may be something concrete about the cultural association between genius and madness. Pointing to the experience of Tesla, who had an extraordinary sensitivity to outside stimuli and would routinely go for long stretches on almost no sleep, she
30 argues that most great innovators have at least a touch of **mania**.

Innovators are also typically blessed (or cursed) with a deep sense of what psychologists call self-efficacy, which is a nice word for what, in other contexts, might be called hubris: the misplaced confidence in one's ability to accomplish whatever

one sets one's mind to. This is crucial because the very nature of breakthrough
35 innovations means that most people will be **skeptical** of their value. Indeed, most
of the people Schilling writes about were, in one sense or another, outsiders in the
fields they helped revolutionize. They were also **idealists**, convinced that they could
change the world. As Schilling puts it, "They are willing to pursue an idea even when
everybody else says it's crazy precisely because they don't need the **affirmation** of
40 others—they believe they are right even if you don't agree." It was that sense of self-
efficacy that allowed Elon Musk to believe he could become the first **civilian** to put
rockets into space, and that allowed Dean Kamen to build a wheelchair that could
climb stairs, even though everyone told him it was impossible.

Part of that willingness to ignore the judgment of others also seems to proceed from
45 what Schilling calls the "marked sense of 'separateness'" that most of her subjects
have felt, which was **manifested** as "a lack of interest in social interaction, a rejection
of rules and norms, and often **isolation** even from family members." This makes it
difficult for innovators to have rich social lives, but also makes it easier for them to
think for themselves.

50 Understanding the characteristics that enabled Einstein to come up with ideas that
others couldn't might help organizations do the same. Encouraging a diversity of
cognitive and social styles and allowing employees to maintain a measure of distance
from one another, rather than insisting on constant connection, will **facilitate**
independent thinking. Letting people come up with ideas and solutions on their own,
55 and then **aggregating** those ideas, is more likely to yield interesting answers than
brainstorming in groups. Casting a wide net when looking for ideas, rather than
talking only to specialists in a field, amplifies the possibilities for unusual approaches.
Finding a way to imbue employees with a real sense of purpose can also be valuable.
An organization doesn't need to find a breakthrough innovator if it can make itself
60 the innovator instead.   (754 words)

Surowiecki, J. (2018, April 9). The quirky secrets of the world's greatest innovators. *strategy+business, 91*. Retrieved from https://www.strategy-business.com/article/The-Quirky-Secrets-of-the-Worlds-Greatest-Innovators?gko=ef650

After You Read

D. Choose the word or phrase that best completes each sentence.

① Rather than collaboration and social setting, the "great person" view of innovation focuses more on _____.
  a) businesses
  b) individuals
  c) groups

② Serial breakthrough innovators are able to come up with _____.
  a) a group of people who can support them
  b) money necessary to fund their projects
  c) important innovations more than once

idealists (n.): people guided more by principles than practicalities

affirmation (n.): proof of something

manifested (v.): became evidence of something

Marie Curie

3 Unlike most people, great innovators get _____.

   a) tremendous pleasure from work

   b) easily distracted by new projects

   c) upset by others not accepting their ideas

4 Thinking of innovative ideas is easier when you _____.

   a) do not need to worry about practicalities

   b) don't have to worry about time

   c) have exceptional working memory

5 There is a common cultural association between _____.

   a) innovators and working people

   b) genius and madness

   c) dreams and inventions

6 Hubris is defined as the _____.

   a) ability to build others' confidence through repeated successes

   b) misplaced confidence in accomplishing whatever you want

   c) first-hand opinions of those around you who you respect

7 Innovators tend to believe _____.

   a) you are wrong even if you agree

   b) agreement does not provide answers

   c) they are right even if you don't agree

8 In terms of rich social lives, innovators are _____.

   a) less likely to have them

   b) secretive about them

   c) more likely to have them

E. The article suggests that letting people come up with ideas and solutions on their own, and then aggregating those ideas, is more likely to yield interesting answers than brainstorming in groups. Why might this be so? Discuss with a partner.

F. The article talks about helping organizations become more innovative by implementing the strategies and conditions common among innovators. Rate the following four strategies in order of importance, with 1 for most important and 4 for least important. Discuss in a group, and convince others of your rankings.

_____ Allow employees to maintain a measure of distance.

_____ Encourage a diversity of cognitive and social styles.

_____ Find ways to give employees a real sense of purpose.

_____ Let non-specialists offer new ideas.

MyBookshelf > My eLab >
Exercises > Chapter 5 >
The Quirky Secrets

FOCUS ON WRITING

Using Register and Tone

When you write, you use different language depending on whom you are writing for and why. For example, the words and sentence structures in a casual email to a friend would be different from what you would use in a scientific article. *Register* is the genre you use and its formality. *Tone* is your attitude, either about what you are writing or the person to whom you are writing.

A. Read the information and consider some of the ways register and tone differ in formal and informal writing. Add examples of your own.

REGISTER AND TONE	IN INFORMAL WRITING	IN FORMAL WRITING
GREETING/ SALUTATION	casual greeting and first name or no name: *Hi Don*, or *Hi,*	*Dear* with title and last name: *Dear Dr. Pratt,*
VOCABULARY	more common words and slang, but avoids professional jargon: *cheap, very, lots of, kneecap, judge* _____ _____	subject-specific words and avoids slang, but may use professional jargon: *inexpensive, more, many, patella, bench* _____ _____
TRANSITION WORDS	simple words: *like, and, so, but, also* _____ _____	complex words: *additionally, as a result, however, in addition, nevertheless* _____ _____
PERSON	first and second person (subjective) more common: *I invented a new app with my friends.* _____ _____	third person (objective) more common: *The team invented a new app.* _____ _____
ACRONYMS, INITIALISMS, AND CONTRACTED FORMS	short forms: *UN, NASA, I'll, won't, don't* _____ _____	full forms: *United Nations, National Aeronautics and Space Administration, I will, will not, do not* _____ _____
SENTENCE STRUCTURE	shortened incomplete sentences and/or simple sentences: *Coming to your office at 4.* _____ _____	complete simple sentences and/or compound and complex sentences: *If you are free, my group will visit your office at 4:00 p.m.* _____ _____

Develop Your Vocabulary: Acronyms like "scuba" are pronounced like words; initialisms like "USA" are pronounced as separate letters. Learn the full forms of popular acronyms and initialisms.

B. Read this email and highlight examples of formal writing that are mentioned in task A. Discuss with a partner.

To:	dr.pratt@tech.uni.edu
Cc:	
Subject:	Advice on an innovation competition

Dear Dr. Pratt,

I am writing to ask if you would be free to speak to two representatives from the Engineering Society (ES). The ES is considering holding an innovation competition and would like your advice on the guidelines. We would also like to invite you to act as judge in the competition.

Please let me know if you would be available, and, if so, would a meeting at your office on Friday at 2:30 p.m. be convenient?

Yours sincerely,

Gabriela García, ES President

MyBookshelf > My eLab > Exercises > Chapter 5 > Focus on Writing

WARM-UP ASSIGNMENT
Write a Formal Email

Write a formal email to your teacher asking for clarification on something in this chapter that interests you.

A. Choose a topic. For example, you might want to know whether a famous living innovator has specific advice for how you can become an innovator in your field. Or you may ask an expert about an innovation idea you have in your field of study or future career.

MY TOPIC: _____

B. Ask your teacher for approval of your choice of topic.

C. Follow the email format you learned in Focus on Writing (page 113), and use the paragraph format for the body of your message. Include a topic sentence that explains the reason you are writing. Ask two questions. Apply proper tone and register.

D. Write your email. Refer to the Models Chapter (page 202) to see another example of a formal email and to learn more about how to write one.

E. Share your email with a partner and ask for feedback.

READING ③ Anyone Can Be an Innovator

What are the skills of an innovator? The ability to think differently is important, as is having a set of skills to help apply new ideas that might come to you. Universities are anxious to find out more about whether innovation can be taught. It signals a change in attitude from innovation being a rarely used eccentric skill, to a skill that most people can use at work and in their daily lives.

| VOCABULARY BUILD | |

In the following exercises, explore key words from Reading 3.

A. Read each bold word in context and write a short definition. Use a dictionary for meanings you cannot guess.

1. Existing theories and previous research on how innovation occurs largely assume that it is an **ingrained** quality of the individual.

   _____

2. Their success was statistically **indistinguishable** from those that were innately drawn to the competition.

   _____

3. Are persuaded innovators less **capable** than those who naturally gravitate to innovative activities?

   _____

4. Innovators in many firms may well depend on their **intrinsic** motivation to succeed in addition to having technical capabilities.

   _____

5. They tested these previously held **notions** by creating a contest for UC San Diego's engineering and computer science students.

   _____

B. Match each key word to its definition.

WORDS		DEFINITIONS
❶ cumulative	_____	a) inborn or natural
❷ induced	_____	b) increasing by addition after addition
❸ innate	_____	c) chosen by the individual participant
❹ self-selected	_____	d) documents for consideration
❺ submissions	_____	e) succeed in getting someone to do something

C. VOCABULARY EXTENSION: Many words have noun, verb, adjective, and adverb forms. Fill in the blanks with the correct form of each one.

NOUN	VERB	ADJECTIVE	ADVERB
submissions			
induction		induced	
		capable	
		innate	
accumulation		cumulative	

MyBookshelf > My eLab > Exercises > Chapter 5 > Vocabulary Review

Before You Read

A. Reading 3 is about an attempt to scientifically answer the question, *Can anyone be an entrepreneur?* Work with a partner to decide how you could create an experiment to test that question.

B. The second paragraph of Reading 3 outlines the approach of the study: creating a contest to collect data. Why might having a contest be a more effective method for finding out information than, for example, studying entrepreneurs in the past?

_____

_____

_____

C. The study subjects were divided between self-selected students (who signed up) and students who did not sign up and were induced (paid to participate). With a partner, think of three reasons why students may not have signed up for the competition, even if they were interested in innovation. While you read, decide whether your reasons would invalidate the study.

1 _____

2 _____

3 _____

Anyone Can Be an Innovator

Innovators aren't born, but they can be made, according to recent research from the University of California San Diego's School of Global Policy and Strategy.

Existing theories and previous research on how innovation occurs largely assume that it is an **ingrained** quality of the individual and that only people with this **innate**
5 ability seek and **attain** jobs that require it. However, economist Joshua S. Graff Zivin and professor of management Elizabeth Lyons tested these previously held **notions** by creating a contest for UC San Diego's engineering and computer science students. The competition, outlined in their National Bureau of Economic Research **working paper**, was designed to answer the question, Are persuaded innovators less **capable**
10 than those who naturally **gravitate** to innovative activities?

attain (v.): achieve something

working paper (n.): a preliminary paper about scientific findings

gravitate (v.): move towards

© ERPI • Reproduction prohibited

116 LEAP 2: Reading and Writing

eligible (adj.): having the right to do or get something

The mobile application contest was advertised through various media on campus and attracted around 100 students. In order to differentiate between **self-selected** innovators and **induced** innovators, a random subset of **eligible** students who did not sign up by the contest deadline were offered a monetary incentive of $100 to participate. In total, 190 students signed up.

Submissions between the two groups were evaluated by technology industry participants who acted as judges for the contest and who had no knowledge of which group the proposals came from. The judges evaluated each application across four categories: **functionality**, user-friendliness, novelty, and potential commercial value.

functionality (n.): the quality of being suited to a purpose

fare (v.): perform in a certain way

Though induced participants were less likely to be drawn from majors that provide the most relevant skills for the competition, such as electrical engineering and computer science, and had lower **cumulative** GPAs, their success was statistically **indistinguishable** from those that were innately drawn to the competition.

Whether innovators can be created, and how they **fare** relative to those who self-select into innovative activities, also has important implications for public and private policy, according to the authors.

"If individuals are being held back by accurate beliefs about their ability to perform, as our results suggest, then efforts to help individuals overcome the psychological barriers that inhibit their participation could potentially enhance innovative output across a wide range of settings," Graff Zivin said. "This shows that psychological barriers, if overcome, could meaningfully contribute to the innovation process."

Contest entries were scored from 1–5 on each category for a total score maximum of 20. The developers of the top three applications were awarded prize money.

impactful (adj.): having a major effect on something

"We selected students at UC San Diego's Jacobs School of Engineering since these students have technical capabilities to produce **impactful** inventions," Lyons said. "In addition, engineers are frequently the targets of interventions to increase innovative activity."

To further explore the psychological factors of innovation, the researchers randomly offered encouragement to subsets of both the induced and self-selected contest participants in order to examine the importance of confidence-building interventions on each sample. While encouragement had no impact on performance on average, and was not differentially important for the induced sample, the authors did find surprising results based on student GPA.

median (adj.): in the middle

Students with above-**median** GPAs performed significantly worse when they received additional encouragement, whereas students with below-median GPAs performed significantly better when they received additional encouragement.

"While our work clearly suggests that innovators can be created through inducement subsidies, whether they will also benefit from confidence-building encouragement of the sort that is standard management practice in many firms may well depend on their **intrinsic** motivation to succeed in addition to having technical capabilities."

Regardless, understanding the conditions under which productivity-enhancing innovation occurs is critical for economic development and can provide novel insights into the rise of new inventions, according to the authors. (586 words)

University of California — San Diego. (2018, April 19). Anyone can be an innovator, research finds: Students given incentives to innovate are just as skilled as the self-motivated. *ScienceDaily*. Retrieved from www.sciencedaily.com/releases/2018/04/180419100151.htm

After You Read

D. Read each statement and indicate whether it is true or false.

STATEMENTS	TRUE	FALSE
❶ The authors of the article believe innovators can be great teachers.	☐	☑
❷ Research on innovation largely assumes it is an innate ability and only people with this ability seek and get jobs that require it.	☐	☐
❸ The research compared a group that was innovative and a group that had to be persuaded to try it.	☐	☐
❹ The contest was advertised through a mobile application.	☐	☐
❺ Technology industry experts were judges for the contest.	☐	☐
❻ The difference between the two groups was statistically significant.	☐	☐
❼ Training people to be innovators has implications for public and private policy.	☐	☐
❽ The study suggests that psychological barriers do not inhibit participation.	☐	☐
❾ Students with above-average marks performed worse with encouragement, while students with below-average marks benefited from encouragement.	☐	☐
❿ Confidence-building encouragement can help people become innovators.	☐	☐

E. Look at the four images in the table and write *high* or *low* for each category. After, discuss your rankings in a group to see if you agree or to understand why you disagree. Use brainstorming techniques to give everyone a chance to share.

CATEGORIES				
❶ FUNCTIONALITY				
❷ USER-FRIENDLINESS				
❸ NOVELTY				
❹ POTENTIAL COMMERCIAL VALUE				

F. Could you be an innovator? Would you want to be? Why or why not? Think of a problem, a product, or a service you might be interested in improving, and share your ideas in a group.

Academic
Survival Skill

Applying Critical Thinking Techniques

Critical thinking means questioning what you read, deciding whether the text contains reliable information and whether it presents a convincing argument. Critical thinking also means deciding if the information in the text is important to you or the task at hand.

A. Apply critical thinking techniques to this paragraph. Then, complete the table by writing examples.

> Understanding the characteristics that enabled Einstein to come up with ideas that others couldn't might help organizations do the same. Encouraging a diversity of cognitive and social styles and allowing employees to maintain a measure of distance from one another, rather than insisting on constant connection, will facilitate independent thinking. Letting people come up with ideas and solutions on their own, and then aggregating those ideas, is more likely to yield interesting answers than brainstorming in groups. Casting a wide net when looking for ideas, rather than talking only to specialists in a field, amplifies the possibilities for unusual approaches. Finding a way to imbue employees with a real sense of purpose can also be valuable. An organization doesn't need to find a breakthrough innovator if it can make itself the innovator instead.

TECHNIQUES	WHAT TO DO	EXAMPLES
CLASSIFY	Identify the type of writing (register). Is it formal or informal? Is it descriptive or persuasive, or a combination of something else?	The writing is *informal and persuasive*.
IDENTIFY BIAS	If the text is persuasive, decide if it is in favour of a particular point of view. If possible, identify how the writer might benefit in some way.	The bias is …
QUESTION THE THESIS	Identify the main argument or arguments. Does the thesis present a new way of examining or explaining something?	The main argument is …
QUESTION SUPPORTING IDEAS	Does the thesis have supporting ideas along with examples and explanations?	One supporting idea is …
QUESTION EVIDENCE	Are there references to support the idea? Is the evidence current and authoritative?	References …
APPLY FINDINGS	Are the findings (conclusions) of the argument meaningful to you? Can you apply them to your existing knowledge or needs (e.g., in writing an essay)?	I (can/can't) apply the information to my existing knowledge or needs.

B. Write the skill you would use to critically evaluate each of these statements.

1 Everyone knows that an asteroid killed the dinosaurs. _____

2 As a bus driver, I know bus drivers should be paid more. _____

3 Callison and Quimby (1984) ask whether tiny dinosaurs were actually fully grown. _____

4 Teachers who are generally happy are also happy on the job. _____

C. Discuss each of the statements in task B with a partner. In terms of thinking critically about the statements, what questions might you have?

FINAL ASSIGNMENT
Write an Email Request for Information

Use what you learned in this chapter to write a formal request for information from one of the authors in the readings.

A. Choose a topic. Review the chapter to find one point of information that you would like to research in greater detail. For example, consider a topic related to an innovation or an innovation technique that could be applied to something of personal interest to you in your field of study or your career.

MY TOPIC: _____

B. Speak with your teacher. Ask for approval of your choice of topic.

C. Using the email format you learned in Focus on Writing (page 113), write your email. Ask three questions. Use the paragraph format for the body of your message. Include a topic sentence that explains the reason you are writing and a closing sentence that summarizes your request. Or you could ask how you might find further information on the topic: books to read, websites to visit, and people to consult.

D. Review Focus on Grammar (page 107) and vary the sentence structure to include at least one example of each sentence type: simple, compound, and complex. Ensure that your email uses proper tone and register (see Focus on Writing, page 113). Refer to the Models Chapter (page 202) to see an example of a formal email and to learn more about how to write one.

E. Proofread your email. Then, share it with a partner and ask for feedback.

F. Make corrections and write a final copy.

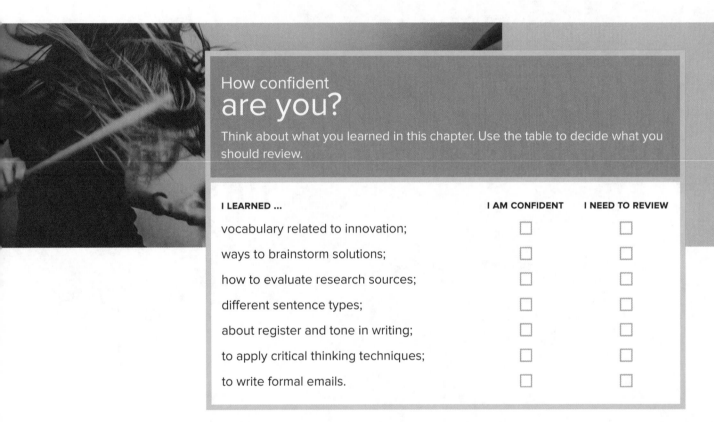

How confident
are you?

Think about what you learned in this chapter. Use the table to decide what you should review.

I LEARNED ...	I AM CONFIDENT	I NEED TO REVIEW
vocabulary related to innovation;	☐	☐
ways to brainstorm solutions;	☐	☐
how to evaluate research sources;	☐	☐
different sentence types;	☐	☐
about register and tone in writing;	☐	☐
to apply critical thinking techniques;	☐	☐
to write formal emails.	☐	☐

CHAPTER 6
A View of the Future

Instead of bringing a travel guide on a trip to Paris, imagine using an augmented reality (AR) device. You can gaze through special AR glasses or point a phone: both overlay information on the object or place you are interested in. From your hotel room, your view of the Eiffel Tower prompts the AR device to supply notes on the Tower's history, ticket prices, elevator wait times, restaurant reviews, and booking information. Looking at the streets, interactive maps guide you there.

What else in the world could AR help you learn?

In this chapter,
you will

- learn vocabulary related to augmented reality and AI;

- identify organizational patterns in texts;

- learn how to summarize text;

- use transitions to ensure unity and coherence;

- review the correct use of articles;

- paraphrase and summarize to avoid plagiarism;

- write summaries.

GEARING UP

A. Look at the photo and then answer the questions.

Source: *A Day Made of Glass*. (2014). Image provided by Corning Incorporated.

1 What advantages might an AR approach have over the same information in books? What disadvantages?

_____

_____

2 AR commonly labels maps with information about locations, including homes. How might this lead to privacy concerns?

_____

_____

3 Facial recognition software identifies people according to features on their face. Why might you want to use this technology?

_____

_____

4 Using AR, a doctor could overlay a picture of your X-ray on a recent injury. How could this be helpful?

_____

_____

B. Discuss the questions and your answers, first with a partner, then in a group.

Below are the key words you will practise in this chapter. Check the words you understand, then underline the words you use. Highlight the words you need to learn.

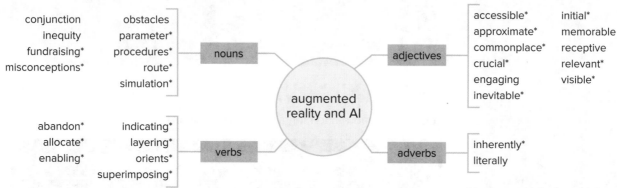

conjunction
inequity
fundraising*
misconceptions*

obstacles
parameter*
procedures*
route*
simulation*

nouns

augmented reality and AI

adjectives

accessible*   initial*
approximate*   memorable
commonplace*   receptive
crucial*   relevant*
engaging   visible*
inevitable*

abandon*
allocate*
enabling*

indicating*
layering*
orients*
superimposing*

verbs

adverbs

inherently*
literally

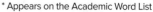

* Appears on the Academic Word List

FOCUS ON
READING

Identifying Organizational Patterns

Being able to recognize organizational patterns in academic writing will help you understand and evaluate the text that is being presented. One way to spot a pattern is to look for commonly used signal words and phrases that are related to a particular organizational pattern. This same skill will also help you when you take notes. For example, if you recognize a chronological pattern, you can take notes on a timeline or, when you see a compare and contrast pattern, on a Venn diagram.

A. Read about organizational patterns and then choose the kind of information best suited for each pattern.

ORGANIZATIONAL PATTERNS	EXPLANATION	SIGNAL WORDS/PHRASES	KIND OF INFORMATION
CLASSIFICATION	organizes text in relation to a group with shared characteristics; often used in definition paragraphs and essays	*for example, for instance, defined as, classified as, part/group*	a) various AR technologies b) map of Canada c) description of oxygen
CHRONOLOGICAL	arranges events according to when they occur in time	*before, initially, then, after, first, second, third, ... finally*	a) places in a town b) history of buildings c) future of bicycles
COMPARE AND CONTRAST	discusses how two or more things are similar or different	*same as, similarly, different than, as opposed to, instead of, however, compared with, although*	a) leader in AR b) leaders' achievements c) one decision by a leader
CAUSE AND EFFECT	shows the relationship between two or more things: the cause or causes and the resulting effect or effects	*because, as a result, for this reason, this led to, consequently, may be due to*	a) directions to a fire b) history of painting c) how accidents happen
PROBLEM/ SOLUTION	introduces a problem and then offers one or more solutions	*the problem is, the question is, one solution/answer is*	a) Nobel Prize winners b) basic singing lessons c) how to avoid an illness

B. Read these excerpts from Reading 1. Which organizational pattern does each use?

ORGANIZATIONAL
PATTERN

1. Augmented reality is hidden content, most commonly hidden behind marker images, that can be included in printed and film media, as long as the marker is displayed for a suitable length of time, in a steady position for an application to identify and analyze it. Depending on the content, the marker may have to remain visible. _____

2. Augmented reality has its origins as early as the 1950s and has progressed with virtual reality since then, but its most significant advances have been since the mid-1990s. _____

3. The idea of having a great deal of information available to you at any time and in any place is inherently appealing in some ways but might be overwhelming in others. _____

FOCUS ON CRITICAL THINKING

Summarizing Text

It's natural for you to summarize what you read, see, hear, and experience. For example, if you read a book and someone asks you what it was about, you don't repeat the book word for word. In academic reading and writing, summarizing is an important skill for note-taking, ensuring that you capture key ideas accurately and concisely.

A. You need reasons to summarize an article. The main reason is to help you remember. With a partner, think of two or more reasons why you might want to summarize an article.

REASON 1: _____

REASON 2: _____

B. Summarizing involves choosing the important parts of a text and deleting those that are not important. In general, adjectives and adverbs are not as important as nouns and verbs. Highlight the important portions of the beginning of Reading 1.

Guide to Augmented Reality
What Is AR?

AR is the process of superimposing digitally rendered images onto our real-world surroundings, giving a sense of an illusion or virtual reality. Recent developments have made this technology accessible using a smartphone.

C. Begin your summary by indicating the writer (or source, if there is no writer), date, and title of the text. The date will often be in the article's reference. In your own words, use the following as a start for your summary of the above paragraph, writing no more than two or three sentences. Then compare your summary with a partner's. Note: A summary should always be shorter than the original.

In "Guide to Augmented Reality," Onvert (2014) explains that ...

_____

_____

_____

_____

Guide to Augmented Reality

A Boeing 747 airplane contains more than four hundred kilometres of wiring connecting countless devices. When something goes wrong, carrying around heavy repair manuals can be a great challenge. In the early 1990s, Boeing engineers met this challenge by creating computer-screen glasses that overlay instructions and wiring diagrams onto the parts of the plane. One of the engineers, Thomas Caudell, was the first to call this "augmented reality."

<table>
<tr><td>

VOCABULARY BUILD

</td><td>

In the following exercises, explore key words from Reading 1.

A. Choose the phrase that best completes each sentence. Key words are in bold.

</td></tr>
</table>

❶ By **superimposing** the engine diagram on the car engine, _____.

    a) it was easier to see what was missing

    b) the customer left a sticky mess

    c) it became impossible to start the car

❷ A mobile phone is more **accessible** than a traditional phone _____.

    a) once you have given your friends your number

    b) as long as you remember to charge it

    c) because you can carry it around with you

❸ The image became **visible** when _____.

    a) we looked away

    b) light shone on it

    c) shadows fell on it

❹ After **indicating** her preference, she asked _____.

    a) which one she should choose

    b) the clerk to package her virtual glasses

    c) whether one was better than the other

⑤ Because he wanted it to be **memorable**, he _____.

    a) tried to forget it entirely

    b) knew he could find it later

    c) repeated it over and over

B. Fill in the blanks with the correct words to complete the sentences.

enabling	engaging	initial	receptive	simulation

① The game was a/an _____ of a person escaping from animals.

② The _____ move in the chess game was taken by the computer.

③ They were interested in _____ kids to do their own programming.

④ We found that older people were just as _____ to AR as younger people.

⑤ The most _____ part of the game was earning points.

Before You Read

A. An old proverb says, "Necessity is the mother of invention." What does this mean and how does it relate to augmented reality?

_____

_____

B. Augmented reality glasses have become controversial because of fears that users might be spying on others around them or recording images and videos. How might this differ from using a phone to do the same thing?

_____

_____

C. Reading 1 mixes organizational patterns. While you read, note in the margin the different patterns the writer uses. For example, the first paragraph uses classification.

Guide to Augmented Reality

What Is AR?

rendered (adj.): drawn by a computer program

AR is the process of **superimposing** digitally **rendered** images onto our real-world surroundings, giving a sense of an illusion or virtual reality. Recent developments have made this technology **accessible** using a smartphone.

5 How Is It Used?

marker images (n.): graphics recognized by a computer for positioning purposes

Augmented reality is hidden content, most commonly hidden behind **marker images**, that can be included in printed and film media, as long as the marker is displayed for a suitable length of time, in a steady position for an application to identify and analyze it. Depending on the content, the marker may have to remain **visible**.

10 It is used more recently by advertisers where it is popular to create a 3D render of a product, such as a car or football boot, and trigger this as an overlay to a marker. This allows the consumer to see a 360-degree image (more or less; sometimes the base of the item can be tricky to view) of the product. Depending on the quality of the augmentation, this can go as far as **indicating** the approximate size of the item, 15 and allow the consumer to "wear" the item, as viewed through their phone.

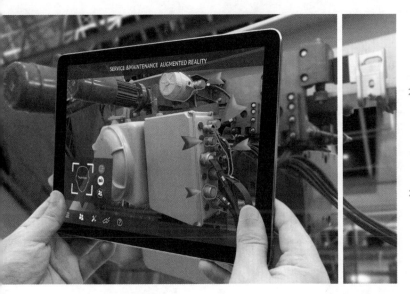

Alternative set-ups include printing out a marker and holding it before a webcam attached to a computer. The image of the marker and the background as seen by the webcam is shown 20 on screen, **enabling** the consumer to place the marker on places such as the forehead (to create a mask) or move the marker to control a character in a game.

In some cases, a marker is not required at all 25 to display augmented reality.

How Does It Work?

Using a mobile application, a mobile phone's camera identifies and interprets a marker, often a black and white **barcode image**. The 30 software analyzes the marker and creates a virtual image overlay on the mobile phone's screen, tied to the position of the camera. This means the app works with the camera to interpret the angles and distance the mobile phone is away from the marker.

barcode image (n.): black and white graphic that alerts the computer or phone to display information

Due to the number of calculations a phone must do to render the image or model 35 over the marker, often only smartphones are capable of supporting augmented reality with any success. Phones need a camera and, if the data for the AR is not stored within the app, a good 3G Internet connection.

Background

origins (n.): beginnings

Augmented reality has its **origins** as early as the 1950s and has progressed with virtual 40 reality since then, but its most significant advances have been since the mid-1990s.

CAD (n.): computer-aided design, used with 3D objects

The technology has been around for many years, used in **CAD** programs for aircraft assembly and architecture, **simulation**, navigation, military and medical procedures. Complex tasks including assembly and maintenance can be simplified to assist in training, and product prototypes can be **mocked up** without manufacturing.

mocked up (v.): drawn or created as a model

45 Augmented reality has been proven very useful on a day-to-day basis when tied with location-based technology. Several apps are available that will show consumers their nearest food outlets or subway transport stations when they raise the app and view their surroundings through the camera.

Their use in marketing is particularly appealing, as not only can additional, detailed 50 content be put within a traditional 2D advert, [but] the results are interactive, cool, **engaging**, and, due to the **initial** novelty, have high viral potential. Consumers react positively to fun, clever marketing, and brands become **memorable**.

The potential audience varies depending on the application of AR. Through a
55 smartphone, it is limited to an audience with suitable handsets and those willing to download an app. With printing a marker for use with a webcam, it is limited to those willing to follow through
60 these steps, though this often opens a wide **demographic**, including children (printing an AR code on a cereal box to play a game, for instance).

demographic (n.): particular group of people

What is certain is that the smartphone
65 population is rising and, with this, the level of processing power is too. More and more consumers are carrying phones capable of displaying augmented reality, and once an app is downloaded and they have scanned their first code, they are far more **receptive** to future appearances of a code—driven by curiosity. As long as the
70 resulting augmented content remains engaging and innovative, consumers will certainly adopt augmented reality as a new and fun twist to **conventional** marketing and services.

conventional (adj.): what is usually done

(713 words)

Onvert. (2014). *What is augmented reality?* Retrieved from http://onvert.com/guides/what-is-augmented-reality/

After You Read

D. Based on your understanding of Reading 1, explain the following phrases.

➊ augmented reality is hidden content: _____

_____

➋ a 3D render of a product, such as a car: _____

_____

➌ place the marker on places such as the forehead (to create a mask):

_____

_____

E. Write about the significance of each of these concepts to augmented reality. Then, discuss with a partner.

➊ interpret angles and distance: _____

_____

➋ a good 3G connection: _____

_____

_____

③ view their surroundings through the camera: _____

_____

④ AR on a cereal box: _____

_____

⑤ phones capable of displaying AR: _____

_____

F. Use what you learned in Focus on Critical Thinking (page 125) to summarize one part of the article, choosing the text between two section headings. Remember to include the author and date: Onvert (2014) explains …

_____

_____

_____

MyBookshelf > My eLab >
Exercises > Chapter 6 >
Guide to Augmented Reality

FOCUS ON WRITING

Ensuring Unity and Coherence

Sometimes you read a paragraph that doesn't seem to make sense. The writer begins on one topic, then switches to an unrelated one. This demonstrates a lack of unity. *Unity* means that the parts of a paragraph need to fit together: a topic sentence with supporting sentences that directly relate to it. *Coherence* is achieved when the supporting sentences are organized in a logical way and are connected.

A. Read this topic sentence. Then, choose those sentences that would give it unity as a paragraph.

> Having a great deal of information available any time and any place is appealing in some ways but might be overwhelming in others.

☐ Although Alexander Graham Bell got a patent in 1876 for the first practical telephone, other researchers before him did important work.

☐ Arbitrary information might even be a dangerous distraction, particularly when you are engaged in other tasks, such as driving.

☐ In other cases, you might simply be exhausted at having advertisements intrude on your thoughts.

☐ Libraries have existed since ancient times, and one of the great losses in history was the destruction of the Library of Alexandria, in Egypt.

☐ Sometimes people talk too much, and it is not particularly interesting to anyone and can be damaging, particularly in a business context.

☐ While it could be helpful to know the best route to take or be warned of poor weather conditions, if such information takes your attention from the road, it might cause an accident.

Stuttgart City Library

B. Coherence can be achieved through techniques that connect ideas between sentences. Read the different techniques and then think of new examples that follow the patterns of the explanations.

TECHNIQUES	EXPLANATION	EXAMPLE
REPETITION	Key words or phrases from the first sentence are repeated in the next sentence.	AR is **new**. **New** ideas scare some people. _____ _____ _____
SYNONYMS	Synonyms (words with the same meaning) are used to connect similar ideas.	AR is **new**. **Original** ideas scare some people. _____ _____ _____
ANTONYMS	Antonyms (words with the opposite meaning) are used to show contrast.	AR is **new**. **Old** ideas comfort some people. _____ _____ _____
NUMBERING	Numbers (or letters) signal different points, usually within a sentence. Numbered items may be developed in following sentences or paragraphs.	There are three reasons AR scares Erica: **1)** loss of privacy; **2)** the expense; and **3)** the learning curve. _____ _____ _____
PRONOUNS	Pronouns refer to the noun in the previous sentence.	AR is new to **Conrad**. New ideas scare **him**. _____ _____ _____
TRANSITION WORDS	Signal words (see Focus on Reading, page 124) can be used to provide transitions between sentences.	AR is becoming popular. **For example**, the global AR market is expected to grow 132 percent in the next five years. _____ _____ _____

C. Read each sentence and then write a second one. Use a different technique to achieve coherence between each pair of sentences. Then, write the technique you used.

1 AR has a role in retail sales.

_____

2 People can use AR apps in stores or at home.

_____

3 You can photograph yourself to try on some clothes.

_____

4 Information about a product might include where it was made.

_____

5 Health-conscious shoppers want nutritional information about their fruits.

_____

MyBookshelf > My eLab > Exercises > Chapter 6 > Focus on Writing

---

READING ❷

How Can Augmented Reality Be Used for Social Good?

Many new tools and applications first become popular as entertainment. Bicycles, for example, were fun long before they became a serious transportation alternative. The same is true of augmented reality, which has been most popular as a game interface but is now emerging as a tool that can be used to help others in many ways.

VOCABULARY BUILD

In the following exercises, explore key words from Reading 2.

A. Highlight the word or phrase in parentheses that best completes each sentence. Key words are in bold.

1 There were many **misconceptions** about augmented reality and virtual reality, but she (didn't know / knew) the difference.

2 Of all the **obstacles** that stand in the way of effective augmented reality, the greatest is (avoiding / finding) an easy way to see it.

3 It was tempting to **abandon** research in augmented reality (when / whether) the headsets were too big and too heavy.

④ There was **literally** no place to use augmented reality (inside / outside) a lab thirty years ago.

⑤ Online **fundraising** for new technologies (can / cannot) allow small companies to create augmented reality applications.

B. Use an arrow (↓) to indicate where the key word in bold should be placed in the sentences (adapted from Reading 2). Check your answers with a partner and explain the meaning of each key word.

① (**conjunction**) A University of Alabama surgical team performed one of the first surgeries in with Google Glass .

② (**inequity**) What if while you did your shopping you could see the of a product's supply chain, the environmental costs, and the context behind each product ?

③ (**layering**) AR enhances the real world by useful or entertaining computer-generated images over it .

④ (**procedures**) AR even has applications for more everyday .

⑤ (**relevant**) It enables students and teachers to pinpoint exactly types of bone, whilst also revealing information about it on screen .

Before You Read

A. Use what you learned in Focus on Critical Thinking (page 125) to highlight the important portions of the beginning of Reading 2. Use your notes to write a short summary, and share it with a partner.

> Augmented reality (AR) mixes fantasy and reality by projecting an AR object over the real world. This allows you to see a mixture of real life and computer-generated life through your device. AR is similar to virtual reality (VR), but different. While VR aims to drop users into a convincing artificial world, AR enhances the real world by layering useful or entertaining computer-generated images over it.

In "How Can Augmented Reality Be Used for Social Good?" Matthews (2017)

_____

_____

_____

B. Social good refers to organized actions that provide some benefit to the public. Examples include charity work, environmental initiatives, and free entertainment and sports events. Choose one kind of social good and consider how AR might be used to make it better. Discuss your ideas with a partner.

C. While you read, take notes on the techniques used to achieve cohesion in some of the paragraphs. For example, in paragraph 1, *this* is a pronoun used to summarize the AR process.

How Can Augmented Reality Be Used for Social Good?

Augmented reality (AR) mixes fantasy and reality by projecting an AR object over the real world. This allows you to see a mixture of real life and computer-generated life through your device.

AR is similar to virtual reality (VR), but different. While VR aims to drop users into 5 a convincing artificial world, AR enhances the real world by **layering** useful or entertaining computer-generated images over it.

AR can be used to create innovative experiences for social good organizations. From interactive learning experiences to **fundraising**, AR is a great way of making social issues **tangible** in ways we've never been able to before.

tangible (adj.): something you can touch

10 Here are some examples [where] … AR [is already being used] to further their cause [the social good].

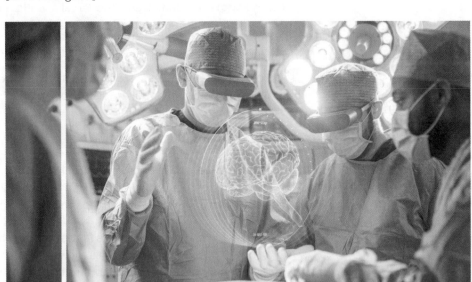

Help with Healthcare

In healthcare, AR could **literally** save lives.

One of the cleverest applications has been ARnatomy's use of the technology in 15 medical education to enable students and teachers to pinpoint exactly types of bone whilst also revealing **relevant** information about it on screen.

This allows medical students to **abandon** heavy textbooks and, even better, manipulate a tangible skeletal model without ever having to meet a real patient.

But it's not just medical students who can benefit from AR. Vipaar is a service for 20 practicing surgeons. Using AR, a **remote** surgeon can project his hands onto the display of an on-site surgeon wearing AR-enabled glasses. This enables him to point and guide the hands of the on-site surgeon, who may be less experienced in a particular type of surgery.

remote (adj.): at a distance

And it's already been put to use. A University of Alabama surgical team performed 25 one of the first surgeries in **conjunction** with Google Glass, a wearable computer with an optical head-mounted display.

AR even has applications for more everyday **procedures**.

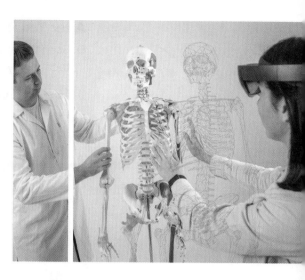

For example, 40 percent of IVs miss on the first attempt at finding a vein, so a
30 medical company called AccuVein has invented an AR scanner that projects over skin and shows nurses and doctors where various veins, valves, and **bifurcations** are in a patient's body.

bifurcations (n.): divisions into two branches

35 This has been used on more than 10 million patients so far and made finding a vein on the first attempt 3.5 times more likely. You could even see it make an appearance in your local
40 doctor's surgery in the near future!

Help People See Again

Most of us will benefit from a different perspective provided to us by AR. But for some people it will literally change the way they see the world.

Most people who are classified as legally blind actually retain some vision but may
45 not be able to pick out faces and **obstacles**, particularly in low light. Because of this, AR could make it easier for some people with sight **impairment** to explore their surroundings.

impairment (n.): being unable to function normally

VA-ST have built software that can be taught to recognize 3D objects and then identify them within a scene. When coupled with their Smart Specs glasses, it provides a new
50 way of enhancing vision for many people who are legally blind or partially sighted.

For people with sight impairments, this can mean the confidence to find lost items or **navigate** unusual environments.

navigate (v.): find your way

Other Uses of AR for Social Good

Here are a few other ideas of AR for social good that we'd love to see.

55 **See the supply chain:** AR is perfectly suited for helping consumers decide what to buy. What if while you did your shopping you could see the **inequity** of a product's **supply chain**, the environmental costs, and the context behind each product? Would it change what you bought?

supply chain (n.): the sequence of production and distribution

first responders (n.): emergency personnel who arrive first on the scene

Respond to emergencies: First responders, police, and firefighters often arrive at
60 **chaotic** scenes of emergencies and need to make sense of the environment and navigate a place they've never been. Could AR help by showing emergency services a virtual map of the emergency site, giving them "X-ray vision" to see underground water and power lines, avoiding potential danger?

chaotic (adj.): in a state of confusion and disorder

empathy (n.): the ability to share and understand the feelings of another

Promote understanding of mental health issues: If you think about it, AR is a lot like
65 experiencing a hallucination. AR could be a good way of reducing **misconceptions** and increasing **empathy** for people who live with symptoms like **psychosis**.

psychosis (n.): a mental disorder where one loses touch with reality

(685 words)

Matthews, B. (2017, September 26). How can augmented reality be used for social good? *Montfort*. Retrieved from https://montfort.io/ar-for-good-how-can-augmented-reality-be-used-for-social-good/

After You Read

D. Scan the article and write notes about each type of social good and the AR technology that is helping it.

SOCIAL GOOD	NOTES
1 FUNDRAISING	*make fundraising tangible for people*
2 HEALTHCARE	
3 EVERYDAY MEDICAL PROCEDURES	
4 HELPING PEOPLE SEE AGAIN	
5 SEE THE SUPPLY CHAIN	
6 RESPOND TO EMERGENCIES	
7 PROMOTE UNDERSTANDING OF MENTAL HEALTH ISSUES	

E. Indicate whether these statements are true or false, according to the text. For those that are false, write a correct statement.

STATEMENTS	TRUE	FALSE
1 AR is the same as VR. _____	☐	☐
2 ARnatomy is used in medical education to enable students and teachers to pinpoint exactly types of bone. _____	☐	☐
3 Using AR in learning about bones is safer than dealing with human patients. _____	☐	☐
4 Vipaar lets one surgeon remotely direct the hands of another surgeon. _____	☐	☐
5 Google Glass allowed for an AR operation on a University of Alabama surgical team member. _____	☐	☐

STATEMENTS		TRUE	FALSE
6 Only 60 percent of attempts to find a vein are successful on the first attempt. _____		☐	☐
7 Someone who is legally blind cannot see anything at all. _____		☐	☐
8 Having a virtual map of an emergency scene would help emergency personnel avoid danger. _____		☐	☐

MyBookshelf > My eLab > Exercises > Chapter 6 > How Can Augmented Reality Be Used for Social Good?

FOCUS ON GRAMMAR

Articles

When you write, using the wrong articles can significantly alter your meaning. It's important to understand articles and use and interpret them correctly. Although there are only two kinds of articles, the definite article *the* and the indefinite article *a* (*an* in front of words beginning with *a, e, i, o, u* sounds), the rules are surprisingly complicated.

An article gives information about a noun. The definite article *the* indicates that one particular item is being discussed. Compare the use of *the* and *a* in these examples.

ARTICLE USE	EXPLANATION
The project is interesting.	*The* refers to a particular project, one that can be seen or is already known. In this case, it is a definite project, so the definite article is the term for *the project*.
A project is fun.	*A* changes the meaning of project, shifting it to a general category; the meaning is that all projects are fun. In this case, there is not a definite project being discussed, so the indefinite article is used.
I have **a** project.	In this case, *a* indicates the singular. You could also say, I have *one* project, which emphasizes the number, e.g., I do *not* have *two* projects.
I like projects.	In this case, no article is used because the noun *projects* is general. Adding an unnecessary article is a common grammatical error.
A student has **a** project. **The** student likes **the** project.	In this two-sentence passage, the indefinite *a* is used when describing the student and project the first time they appear, but as the discussion continues, the student and the project are known and therefore definite.
All of/Most of/None of/ Some of **the** projects are finished.	The definite article follows *all of, most of, none of,* and *some of.*
All/Most/No/Some projects are interesting.	With *all, most, no,* and *some,* no article is necessary.

A. Fill in the blanks with the correct articles to complete the sentences: *a*, *an*, *the*, or *X* if no article is needed. Then, discuss your answers with a partner.

1. Your AR simulates _____ X-ray view of your car.

2. Imagine _____ day with augmented reality combined with _____ artificial intelligence.

3. On _____ way to work, you get _____ flat tire and have to fix _____ tire before anything else.

4. If such information takes your attention from the road, it might cause _____ accident.

5. In _____ future, if you could access _____ knowledge so easily, you would be motivated to learn.

Use what you learned about articles when you write assignments.

MyBookshelf > My eLab > Exercises > Chapter 6 > Grammar Review

Academic
Survival Skill

Avoiding Plagiarism

Plagiarism is using the words or ideas of others as your own. In an academic context, plagiarism is a serious offence and can lead to being expelled from a course or an institution. In the digital age, it's easy to plagiarize (copy and paste), but it's also easy to detect plagiarism (copy and search). Three ways to avoid plagiarism are to quote with citations, to paraphrase, and to summarize.

When you quote the words of another writer, the quote is set off by quotation marks, followed by an in-text citation, including a page or paragraph number and a full reference at the end. When you quote the ideas of another writer, the ideas are paraphrased, followed by an in-text citation and a full reference, but you do not need to provide a page or paragraph number.

This excerpt is from page 143 of this book: Beatty, K. (2019). *LEAP 2: Reading and Writing*. Montreal: Pearson. Write it as a quote.

> It may be fine to recognize a friend, but would it be okay for facial recognition software to identify you to strangers, sharing details of your life? How much do you want a stranger to know about you?

_____

_____

_____

_____

_____

_____

When you paraphrase, you are expressing another writer's words or ideas in your own words. A paraphrase is similar to a summary, but unlike a summary, it does not necessarily shorten the text. A paraphrase takes the original

sentence, or sentences, and states them in another way, making the meaning clearer. When you paraphrase, do not simply use a series of synonyms to replace key words.

Read this excerpt from Reading 3 (page 142), and then read the example paraphrase.

ORIGINAL EXCERPT	PARAPHRASE
Social media tools already track your preferences and use them to tailor **advertisements** on the websites you skim. But tracking your location and the things you glance at in the real world could be an enormous invasion of your and others' **privacy**.	Beatty (2019) writes that, when you use **social media**, the Web notes your interests and delivers **advertisements** accordingly. If you use AR outside, the things you look at may also be noted. This might lead to **privacy** concerns.

As with a paraphrase, a summary conveys the words or ideas of another, but unlike a paraphrase, a summary is much shorter than the original text, approximately one-quarter to one-third the length of the original text. Before you summarize, read the entire text and try to understand its overall meaning. While you read, take notes or highlight key points. Then, write the summary in your own words. Keep a copy of the original, with references, and refer to it when you finish, ensuring that your summary has not accidentally plagiarized original content.

To write a summary, follow these steps.

- Skim the text to get a general understanding. Then, read it in detail, asking yourself *who*, *what*, *when*, *where*, *why*, and *how* questions. Highlight key points.

- If the text is long, write notes on different sections—for example, sections with subheadings. Write notes in your own words. Keep in mind why the information is important or worth knowing, but don't add personal opinions.

- Ignore unimportant details.

- Write a topic sentence that explains what the summary is about. Include the author's name as well as the title and the source of the text.

- Review your summary to ensure you have achieved unity and coherence. Refer to Focus on Writing (page 130).

WARM-UP ASSIGNMENT
Write a Short Summary

Write a short summary of the article below, titled "HUDs in Your Future."

A. Read the article and, using information from Academic Survival Skill, write a summary. Ensure your summary avoids plagiarism by citing author, date, and page number and by paraphrasing main ideas. Refer to the Models Chapter (page 203) to see an example of a summary and to learn more about how to write one.

HUDs in Your Future

One area where augmented reality has been used for some time is in heads-up displays (HUDs) in military aircraft. The displays appear on the windshield before the pilot's eyes so there is no need to look down at a set of control indicators, such as those for speed, direction, and fuel. For a jet fighter, this is important because a target, such as an enemy jet, may be in front of the pilot and moving quickly out of range in the space of a distracted glance.

Source: TechMASH. (2014). Car HUDs from Microvision. Photo Courtesy of MicroVision Incorporated.

The same technology is now being adapted for use in cars, allowing drivers to see fuel levels and speed as well as global positioning system (GPS) data mapping routes to drive. The system can also indicate important traffic information: speed zones, stop signs, or updates on roads that are closed or busy.

McLean, M. (2015). *Focused forward: Heads-up display applications*. Halifax, NS: RareLeaf Press.

Use feedback from your teacher and classmates on this Warm-Up Assignment to improve your writing.

B. Compare summaries with a partner. Did you write a topic sentence that explains what the summary is about? Did you include the author's name as well as the title and the source of the text? Did you paraphrase the original text? Is your summary coherent?

C. Make corrections and write a final copy.

READING ③   AR + AI = New Life

Like many other inventions, AR was predicted in science fiction. After finishing *The Wizard of Oz*, Frank L. Baum (1856–1919), in 1901, wrote a novel about a Demon of Electricity who gives a boy a pair of glasses that he explains will overlay symbols for the qualities of anyone the boy looks at: G for good, E for evil, W for wise, and so on. Today, we would call this technology *facial recognition software*. Although we can't yet use technology to measure people's characters, we can overlay web-based information about them.

VOCABULARY BUILD

In the following exercises, explore key words from Reading 3.

A. Write a definition for each of these words. For words you are not sure of, look at their context in the reading. Use a dictionary to check your answers.

1 commonplace: _____

2 inevitable: _____

3 inherently: _____

4 orients: _____

5 parameter: _____

B. Choose the word or phrase that best completes each sentence. Key words are in bold.

1 When I say that we have to **allocate** funds, we have to _____.
  a) forget about money
  b) put some money aside
  c) hire volunteers

2 The choice of a new AR app can be **arbitrary** if there are _____.
  a) no opportunities to play it
  b) many similar ones around
  c) no other choices available

3 For AR to become universal, it's **crucial** that _____.
  a) it can be used in video games
  b) virtual reality loses its appeal
  c) it works on mobile phones

4 An AR program typically **orients** the images to _____.
  a) where you are looking
  b) your home and office
  c) the last place you were

5 An AR program can help you plan your **route** _____.
  a) as long as you are only walking
  b) if you are only travelling virtually
  c) by providing data along the way

C. VOCABULARY EXTENSION: Like augmented reality, two phrases used in Reading 3, *artificial intelligence* and *paradigm shift*, are collocations—commonly associated words. Use the following words to construct pairs of words that naturally go together. Use each word only once. Check your answers in Reading 3.

arrival	frequency	information	radio	speech	time
commands	identity	~~list~~	~~shopping~~	theft	weather

1 ____ *shopping list* ____ **4** _____

2 _____ **5** _____

3 _____ **6** _____

Develop Your Vocabulary: Keep a list of short forms (acronyms and initialisms) and their meanings. Review them regularly until memorized.

MyBookshelf > My eLab > Exercises > Chapter 6 > Vocabulary Review

Before You Read

A. In Baum's story, the boy who receives the glasses decides not to use them to examine his family members, fearing the glasses might reveal qualities that go against the goodness he sees in his loved ones. What message does this story send about augmented reality?

_____

_____

B. Reading 3 begins with a fictional day in which one person uses AR and AI extensively. Discuss with a partner how you each might use AR and AI on a typical day.

C. While you read, note the organizational pattern in the complete text, as well as in each paragraph.

AR + AI = New Life

Imagine a day with augmented reality (AR) combined with artificial intelligence (AI). You wake up and immediately put on AR glasses that show a ghostly image of your schedule. A global positioning system (GPS) sensor recognizes your window and overlays the day's **crucial** weather information.
5 It's going to be cool and rainy. As you decide what to wear, miniature radio frequency identification tags (RFID) embedded in your clothes work with your AI to transmit information about sales at two of your favourite stores. As you decide what to have
10 for breakfast, your glasses scan barcode images on your cereal package and milk container and list calories and other nutritional information. The milk is almost past its shelf life, so your AI program asks if you want to add milk to your shopping
15 list. "Yes." The AI in your glasses recognizes speech commands.

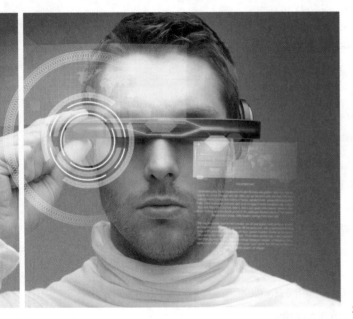

glance (v.): look quickly

It is time to go to work, but you are unsure whether to take your car or **allocate** extra time for the bus. A **glance** at your bus pass alerts your AI to consult
20 with your calendar and local road maps and estimate your approximate arrival time. Your AI discovers your bus has broken down, so you decide to take the car. But, on the way to work, you get a flat tire and have to fix it. You have never done this before, but your AR glasses see the tire and the AI program recognizes that it is flat. Your AR simulates an X-ray view of your car so you
25 can see the location of the spare tire and tools. A short Web video lets you begin the tire replacement process, and soon you arrive at work. Along the way, the AI program **orients** you to the best **route** to take but does not display sales at the stores you pass because your AI recognizes you are late.

Arriving at work, you see a colleague, and the AI's facial recognition program tells
30 you that not only has your friend been promoted recently but also today is her birthday. You congratulate her and suggest lunch to celebrate. Your AI hears the word _lunch_ and explores price and location **parameters** to display local restaurant

suggestions. You agree on a place, and as you walk to your desk, your AR glasses are
35 already displaying your work emails.

This start of an AR- and AI-enabled day is not all science fiction. Many of these ideas are already in use and some are likely to become **commonplace** in the coming years (Bonsor
40 & Chandler, 2018; Hill, 2014; Widder, 2017). But, as with any technology, **barriers** stand in the way including **information overload**, privacy, and security.

The idea of having a great deal of information
45 available to you any time and any place is **inherently** appealing in some ways but might be overwhelming in others. **Arbitrary** information might even be a dangerous distraction, particularly when you are engaged
50 in other tasks, such as driving. While it could be helpful to know the best route to take or be warned of poor weather conditions, if such information takes your attention from the road, it might cause an accident. In other cases, you might simply be exhausted at having advertisements **intrude** on your thoughts.

55 Social media tools already track your preferences and use them to tailor advertisements on websites you skim. But tracking your location and the things you glance at in the real world could be an enormous **invasion** of your and others' privacy. It may be fine to recognize a friend, but would it be okay for facial recognition software to identify you to strangers, sharing details of your life? How much do you want a stranger to
60 know about you?

These questions are particularly important in terms of security. If your face can be matched to your home or place of work, thieves not only know where you are but might also be able to engage in **identity theft**, falsely making purchases using your financial information. What if such AI and AR systems are **hacked** and trusting
65 individuals given false and dangerous travel information?

Samuel Johnson (1709–1784) described two kinds of knowledge, knowing something or knowing where you could find information about it. In the future, if you can access knowledge so easily, will you be motivated to learn and to think and remember?

What is without question is that an **inevitable** combination of AI and AR will create
70 a **paradigm shift** that will disrupt your life from the moment you wake until the moment you fall asleep. (765 words)

barriers (n.): obstacles that prevent movement or access

information overload (n.): exposure to too much information

intrude (v.): enter uninvited or unwelcome

invasion (n.): entry and attack on another's area

identity theft (n.): illegal use of another person's personal information

hacked (v.): access another's computer without permission

paradigm shift (n.): a fundamental change or shift in approach or thinking

References

Bonsor, K., & Chandler, N. (2018). How augmented reality works. *How Stuff Works*. Retrieved from http://computer.howstuffworks.com/augmented-reality.htm

Hill, S. (2014, March 15). Get past the gimmicks and gaze upon the future of augmented reality apps. *Digital Trends*. Retrieved from http://www.digitaltrends.com/mobile/future-ar-mobile/#ixzz376wQUWz6

Widder, B. (2017, April 19). Best augmented-reality apps. *Digital Trends*. Retrieved from https://ca.news.yahoo.com/best-augmented-reality-apps-171552673.html

After You Read

D. Read the events and predict when they are likely to happen. Write the numbers on the timeline. Then, discuss in a group.

NOW	IN A YEAR	IN FIVE YEARS	IN TEN YEARS	IN A CENTURY	NEVER

1. AI adds items to your shopping list.
2. AI makes suggestions for your daily travel plans.
3. AR programs scan barcode images on your food packages.
4. AR/AI gives X-ray views of your car and other appliances.
5. Facial recognition software provides information about friends and colleagues.
6. GPS-based weather reports are available for your exact location.
7. Most people wear AR glasses.
8. RFID tags report on store sales.
9. False travel instructions cause accidents.
10. Thieves steal AR and AI data.

MyBookshelf > My eLab >
Exercises > Chapter 6 >
AR + AI = New Life

E. Reading 3 ends with the suggestion that "the inevitable combination of AI and AR will create a paradigm shift that will disrupt your life from the moment you wake until the moment you fall asleep." In what ways might artificial intelligence and augmented reality become bigger parts of your life? Discuss in a group.

FINAL ASSIGNMENT
Write a Summary

Use what you learned in this chapter to write a summary of one of the readings.

A. Choose which reading you will summarize.

☐ Reading 1 Guide to Augmented Reality

☐ Reading 2 How Can Augmented Reality Be Used for Social Good?

☐ Reading 3 AR + AI = New Life

B. Review the reading and its exercises.

C. Follow the steps for summarizing found in Focus on Critical Thinking (page 125) and Academic Survival Skill (page 138).

D. Write your summary. Paraphrase at least two important points and give in-text citations. Refer to the Models Chapter (page 203) to see an example of a summary and to learn more about how to write one.

E. Proofread your summary. Make sure your paragraphs are unified and coherent. Check your use of articles. Then, share your summary with a partner for feedback.

F. Make corrections and write a final copy.

How confident
are you?

Think about what you learned in this chapter. Use the table to decide what you should review.

I LEARNED ...	I AM CONFIDENT	I NEED TO REVIEW
vocabulary related to augmented reality and AI;	☐	☐
to identify organizational patterns in texts;	☐	☐
how to summarize text;	☐	☐
to use transitions to ensure unity and coherence;	☐	☐
the correct use of articles;	☐	☐
how to paraphrase and summarize to avoid plagiarism;	☐	☐
to write summaries.	☐	☐

CHAPTER 7

Education for All

Many people enter the workforce without a college or university degree, but, increasingly, those who attend academic institutions are finding that they need not just one but two degrees to get the best jobs. These students either extend the years they spend at school or find alternative programs to complete second degrees while they work. As has always been the case, some people study purely for personal interest, without intending to pursue a job in the field. All of this is creating opportunities for online education providers.

What would you like to study for your own interest?

In this chapter, you will

- learn vocabulary related to individual learning;
- interpret visual elements;
- consider implications and consequences;
- review pronoun-antecedent agreement;
- learn how to explain processes;
- explore ways to work in a group;
- write a process paragraph and give a presentation.

GEARING UP

A. Look at the map and then answer the questions.

Territory size by the proportion of those enrolled in tertiary education

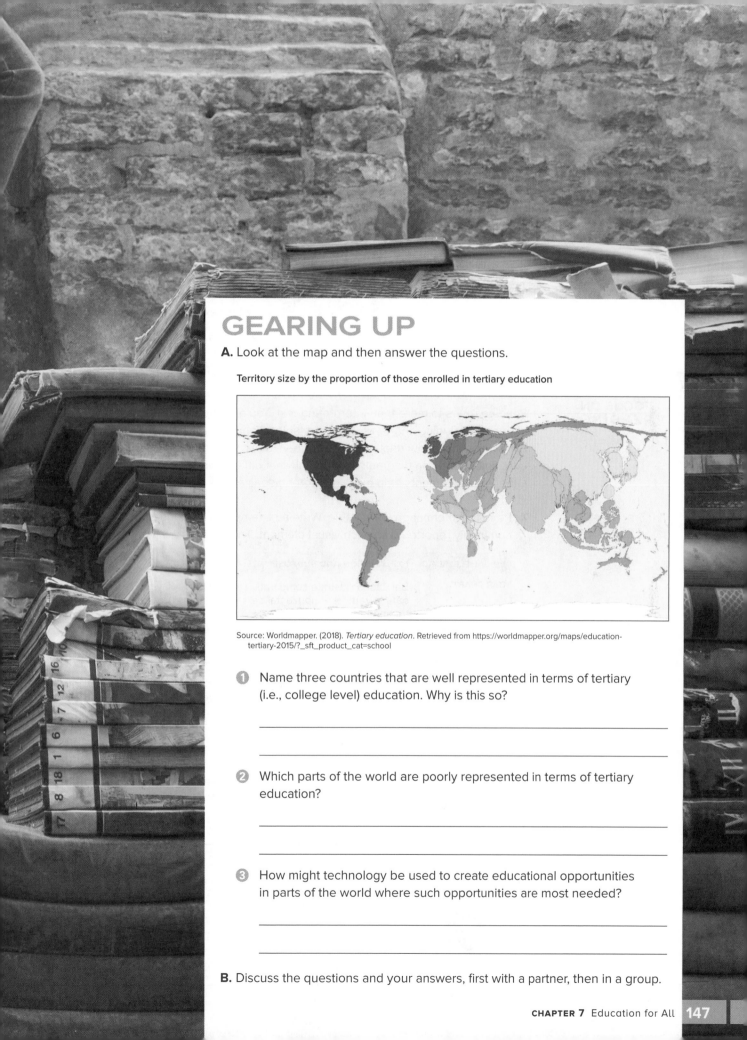

Source: Worldmapper. (2018). *Tertiary education*. Retrieved from https://worldmapper.org/maps/education-tertiary-2015/?_sft_product_cat=school

1. Name three countries that are well represented in terms of tertiary (i.e., college level) education. Why is this so?

   _____

   _____

2. Which parts of the world are poorly represented in terms of tertiary education?

   _____

   _____

3. How might technology be used to create educational opportunities in parts of the world where such opportunities are most needed?

   _____

   _____

B. Discuss the questions and your answers, first with a partner, then in a group.

Below are the key words you will practise in this chapter. Check the words you understand, then underline the words you use. Highlight the words you need to learn.

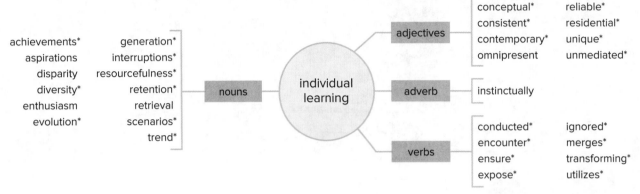

achievements*
aspirations
disparity
diversity*
enthusiasm
evolution*

generation*
interruptions*
resourcefulness*
retention*
retrieval
scenarios*
trend*

nouns

individual learning

adjectives

conceptual*   reliable*
consistent*   residential*
contemporary*   unique*
omnipresent   unmediated*

adverb

instinctually

verbs

conducted*   ignored*
encounter*   merges*
ensure*   transforming*
expose*   utilizes*

* Appears on the Academic Word List

FOCUS ON
READING

Interpreting Visual Elements

Reading refers to more than interpreting text. You also interpret various visual elements, including charts, graphs, and tables. You have already encountered mind maps that show relationships between ideas, timelines that record events over time, and Venn diagrams that reveal what different ideas have in common. Other visual elements help explain different ideas and relationships.

A. Read the information in the table. Write an example of the kind of data commonly reported with each visual element. Then, discuss with a partner.

VISUAL ELEMENTS	EXPLANATION AND PURPOSE
BAR CHART	Bar charts illustrate comparative amounts: display numerical data in vertical or horizontal bars with lengths proportional to amounts. Example: *money budgeted for education in different countries*
FLOW CHART	Flow charts show a sequence of related events and consequences connected by lines and/or arrows. Example: _____
GANTT CHART	Gantt charts schedule project tasks on a timeline that shows where tasks start and stop and how they overlap other tasks. Example: _____
ILLUSTRATION	Illustrations are pictures or diagrams that help explain or demonstrate ideas in a text. Illustrations are less likely to be based on numerical data. Example: _____

VISUAL ELEMENTS	EXPLANATION AND PURPOSE
LINE GRAPH	Line graphs connect data points that represent changes in amounts over time between two or more factors. Example: _____ _____
MAP	Maps show geographical information and symbols (usually explained in a legend) that highlight how certain features are distributed. Example: _____ _____
PIE CHART	Pie charts are circles divided into sections that represent amounts that are relative percentages of the whole. Example: _____ _____

B. Which visual element would you use to represent each kind of information?

1 number of female versus male university students entering college each year for ten years _____

2 current distribution of universities in South America _____

3 increase in spending on computers and phones over the last ten years _____

4 steps involved in enrolling in several college programs _____

5 percentage of reasons for taking online learning courses _____

6 times necessary for students to complete different jobs to finish a project _____

FOCUS ON CRITICAL THINKING

Considering Implications and Consequences

In a fable, a farmer's horse escapes. "Who knows if it's good or bad?" asks the farmer. The lost horse returns with several wild ones, which seems like good news, until the farmer's son breaks his leg riding one. In turn, this bad news turns into good news when a passing army recruits all young men from the village except the farmer's son. *Implications* follow from thoughts—what we might imagine might happen. *Consequences* follow from actions, what actually happens. Two important critical thinking skills are imagining implications and identifying consequences.

A. The following paragraph from Reading 1 outlines the advantages of online learning. Imagine you took an online degree. What two positive and two negative implications might your studies have? Write your answers and then compare them with a partner to see if you agree.

> There are many common-sense advantages to the online course approach, including the wide flavour of degree programs and classes offered, flexible study times, and the ability for students to balance between a career and education.

POSITIVE IMPLICATIONS
❶
❷

NEGATIVE IMPLICATIONS
❶
❷

B. In a group, share your positive and negative implications, and consider whether the positive ones outweigh the negative ones. Give reasons to support your conclusions.

C. Consequences are the positive and negative outcomes of actual actions, not just ideas. Consider the following five points, and write a consequence related to education that has happened because of each one. After, compare your answers in a group. Which consequences have been positive, and which have been negative? Why?

POINTS	CONSEQUENCES
❶ 1801: The invention of the blackboard	*a more flexible and interactive way to share information*
❷ 1917: The first educational radio classes	
❸ 1959: Introduction of the photocopier	
❹ 1969: The beginning of ARPANET, which led to the Internet	
❺ 1998: Google founded	

READING ❶

To Adapt MOOCs, or Not? That Is No Longer the Question

A Massive Open Online Course (MOOC) is a modern way of teaching and learning. Although there are different forms, the basic idea involves professors recording a set of lectures and setting discussion questions and computer-based tests. Students watch the lectures, participate in discussion forums with other students, and then complete the automatically marked tests or peer mark assignments, without any contact with the professor. Students are not given traditional university credit, in part because professors cannot guarantee that the student writing the test is the same student who took the course.

In the following exercises, explore key words from Reading 1.

A. Draw an arrow (↓) to indicate where in each sentence the word in parentheses should be placed.

1. (ignored) The student the party invitation to finish her project instead.

2. (trend) A recent has seen students using only computers to take notes in class.

3. (retention) Reading appears to be higher with paper books than with e-books.

4. (residential) Traditional programs are still popular despite the rise of online programs.

5. (disparity) Throughout history, there has always been a between educational opportunities for the rich and the poor.

B. Choose the phrase that best completes each sentence. Key words are in bold.

1. A scientist **utilizes** a variety of _____ the spread of viruses.
   a) ways to encourage
   b) books to ignore
   c) tools to investigate

2. By promoting **diversity** in the workplace, governments _____.
   a) can restrict the number of job applicants
   b) encourage the best people to get jobs
   c) frequently ignore the contributions of others

3. In order to be **consistent**, the teacher _____.
   a) marked all the mid-term exams in the same way
   b) developed a different approach for each student
   c) applied a variety of approaches when marking

4. The computer was not **reliable** _____.
   a) so everyone bought one
   b) and was replaced
   c) but only when used

5. There has been an **evolution** in learning materials, that is, we've _____.
   a) gone from computers to books
   b) replaced computers with pencils
   c) gone from books to computers

Before You Read

A. One commercial MOOC provider, Coursera, approached Princeton University professor Mitchell Duneier about licensing his course so other colleges could use the content to save money. Why do you think he refused?

_____

_____

B. According to Yvonne Belanger (2012), although many students sign up for MOOCs, a surprising number fail to complete their studies. Look at the student participation numbers for a Duke University course on bioelectricity, and then discuss with a partner why the completion rate might be so low.

STUDENTS WHO ...	NUMBER
enrolled	12,461
watched a video	7593
answered at least one question correctly on both week 1 quizzes	1267
attempted the final exam	358
passed, earning a certificate	313

Reference

Belanger, Y. (2012, December 4). *Duke's first MOOC: A very preliminary report.* Retrieved from Duke Center for Instructional Technology: http://cit.duke.edu/blog/2012/12/bioelectricity-preliminary-report/

C. While you read, highlight information that could be represented using a visual element. Indicate which visual element would be the most suitable.

To Adapt MOOCs, or Not? That Is No Longer the Question

Online education is certainly not a new approach for learning and teaching in globally disparate environments; it is an approach that has been steadily evolving for years. Massive Open Online Courses (MOOCs) are a logical product of this **evolution**. Online course offerings are one of the most effective and efficient delivery methods for
5 contents and skills globally. There are many common-sense advantages to the online course approach, including the wide flavour of degree programs and classes offered, flexible study times, and the ability for students to balance between a career and education. Although the online movement is growing dramatically, leading to more creative philosophies such as MOOCs, it cannot be considered a true revolution. Yet
10 it cannot be **ignored** for the simple reason that it promotes sharing information worldwide and has created many opportunities for teaching and learning in a variety of disciplines [1, 8, 9, 10].

According to a recent worldwide survey, the adoption
15 of MOOCs is on the rise [2, 3]. Here are a few important responses to the **trend** that should cause universities to seriously pay attention to MOOCs:

- 90 percent of schools offer or plan to offer online courses in the next three years—74 percent offer
20 them today.
- 2013—Only 13 percent of schools offer MOOC; but 43 percent plan to offer MOOCs by 2016.
- Only 44 percent of schools are planning to offer MOOC credits.

25 • 83 percent of schools would consider joining an online education group such as edX, Coursera, or Udacity.

• 67 percent of schools believe that MOOCs will never replace traditional, **residential** classes; 5 percent said yes within five years [quoted directly from the survey results in 3].

30 Thus, "To adopt MOOCs or not?" is no longer a question. It is a logical outcome of the ongoing evolution of distance learning.

...

Advantages and Disadvantages

elite (adj.): highest-level group

1. *Motivation.* MOOCs currently and generally are developed by **elite** universities 35 using prominent professors [4]. The consequences of this approach are two-fold: (i) it serves as a great global marketing technique for universities and (ii) provides opportunities for faculty involved to sell course materials, textbooks, and other related items. On the other hand, student motivation to take these types of courses includes curiosity or getting certificates from the elite universities, boosting their

ego (n.): sense of self-esteem

40 **ego** and possibly their resumes.

2. *Enormous enrolment.* MOOCs have the potential to engage a large number of students—thousands—to take a single course. For instance, Stanford's course on artificial intelligence, taught by two "celebrity professors," attracted 150,000 students. The

intimidating (adj.): frightening or worrying

45 class size may be **intimidating** to instructors, and the common tasks of regular interaction and evaluation are almost impossible; however, a recent report demonstrates the massiveness of MOOCs is a net **boon**, because it can energize

boon (n.): something helpful

50 students and faculty experiences [8, 9].

3. **Retention.** One of the major challenges of MOOCs is drop rate [7]. Since students do not invest any financial resources, it is easy for them to drop a course at any time without any of the 55 consequences that they would have faced with traditional courses. Courses commonly only have a 10–20 percent completion rate [5, 11]—a few

anecdotal (adj.): based on personal experience

anecdotal reports denote as low as 2 percent completion rate.

60 4. **Diversity** *and* **disparity.** Students who are taking MOOC courses inherently represent wider and larger diversity compared with traditional structured curriculum courses. MOOCs experience a wider variety of elements such as background education and specific knowledge and skills, just to list a few. While, like the traditional online courses,

magnitude (n.): great size or extent

65 students geographically present disparity, naturally the **magnitude** is much larger with the MOOCs offerings [9].

5. *Interaction and feedback.* Almost no one in a MOOC receives individual interaction or attention from an expert. Lack of **consistent** review and grading system further weakens the already non-existent interaction, which ultimately provides

70   unacceptable feedback compared with traditional learning [6]. Generally, the
      evaluation of students' work **utilizes** guided peer assessment, which, in turn, opens
      up new safety and privacy issues [8].

      …

      6. *Success rate.* While thousands enrol for the MOOC courses, the completion rate is
75   extremely low; this makes it challenging to determine whether MOOCs are successful
      [4, 5]. Studies report completion rates of between 10 percent and 20 percent
      (80–90 percent non-completion rate), and an even smaller rate of students actually
      receive certificates. It must be noted that "completion" is different from "learning,"
      and yet there are no **reliable** data to support the MOOCs learning outcomes.

80 …

      While MOOCs are in their infancy and need resources and time to evolve into a fully
      effective and efficient educational platform, their potential and movement cannot
      be ignored.

                                                                          (742 words)

References

[1] Martin, F. G. (August 2012). Will massive open online courses change how we teach? *Communications of the ACM, 55*(8), 26–28.

[2] Vihavainen, A., Luukkainen, M., & Kurhila, J. (2012). Multi-faceted support for MOOC in Programming. *ACM Joint Conference SIGITE/RIIT*. Calgary, Alberta.

[3] Afshar, V. (2017, December 6). Adoption of massive open online courses [worldwide survey]. *Huffpost.* Retrieved from http://www.huffingtonpost.com/vala-afshar/infographic-adoption-of-m_b_3303789.html

[4] Sahami, M., Martin, F. G., Guzdial, M., & Parlante, N. (2013, March). The revolution will be televised: Perspectives on massive open online education. *Proceeding of the 44th ACM Technical Symposium on Computer Science Education* (pp. 457–58). Denver, Colorado. doi:10.1145/2445196.2445330

[5] Malan, D. J. (2013, June). Implementing a massive open online course (MOOC) [tutorial presentation]. *Journal of Computing Sciences in Colleges, 28*(6), 136–137.

[6] Carlson, R. (2000). Assessing your students: Testing in the online course. *Syllabus, 12*(7), 16–18.

[7] Kelly, M. (2013, May 7). To MOOC or not to MOOC? What's in it for me? *Edwired.org.* Retrieved from http://edwired.org/to-mooc-or-not-to-mooc-whats-in-it-for-me/

[8] Head, K. (2013, April 29). Massive open online adventure. *The Chronicle of Higher Education.* Retrieved from http://chronicle.com/article/Massive-Open-Online-Adventure/138803/

[9] Roth, M. (2013, April 29). My modern experience teaching a MOOC. *The Chronicle of Higher Education.* Retrieved from http://chronicle.com/article/My-Modern-MOOC-Experience/138781/

[10] Major players in the MOOC universe. (2013, April 29). Retrieved from http://chronicle.com/article/The-Major-Players-in-the-MOOC/138817/

[11] Jordan, K. (2015, June 12). MOOC completion rates: The data. *Katy Jordan: Researching Education and Technology.* Retrieved from http://www.katyjordan.com/MOOCproject.html

North, S. M., Richardson, R., & North, M. M. (2014). To adapt MOOCs, or not? That is no longer the question. *Universal Journal of Educational Research, 2*(1), 69–72. doi: 10.13189/ujer.2014.020108

After You Read

D. Answer the questions and then compare answers with a partner.

1 What do the writers believe are the advantages of online learning?

_____

_____

_____

2 Why do the writers feel there is no question that MOOCs will be adopted?

_____

_____

3 When MOOCs are free, how can universities make money from them?

_____

_____

4 MOOC courses are often not accepted as credit courses because students cannot be properly assessed. What problems with assessment do the writers point out?

_____

_____

E. Explain the significance of each number.

1 150,000 _____

_____

2 2 percent _____

_____

3 43 percent _____

_____

4 5 percent _____

_____

5 between 10 percent and 20 percent _____

_____

F. Imagine that all university education moved online. What would be one positive implication and one negative one? What has been the most positive consequence of online learning with MOOCs? Discuss your answers in a group to see if others agree.

POSITIVE IMPLICATION: _____

NEGATIVE IMPLICATION: _____

POSITIVE CONSEQUENCE: _____

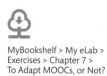

MyBookshelf > My eLab > Exercises > Chapter 7 > To Adapt MOOCs, or Not?

FOCUS ON GRAMMAR

Pronoun-Antecedent Agreement

When you read a text, notice when a pronoun takes the place of a noun. The most common pronouns are personal pronouns that replace the subject or the object of a sentence. The noun to which a pronoun refers is called the *antecedent*. Pronouns and antecedents must agree in gender (male, female, or neutral), case (subject, object, or possessive), and number (singular or plural).

▶

A. Look at the table and fill in the missing pronouns.

	SUBJECT	OBJECT	POSSESSIVE ADJECTIVES	POSSESSIVE PRONOUNS
first-person singular	I		my	mine
second-person singular		you	your	yours
third-person singular	he/she/it	him/her/it	his/_____ /its	his/hers/its
first-person plural	we	us		ours
second-person plural	you	you	your	
third-person plural	they		their	theirs

Note: Two singular subjects connected by a conjunction are treated as plural. The teacher **and** the student wrote **their** ideas on the board.

B. Highlight the pronoun in parentheses that best completes each sentence.

1. John found (my / me / mine) book and put (its / it / us) on (you / your / yours) desk.

2. People freely give (they / them / their) time and expertise to share what (he / they / them) know.

3. When students solve problems, (our / they / us) are rewarded with harder problems.

4. The just-in-time learning model implies (you / me / them) can wait to learn something until just before (us / you / their) need to use (them / it / theirs).

5. Millions experience Internet-based learning in informal ways when (we / they / us) use online tutorial videos.

Indefinite Pronouns

An indefinite pronoun does not refer to any person or thing in particular. Indefinite pronouns can be singular or plural, or both. Plural indefinite pronouns include: *several*, *both*, *few*, and *many*. Singular indefinite pronouns include: *anybody*, *anyone*, *everybody*, *everyone*, *no one*, *nobody*, *somebody*, *someone*, *either*, *neither*.

Gender

Although we consider it sexist, *his* and *he* are often used in situations where the gender might be either male or female.

Every girl and boy should pick up **his** book and decide where **he** can keep it.

Male and female pronouns can be used to avoid offence but can sound awkward, and the traditional order of pronouns (*his/her* and *he/she*) can also appear sexist.

Every girl and boy should pick up **his** or **her** book and decide where **he** or **she** can keep it.

Find ways to avoid gender-biased writing. Change *his* or *her* to *a* if no meaning is lost. Note changes in the pronouns as well as the plural of some nouns.

Students should pick up **their** book**s** and decide where **they** can keep **them**.

Visit My eLab
Documents to review
other types of pronouns:
demonstrative,
interrogative, relative,
reflexive, and intensive.

MyBookshelf > My eLab >
Exercises > Chapter 7 >
Grammar Review

C. Rewrite these sentences to make them gender-neutral. Change pronouns and make nouns plural where necessary.

1. Each classmate can sign his name to join the debate team.

   _____

2. Everybody should choose his seat at the table.

   _____

3. Each student should write his name.

   _____

READING ❷   The SOLE of a Student

SOLE = Self-Organized
Learning Environment

A *polymath* is someone with knowledge in a variety of areas. Sugata Mitra has been called a polymath because of his work in adding to the understanding of molecules, semiconductors, sense organs, computer networking, and Alzheimer's disease. His work has led him to an interest in what he calls "minimally-invasive education," where students are largely left to learn by themselves.

VOCABULARY BUILD

In the following exercises, explore key words from Reading 2.

A. Fill in the blanks with the words from the box.

conducted	ensure	instinctually	merges	transforming

1. A new educational model _____ technology with students' natural creativity.

2. Just as computers once did, mobile phones are _____ educational opportunities.

3. Experiments have been _____ to find the best ways to help students remember.

4. It is important to _____ that students' needs are met, regardless of teaching style.

5. People almost _____ choose older universities, even though there are better, more modern options.

B. Highlight the word or phrase in parentheses that best completes each sentence. Key words are in bold.

1. Preschool education may be largely **unmediated** if parents (make / don't make) decisions about their child's learning.

2. Regardless of any kind of education, an **omnipresent** factor is (assessments / mathematics).

3. **Contemporary** thinking on education tends to focus on (innovations / traditions).

④ Traditionally, the **retrieval** of knowledge was done using your notes or (computers / textbooks).

⑤ Poor nations must rely on **resourcefulness** to overcome what they cannot (afford / waste) in their schools.

Before You Read

A. You have learned many things on your own or without a formal teacher. Write a list and compare it with a partner's list. Which techniques have you used to learn on your own?

B. Read this excerpt from Reading 2 and consider the approach used in the experiment. Then, write three benefits and three problems on a separate page. Discuss your answers in a group.

> I conducted an experiment called the "hole in the wall." By installing Internet-equipped computers in poor Indian villages and then watching how children interacted with them, unmediated, I first glimpsed the power of the cloud [i.e., the Internet]. Groups of street children learned to use computers and the Internet by themselves, with little or no knowledge of English and never having seen a computer before. Then they started instinctually teaching one another.

C. In the first paragraph of Reading 2, Mitra sets up the ideas that follow by asking "How do we spark creativity, curiosity, and wonder in children?" While you read, take notes on how Mitra tries to answer that question in each paragraph and in the flow chart.

The SOLE of a Student

pedagogical (adj.): educational

philosophized (v.): thought about deeply

From Plato to Aurobindo, from Vygotsky to Montessori, centuries of educational thinking have vigorously debated a central **pedagogical** question: how do we spark creativity, curiosity, and wonder in children? But those who **philosophized** pre-Google were prevented from wondering just how the Internet might influence
5 the **contemporary** answer to this age-old question. Today, we can and must; a generation that has not known a world without vast global and online connectivity demands it of us.

military-industrial machine (n.): the military and industry working together for economic reasons

zenith (n.): top point or peak

Victorians (n): people who lived under Queen Victoria's rule (1837–1901)

churned (v.): mixed

robust (adj.): strong

But first, a bit of history: to keep the world's **military-industrial machine** running at the **zenith** of the British Empire, **Victorians** assembled an education system to
10 mass-produce workers with identical skills. Plucked from the classroom and plugged instantly into the system, citizens were **churned** through an educational factory engineered for maximum productivity.

Like most things designed by the Victorians, it was a **robust** system. It worked. Schools, in a sense, manufactured generations of workers for an industrial age.

relics (n.): objects from the past

salient (adj.): most noticeable

15 But what got us here won't get us there. Schools today are the product of an expired age; standardized curricula, outdated pedagogy, and cookie-cutter assessments are **relics** of an earlier time. Schools still operate as if all knowledge is contained in books, and as if the **salient** points in books must be stored in each human brain—to be used when needed. The political and financial powers controlling schools decide
20 what these salient points are. Schools **ensure** their storage and **retrieval**. Students are rewarded for memorization, not imagination or **resourcefulness**.

Today we're seeing institutions—banking, the stock exchange, entertainment, newspapers, even health care—capture and share knowledge through strings of zeros and ones inside the evolving
25 Internet … "the cloud." While some fields are already far advanced in understanding how the Internet age is **transforming** their structure and substance, we're just beginning to understand the breadth and depth of its implications on the future of education.

Unlocking the power of new technologies for self-guided education
30 is one of the twenty-first-century superhighways that need to be paved. Profound changes to how children access vast information is yielding new forms of peer-to-peer and individual-guided learning. The cloud is already **omnipresent** and indestructible, **democratizing** and ever changing; now we need to use it to spark
35 the imaginations and build the mental muscles of children worldwide.

democratizing (adj.): making equal for all

This journey, for me, began back in 1999, when I **conducted** an experiment called the "hole in the wall." By installing Internet-equipped computers in poor Indian villages and then watching how children interacted with them, **unmediated**, I first glimpsed
40 the power of the cloud. Groups of street children learned to use computers and the Internet by themselves, with little or no knowledge of English and never having seen a computer before. Then they started **instinctually** teaching one another. In the next five years, through many experiments, I learned just how powerful adults can be when they give small groups of children the tools and the **agency** to guide their own
45 learning and then get out of the way.

agency (n.): action or intervention

Learning dynamics

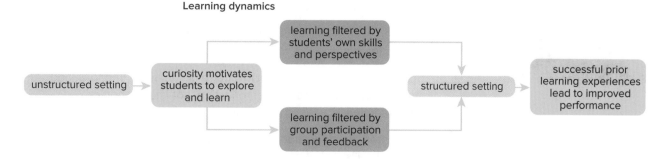

It's not just poor kids that can benefit from access to the Internet and the space and time to wonder and wander. Today, teachers around the world are using what I call "SOLEs," "self-organized learning environments," where children group around Internet-equipped computers to discuss big questions. The teacher **merges** into the
50 background and observes as learning happens.

I once asked a group of ten-year-olds in the little town of Villa Mercedes in Argentina: Why do we have five fingers and toes on each limb? What's so special about five? Their answer may surprise you.

theology (n.): study of religion

amphibians (n.): creatures who live in the water and on land

The children arrived at their answer by investigating both **theology** and evolution,
55 discovering the five bones holding the web on the first **amphibians'** fins, and studying geometry. Their investigation resulted in this final answer: the strongest web that can be stretched the widest must have five supports.

…

We need a curriculum of big questions, examinations where children can talk, share,
60 and use the Internet, and new, peer-assessment systems. We need children from a
range of economic and geographic backgrounds and an army of visionary educators.
We need pedagogy free from fear and focused on the magic of children's innate quest
for information and understanding.

(696 words)

Mitra, S. (2013, February 28). The SOLE of a student. *NDTV*. Retrieved from http://www.ndtv.com/article/world/the-sole-of-a-student-ted-winner-sugata-mitra-s-blog-336014

After You Read

D. Correctly number the sentences to make a summary of Reading 2.

_____ A computer placed in a public space showed how children used it and interacted to learn.

___10___ Example: Children determined that the norm of five fingers is based on building the strongest webs.

___1___ Debate: How do we spark creativity, curiosity, and wonder in children?

_____ In self-organized learning environments (SOLEs), children group around Internet-equipped computers to discuss big questions, and the teacher observes.

_____ Many non-educational institutions are being transformed by the Internet.

_____ People are exploring how an Internet-enabled world can help learning.

_____ School pedagogy is outdated.

_____ Children access vast information through peer-to-peer and individual-guided learning.

_____ Schools still operate as if all knowledge is contained in books, and students are rewarded for memorization, not imagination or resourcefulness.

_____ The Victorians' education system mass-produced workers with identical skills.

MyBookshelf > My eLab >
Exercises > Chapter 7 >
The SOLE of a Student

E. Draw a Venn diagram on a separate page with OLD SCHOOLS as the label for one circle and NEW SCHOOLS as the label for the other. Decide where each sentence in task D belongs and write the number in the appropriate circle, including the overlap between the two circles.

FOCUS ON WRITING

Explaining Processes

The flow chart on page 159 shows a process in a graphic way. A process paragraph, with or without a flow chart, is a descriptive way to explain how something is done or how something happens. For example, a process paragraph might explain developments in the evolution of computers or the steps for what to do if one is not working. Writing about process involves a sequence of steps along with definitions of any technical terms.

▶

A. Read the steps required to write a process paragraph.

STEPS	EXPLANATION	EXAMPLE
CHOOSE A TOPIC	Choose a topic that you understand well and write it in the form of a title.	*How to Brainstorm*
CONSIDER YOUR AUDIENCE	Consider who will be reading your process paragraph and decide how much background information you will need to give.	*college students*
BREAK THE PROCESS INTO STEPS	Use flow chart arrows to briefly outline the steps.	*define problem → appoint reporter → each member speaks → review ideas → discuss → decide*
WRITE A TOPIC SENTENCE	A topic sentence should state what you are going to explain, and why.	*Brainstorming is a skill for generating new ideas that will help you solve problems creatively.*
DEFINE KEY TERMS	Technical terms might need to be defined at the beginning or as part of the step where they appear.	*Brainstorming is a group-thinking activity based on not rejecting others' ideas.*
WRITE THE STEPS IN A LOGICAL ORDER	Write the steps in the correct order. Use transition words to signal the order of steps: *first, begin by, before, next, then, as soon as, finally.* Review the steps to make certain you are not missing any.	*First, define the problem being discussed. Next, appoint a reporter who will record everyone's ideas. Then, let each person offer ideas without interruption or criticism. Finally, when everyone has offered ideas, review and discuss how practical each one is for solving the problem.*
CONCLUDING SENTENCE	Process paragraphs do not need a concluding sentence. However, sometimes a concluding sentence is used to offer encouragement or to give a suggestion of where to find additional information on the topic.	*This is only one of many ways to brainstorm. Look online for others and make brainstorming part of your future group-thinking process.*

B. Number these steps in the correct order to form a process paragraph on how to solve a problem with creative thinking. Highlight the transition words.

_____ After you have had enough time to reflect, be open to surprising ideas and make sure you write them down to study after.

_____ Begin by immersing yourself in the problem you are trying to solve. Find out as much as possible about the problem.

_____ Creative thinking is a way to solve problems that everyone should practise.

_____ Finally, become critical. Challenge your ideas and look for errors; this process can help you spot problems and develop solutions.

___*1*___ How to Solve a Problem with Creative Thinking

_____ Next, step away, giving yourself time to reflect on what you learned.

C. Write a concluding sentence for the process paragraph in task B.

_____

_____

_____

MyBookshelf > My eLab > Exercises > Chapter 7 > Focus on Writing

WARM-UP ASSIGNMENT
Write a Process Paragraph

Write a process paragraph that describes the steps needed to teach someone something new, such as those involved in learning a special skill in your academic discipline, a sport, a game, how to fix something, or how to cook something. Follow the steps outlined in Focus on Writing (page 160).

A. Choose a topic—something you know about that you can easily explain. Your audience will be your class. Use this flow chart to briefly outline the steps.

B. Write your paragraph. Use transition words to signal the order between steps. Pay attention to your use of pronoun-antecedent agreement. Refer to the Models Chapter (page 206) to see an example of a process paragraph and to learn more about how to write one.

C. Add a title and a concluding sentence explaining where students can find more information on your topic.

D. Proofread your paragraph to make sure you have not missed any steps. Then, share your paragraph with a partner and ask for feedback.

Use feedback from your teacher and classmates on this Warm-Up Assignment to improve your writing.

 **READING ❸**   ## A Personal Education

Modern technology may have convinced you that learning is mostly about collecting facts and that those facts are only as far away as an online search on your phone. If that's true, then there's no point in learning some things at all. This is especially true as you individualize your learning, choosing topics of personal interest that you want to study in depth. However, to do so, you need a set of strategies.

In the following exercises, explore key words from Reading 3.

A. Read each sentence and use the context to help you choose the best definition for the word in bold.

1. Check your small **achievements** off a list and reward yourself as you meet mini-goals.
   a) things that you are evaluated on
   b) the things that you accomplish in life

2. Students who took notes on laptops performed worse on **conceptual** questions.
   a) based on theory
   b) based on memorization

3. It's also important to find various ways to **expose** yourself to your topic.
   a) meaningfully encounter
   b) temporarily withdraw from

4. Immersing yourself in learning involves avoiding **interruptions**; turn off your phone!
   a) discussions with others
   b) breaks in concentration

5. Today the focus is more on letting students pursue their **unique** passions.
   a) something universal
   b) something individual

B. Fill in the blanks with the correct words to complete the paragraph.

aspirations	encounter	enthusiasm	generation	scenarios

Each _____ has different attitudes toward education.

Your parents' _____ may have focused on getting a job.

But the employment _____ for you are likely to be more

fluid. Regardless of your _____ for a particular career,

it may be one that begins to disappear by the time you graduate. The best

strategy is to build up a range of skills that will enable you to face any

challenge you _____.

C. VOCABULARY EXTENSION: Many words contain a root word that is sometimes easier to understand. Which of the following have complete root words within them with similar meanings? Write the root words and a definition for each one.

KEY WORDS	ROOT WORDS	DEFINITIONS
1 achievements	*achieve*	*reach an objective*
2 conceptual		

KEY WORDS	ROOT WORDS	DEFINITIONS
❸ encounter		
❹ expose		
❺ interruptions		

MyBookshelf > My eLab >
Exercises > Chapter 7 >
Vocabulary Review

Before You Read

A. Compare one important thing you have learned in a traditional way, either in school or outside of school, with one important thing you learned in a non-traditional way. Discuss the advantages and disadvantages of traditional and non-traditional learning with a partner.

B. What are three key strategies you use for remembering what you learn? Compare your strategies in a group and discuss which are the most effective. Ask yourself which ones you should adopt.

STRATEGY 1: _____

STRATEGY 2: _____

STRATEGY 3: _____

C. As you read, consider what you learned in Focus on Reading (page 148), and think about what type of chart would be good for organizing the points in Reading 3. Would your choice of chart be good for note-taking? Why or why not?

_____

_____

_____

_____

A Personal Education

Science fiction is extremely fond of depicting the future of education. In the simplest, and most unlikely **scenarios**, a young student takes a pill and suddenly has a brain full of decades' worth of knowledge. In many other science fiction scenarios, a student is taught everything worth knowing by a wise computer, often in the form
5 of a robot.

Some future educations involve virtual reality where a student may play games battling aliens (Card, 1994). Lee and Hammer (2011) describe this as the **gamification** of learning that allows students "to experiment with rules, emotions, and social roles" (p. 2). But, often in science fiction, students only observe, such as this description of
10 a virtual visit to Egypt:

> During our world history lesson that morning, Mr. Avenovich loaded
> up a standalone simulation so that our class could witness the discovery
> of King Tut's tomb by **archaeologists** in Egypt in AD 1922. (The day
> before, we visited the same spot in 1334 BC and had seen Tutankhamen's
> 15 empire in all its glory.) (Cline, 2011, p. 48)

gamification (n.): turning something into a game

archaeologists (n.): those who study human history and prehistory through excavations

The writer goes on to describe travelling through a human heart in biology class, visiting the Louvre Museum in Paris in art class, and standing on one of Jupiter's moons in astronomy class.

20 What these and other scenarios often lack is an understanding of the process of education. More than half a century ago, Bruner (1960) wrote that "Each **generation** gives new form to the **aspirations** that shape education in its time" (p. 1). His idea was

25 that education is not a fixed process with the content to be learned and the same objectives to be pursued. While schools were once concerned with training most students to become clerks and factory workers, today the focus is more on letting students pursue

30 their **unique** passions. DeMers (2017) outlines a nine-step process for learning almost anything on your own.

1. Talk to an expert.

ironically (adv.): happening in an unexpected way

Ironically, the first step is to follow one of the oldest ways of learning: find a mentor. A mentor is someone who has learned what you want to learn and may be able to

35 share strategies and shortcuts. If you want to learn mountain climbing, an expert might share key safety tips.

2. Immerse yourself in learning.

Immersing yourself in learning involves avoiding **interruptions** (turn off your phone!) to focus on what you need to learn. It's also important to find various ways to **expose**

40 yourself to your topic. For example, if you want to learn to play the guitar, listen to recordings, go to concerts, and read guitar books and magazines.

3. Time your learning.

When you are learning something new, your attentiveness can begin to wander. It is better to schedule multiple short sessions of twenty to thirty minutes to maintain

45 your peak focus.

4. Take notes.

Taking notes is a way to help preserve ideas in your mind, but use a pen and paper, not a computer. Mueller and Oppenheimer (2014) explain,

shallower processing (n.): considering something with less reflection

> … even when laptops are used solely to take notes, they may still be
> 50 impairing learning because their use results in **shallower processing**.
> In three studies, we found that students who took notes on laptops
> performed worse on **conceptual** questions than students who took
> notes longhand. (p.1)

5. Focus on the key ideas.

55 Once you've sorted out how to learn, focus on the key ideas. You can pick up other details later.

6. Look for feedback.

As you learn, it's important to get feedback to ensure you are on the right path, and not just practicing mistakes.

hardwire (v.): make behaviours or beliefs standard

60 **7. Make time to practice.**

Whatever you learn, you can also forget. Use practice to **hardwire** new ideas into your mind.

8. Share.

When you learn something new, share it with others or even try to teach them what 65 you have learned. Not being able to do so, or having people not comprehend your explanations, is a way to see what you may not have mastered in your learning.

9. Avoid the dip.

setback (n.): a reversal in progress

tedious (adj.): boring

Author Seth Godin defines the dip as a temporary **setback** that can be overcome with persistence. When you are learning something new, you often **encounter** a dip in 70 **enthusiasm** because the work can seem difficult or even **tedious**. The point is to find a reason—any reason—for continuing. These reasons might include checking your small **achievements** off a list and rewarding yourself as you meet mini-goals.

Until an education pill is developed, these nine steps may be the best way to learn on your own.

(749 words)

References

Bruner, J. (1960). *The process of education.* Cambridge, MA: Harvard University Press.

Card, O. S. (1994). *Ender's game.* New York: Tom Doherty Associates.

Cline, E. (2011). *Ready player one.* New York: Random House.

DeMers, J. (2017, August 31). The 9 steps that will help you learn anything. *Entrepreneur.* Retrieved from https://www.entrepreneur.com/article/299219

Lee, J. J., & Hammer, J. (2011). Gamification in education: What, how, why bother? *Academic Exchange Quarterly, 15*(2). Retrieved from https://www.researchgate.net/publication/258697764_Gamification _in_Education_What_How_Why_Bother

Mueller, P. A., & Oppenheimer, D. M. (2014, April 23). The pen is mightier than the keyboard: Advantages of longhand over laptop note taking. *Psychological Science, 25*(6), 1159–68. doi:10.1177/09567 97614524581

After You Read

D. Review your notes, and use what you learned in Focus on Critical Thinking (page 149) to imagine possible implications if you adopt each of the points in Reading 3.

POINTS	POSSIBLE IMPLICATIONS
❶ TALK TO AN EXPERT	*The expert might introduce you to other people in the field.*
❷ IMMERSE YOURSELF IN LEARNING	
❸ TIME YOUR LEARNING	
❹ TAKE NOTES	
❺ FOCUS ON THE KEY IDEAS	

POINTS	POSSIBLE IMPLICATIONS
❻ LOOK FOR FEEDBACK	
❼ MAKE TIME TO PRACTISE	
❽ SHARE	
❾ AVOID THE DIP	

MyBookshelf > My eLab > Exercises > Chapter 7 > A Personal Education

E. Reflect on your answers to task A (page 164). Of the things you identified that you had learned, which might you try to learn differently after reviewing the points in Reading 3? Why? Discuss your answers in a group.

Academic
Survival Skill

Working in a Group

Being able to work effectively as a group is a valuable achievement. Group work skills are always useful, whether organizing projects with friends, fellow students, volunteers, or co-workers. Part of working in a group is making sure each group member shares a common goal and has a plan for reaching it. Group members may sometimes have personal priorities that interfere with the goal. Good group members learn to manage each other, ensuring that conflict is recognized and quickly handled.

A. Read the steps with a partner. Compare them with group projects you have participated in. Discuss similarities and differences, and add to the questions.

STEPS IN A GROUP PROJECT	QUESTIONS
❶ Define the assignment; make sure everyone has a common understanding.	What exactly is the teacher asking for in this assignment? What additional information does the group need?
❷ Negotiate to divide the work into smaller equal tasks.	What is a fair way to divide the work?
❸ Define roles for each group member based on interests, strengths, and skills.	Who will do which task? Do any of the group members have special skills?
❹ Organize a timeline to get the work done in a sequential manner.	Is there an order in which things need to be done? Do some tasks need to be finished before other tasks can be started?
❺ Keep track of progress and report to the group, dealing with conflicts promptly.	Are you using a Gantt chart or some other way to organize your schedule? Do you need help from another group member, or do other group members need more help or time?
❻ Evaluate how well you worked together to improve for next time.	Was the process of working together efficient and effective for everyone? What should be changed? What could have been done to make working together better?

B. Use the information in this paragraph to complete the Gantt chart.

> We will begin the project on April 23 and spend four days designing the questionnaire. As soon as the questionnaire is finished, we will spend two days using it to collect information. Then, on the 29th, we can begin work on the computer presentation. This work will continue until May 5, but during this time, from April 30 to May 3, work can be done on the handouts. While the handouts are being made, the poster should be designed. Poster design will also go on from April 30 to May 3, but the person who makes the posters should put them up on May 5. We will have a meeting to practise the presentation on the evening of May 5. The presentation is on May 6. A meeting to evaluate how our working together went will be held on May 7.

ACTIVITIES	APRIL								MAY						
	23	24	25	26	27	28	29	30	1	2	3	4	5	6	7
DESIGN QUESTIONNAIRE	■	■	■	■											
COLLECT INFORMATION															
WORK ON COMPUTER PRESENTATION															
PREPARE HANDOUTS															
DESIGN AND PLACE POSTERS															
PRACTISE PRESENTATION															
PRESENTATION															
EVALUATION MEETING															

C. Discuss the Gantt chart in a group. Which tasks would be the easiest to complete? Which tasks would be the hardest? Decide who in your group would take on which task based on individual strengths or skills.

FINAL ASSIGNMENT

Write a Process Paragraph and Give a Presentation

Working in a group, use what you learned in this chapter to write two (or more) paragraphs outlining a process. Then, present the process to the class.

A. Form a group of three or four students and, as a group, choose a topic related to education.

☐ How do students choose a discipline or program to study?

☐ How were the first universities established?

☐ How do different students plan their study schedules?

☐ How does a particular type of book organize information?

☐ ANOTHER TOPIC: _____

B. Ask your teacher for approval of your choice of topic.

C. Follow the steps in Academic Survival Skill: assign roles, divide work among group members, and prepare a Gantt chart to schedule task times and deadlines, with the start date and the presentation date. Tasks might include research, writing, visual elements, preparation of the presentation, and giving the presentation in front of the class.

D. For the written work, review Focus on Writing (page 160) and Focus on Grammar (page 155). For visual elements, review Focus on Reading (page 148). Refer to the Models Chapter (page 206) to see an example of a process paragraph and to learn more about how to write one.

E. Work to complete assigned tasks and monitor progress as a group.

F. Practise your presentation, and then deliver it to the class.

G. After the presentation, meet as a group to discuss feedback from the class and your teacher and to evaluate how well you worked together as a group and what could be improved for next time.

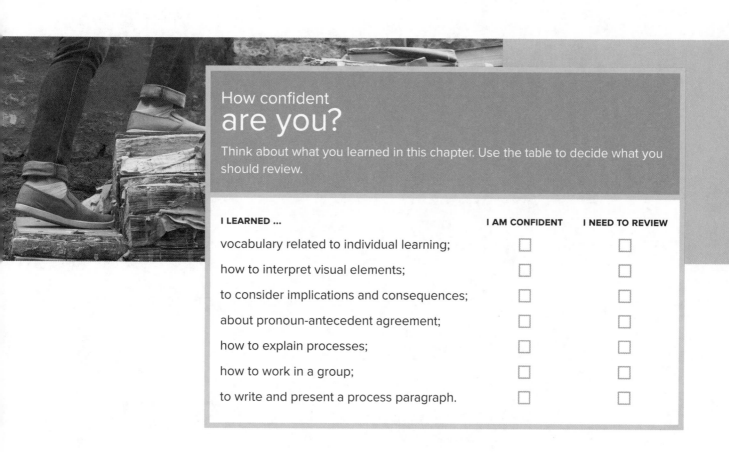

How confident
are you?

Think about what you learned in this chapter. Use the table to decide what you should review.

I LEARNED ...	I AM CONFIDENT	I NEED TO REVIEW
vocabulary related to individual learning;	☐	☐
how to interpret visual elements;	☐	☐
to consider implications and consequences;	☐	☐
about pronoun-antecedent agreement;	☐	☐
how to explain processes;	☐	☐
how to work in a group;	☐	☐
to write and present a process paragraph.	☐	☐

CHAPTER 8

Rights and Obligations

The basic obligation of every government is to care for its citizens, ensuring that they can enjoy their rights. Of increasing concern is a question of the role of governments, businesses, and individuals in protecting one right in particular: privacy. With the rise of a digital culture, your private information is increasingly at risk of being shared with those who can misuse it, particularly to steal from you and to damage your reputation, such as through online bullying. The opposite is also true; governments and organizations sometimes hide information that they should share with the public.

How important is your private information?

In this chapter, ## you will

- learn vocabulary related to privacy and the law;

- distinguish fact from opinion;

- identify and use persuasive techniques;

- use the active and passive voice;

- explore the persuasive essay format;

- learn how to prepare for an exam;

- write an introductory paragraph and a persuasive essay.

GEARING UP

A. Look at the diagram and then answer the questions.

Nine aspects of human rights

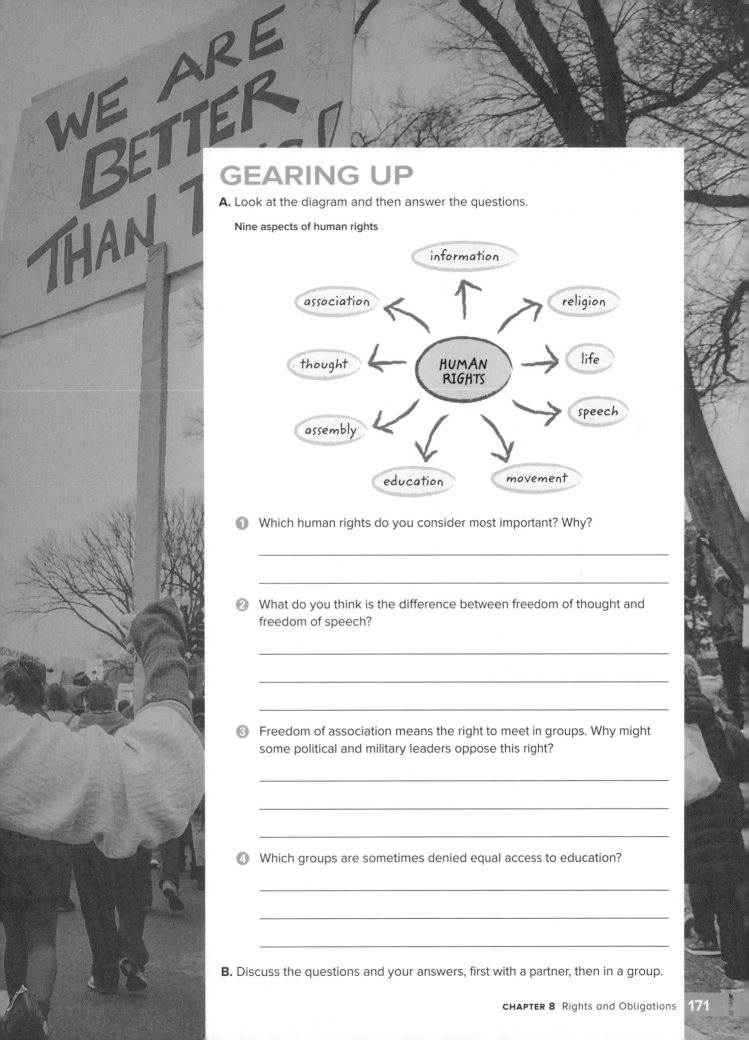

1 Which human rights do you consider most important? Why?

_____

_____

2 What do you think is the difference between freedom of thought and freedom of speech?

_____

_____

_____

3 Freedom of association means the right to meet in groups. Why might some political and military leaders oppose this right?

_____

_____

_____

4 Which groups are sometimes denied equal access to education?

_____

_____

_____

B. Discuss the questions and your answers, first with a partner, then in a group.

Below are the key words you will practise in this chapter. Check the words you understand, then underline the words you use. Highlight the words you need to learn.

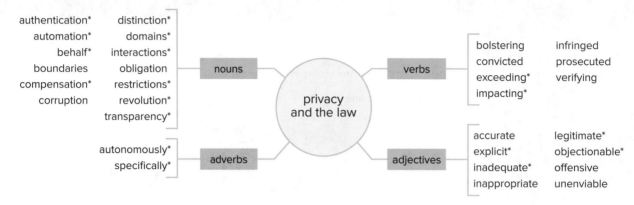

nouns
authentication*
automation*
behalf*
boundaries
compensation*
corruption
distinction*
domains*
interactions*
obligation
restrictions*
revolution*
transparency*

adverbs
autonomously*
specifically*

privacy and the law

verbs
bolstering
convicted
exceeding*
impacting*
infringed
prosecuted
verifying

adjectives
accurate
explicit*
inadequate*
inappropriate
legitimate*
objectionable*
offensive
unenviable

* Appears on the Academic Word List

FOCUS ON READING

A famous person's opinion is still just an opinion, especially if the person is not an expert on the topic.

Distinguishing Fact from Opinion

One important critical skill to develop is the ability to distinguish fact from opinion. A fact is something that has been scientifically investigated and proven to be true, or something that is accepted because it has occurred in history. For example, "the Earth revolves around the sun" is a fact, even though most Europeans believed the opposite until the 1540s. Proof came from observation and mathematics. An opinion is something that cannot be proven or may simply be an idea that differs from person to person. You may think solar flares are the greatest threat facing Earth, but your belief does not make it a fact. Opinions are debatable; facts are not. When trying to distinguish fact from opinion, ask questions.

A. Read these comparisons of facts and opinions. Then, write an example of your own.

QUESTIONS	FACTS	OPINIONS
IS IT TRUE?	A fact is scientifically proven or agreed upon by experts: *Newspapers are printed on paper.* Example: _____ _____	An opinion is a personal belief that may not be shared by others: *Newspapers are too expensive.* Example: _____ _____
DOES IT EXIST?	Facts can be observed first-hand by anyone: *Loch Ness is a lake in Scotland.* Example: _____ _____	Opinions cannot be observed or supported by proof: *The Loch Ness monster is a prehistoric creature.* Example: _____ _____
HAS IT OCCURRED?	Even if something cannot be observed today, it can be established through logical thinking: *Fossils tell us dinosaurs once existed.* Example: _____ _____	An opinion lacks evidence or scientific credibility: *Early humans hunted dinosaurs.* Example: _____ _____

B. Decide whether these statements are fact or opinion. Discuss your answers with a partner.

1. Earth is home to billions of people. _____

2. The press has never been fair in reporting the news. _____

3. The first person to step onto the moon was Neil Armstrong. _____

4. A full moon affects a person's mood. _____

5. The moon's gravitational forces influence the tides. _____

C. Comparative and superlative adjectives can signal opinions, as can statements that feature phrases such as "I believe" or "everyone knows." Numerical data—statistics and dates—often indicate facts. Consider the words and phrases in bold, and indicate which would signal a fact and which an opinion. Discuss your reasons with your partner.

STATEMENTS	FACT	OPINION
1. Exactly **37 percent** of the class are members of a gym.	☐	☐
2. The **worst** thing to do for a cold is to overeat.	☐	☐
3. The flower is sort of a **greyish purple**.	☐	☐
4. Many of the store's employees are **mean**.	☐	☐
5. Orange juice is **better** for you than apple juice.	☐	☐
6. The house has several **glass** windows.	☐	☐
7. The kangaroo is the **quickest** animal in the world.	☐	☐
8. Cheetahs run at speeds of **120 kilometres per hour**.	☐	☐

D. *Reasonable* or *valid* opinions are supported by facts. *Invalid* opinions are not supported by facts. Choose the phrase that makes each sentence a valid opinion.

1. Bananas are a healthier choice for runners than apples because bananas _____.
   a) contain high levels of potassium
   b) can be eaten more quickly

2. London is the most popular city in the world _____.
   a) because it is so beautiful and has wonderful museums and art galleries
   b) based on its ranking for the highest number of tourist visits

3. At most, people can remember five to seven things at the same time, based on _____.
   a) a few friends of different ages I asked
   b) a study by George A. Miller in a 1956 issue of *Psychology Review*

4 Most real estate agents aren't as concerned with their clients' money as with their own, _____.

    a) measured by how much longer agents wait to sell their own versus clients' homes

    b) because everyone naturally looks after their own interests before the needs of others

FOCUS ON CRITICAL THINKING

Identifying Persuasive Techniques

Think of a strong opinion you have. What would make you change your mind about it? The art of persuasion is about changing people's minds with a mix of persuasive language and supporting facts. Persuasive writing needs to capture readers' attention, encourage them to consider new ideas, and help them make decisions that they realize make more sense or that will benefit them. Identifying persuasive techniques when you read can help you better understand arguments.

A. Persuasive text is more effective if it explains the context of an argument, explains why there is a problem, and offers supporting examples, usually in the form of facts. Read the following sentences from Reading 1 and identify the role of each one.

SOLUTIONS	CONTEXT	PROBLEMS	EXAMPLES
1 As a result, the distinction between private and public spheres is blurring and the individual's right to privacy is being threatened.	☐	☐	☐
2 *Business Insider* projects there will be 34 billion devices connected to the Internet by 2020.	☐	☐	☐
3 In hiring practices, for example, algorithms mimic human decision-making, which can be based on bias.	☐	☐	☐
4 However, not all data is created equal, nor is it equally available across geographies and demographics.	☐	☐	☐
5 Millions of us are giving away our private data without even realizing, despite many of us valuing privacy more than ever.	☐	☐	☐
6 The biggest sources of risk for data-related discrimination are inadequate data availability and biased or error-ridden data.	☐	☐	☐

> ❗ *Be critical of weak rhetorical questions with obvious answers, such as "Do you want to be rich?"*

B. A key technique in persuasive writing is asking rhetorical questions that are aimed to make the reader think rather than provide a quick answer. Rhetorical questions make readers question what they know about a topic and their assumptions or opinions they may have. Reread the first three sentences in task A and write a rhetorical question about each one.

RHETORICAL QUESTION 1: *Do you think your data is safe?* _____

RHETORICAL QUESTION 2: _____

RHETORICAL QUESTION 3: _____

C. A persuasive text starts with a thesis statement that includes the writer's point of view (or opinion) and facts that support it. The phrase *testing your thesis* refers to looking at your own persuasive argument and trying to imagine what facts would support the opposite point of view. In a persuasive essay, it's common to identify the opposite point of view and then use facts to explain why arguments for it are faulty. Work with a partner to fill in the table.

PERSUASIVE ARGUMENT (OPINION)	OPPOSITE POINT OF VIEW (OPINION)	WHY THE OPPOSITE POINT OF VIEW IS WRONG (FACTS)
1 Privacy is overrated.	*Privacy is underrated.*	*Losing private bank information can lead to financial problems.*
2 Home Internet connected devices (ICDs) are entertaining and useful.		
3 Stores cannot be trusted with the private information they collect about you.		

READING 1 — How Are Today's Biggest Tech Trends Affecting Our Human Rights?

More than at any other time in history, technology is changing society and creating new challenges for human rights. These include questions not asked before, such as whether businesses or governments need to compensate human workers when their jobs are taken by machines. The answers to these and other questions may be difficult, but you need to consider your future in light of them.

VOCABULARY BUILD

In the following exercises, explore key words from Reading 1.

A. Choose the phrase that best completes each sentence. Key words are in bold.

1 The **automation** of many apps to collect private information means _____.

    a) it can be done far more efficiently

    b) robots are directly employed

    c) no one knows how it's being used

2 The term **domains** is used to describe a kind of _____.

    a) place not found on computers

    b) the identities of companies

    c) neighbourhood on the Internet

3 The likelihood of your personal information **impacting** your buying decisions _____.

    a) cannot be measured

    b) is extremely high

    c) is about 50 percent

4 Social media has produced a **revolution** in the way _____.

    a) marketing professionals can identify potential shoppers

    b) political groups refuse to follow government policies

    c) the Internet has been able to keep many groups quiet

5 In asking for greater **transparency**, governments would like to see _____.

    a) a reduction in the number of public complaints

    b) companies have more opportunities for privacy

    c) users made aware of how their information is used

B. Fill in the blanks with the correct words to complete the paragraph.

authentication	autonomously	distinction	exceeding	interactions

Most websites are already _____ their advertised purpose by collecting information on users. By asking for personal details, supposedly for _____, they are blurring the _____ between a business that supplies information and one that merely collects it. Working _____, bots use your personal details and connect them with other details about you, including photos. Eventually, all your online _____ are monitored and will be sold to marketing companies.

Before You Read

A. Reading 1 begins with a reference to the Fourth Industrial Revolution. With a partner, look at the innovations in the table and decide which revolution produced each one.

INNOVATIONS	FIRST	SECOND	THIRD	FOURTH
❶ 3D printing	☐	☐	☐	☑
❷ digital technologies	☐	☐	☐	☐
❸ growth of large factories	☐	☐	☐	☐
❹ industrial robots	☐	☐	☐	☐
❺ internal combustion engine	☐	☐	☐	☐
❻ Internet	☐	☐	☐	☐
❼ light bulb	☐	☐	☐	☐
❽ personal computer	☐	☐	☐	☐
❾ rail travel	☐	☐	☐	☐

INNOVATIONS		FIRST	SECOND	THIRD	FOURTH
⑩	self-driving vehicles	☐	☐	☐	☐
⑪	steam engine	☐	☐	☐	☐
⑫	telephone	☐	☐	☐	☐

B. In the first paragraph of Reading 1, the writer says that the Fourth Industrial Revolution has the potential to both challenge and uphold human rights. Think of one way each might happen.

① CHALLENGE HUMAN RIGHTS:

_____

_____

② UPHOLD HUMAN RIGHTS:

_____

_____

C. While you read, highlight the writer's opinions.

How Are Today's Biggest Tech Trends Affecting Our Human Rights?

As a technological **revolution**, the Fourth Industrial Revolution is changing the way we live, work, and interact with one another. It also has the potential to both challenge and uphold human rights. How are today's three biggest technological trends **impacting** these rights?

5 ## Automation and the Right to Fair and Decent Work

The increasing use of AI and **automation** is disrupting the global jobs market and significantly impacting the right to fair and decent work. Experts estimate that, by 2020, 85 percent of all customer **interactions** will be handled without a human agent, with support coming in the form of

10 **chatbots** and self-service technologies. The **OECD** estimates that AI is currently meeting or **exceeding** human performance in a significant number of **domains**.

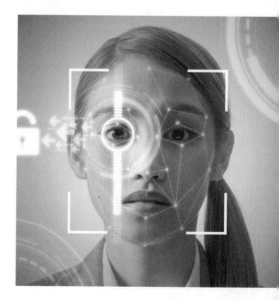

A subset of AI, **machine learning** (ML), is
15 expanding rapidly, unlocking pathways to increasingly efficient, accurate, and powerful processes ranging from diagnosing cancer to enabling self-driving cars. Data is the key ingredient that makes machine learning
20 possible. Companies like HireVue are using AI and **facial analysis** to measure tone and delivery, for example, to make the hiring process more efficient.

chatbots (n.): computer programs designed to simulate conversation with humans

OECD (n.): Organization for Economic Cooperation and Development

machine learning (n.): a form of data analysis that allows computers to learn

facial analysis (n.): a computer program that interprets facial expressions

However, not all data is created equal, nor is it equally available across geographies
25 and demographics. The biggest sources of risk for data-related discrimination are
inadequate data availability and biased or error-ridden data. In hiring practices, for
example, algorithms mimic human decision-making, which can be based on bias.

The Internet and the Right to Freedom of Expression

The Internet provides huge opportunity for individuals to exercise the right to **freedom**
30 **of opinion and expression** through communication and exchange of ideas. More
than 3 billion people now use the Internet, a 2.3 billion rise since 2000.

Yet governments around the world shut down the Internet more than fifty times in
2016, according to the United Nations—**suppressing** elections, slowing economies,
and limiting free speech.

35 ## The Internet of Things and the Right to Privacy

The Internet of Things is perforating domains that were
previously private. As a result, the **distinction** between private
and public spheres is blurring and the individual's right to
privacy is being threatened. *Business Insider* projects there
40 will be 34 billion devices connected to the Internet by 2020.
All of those devices have the ability to interact with and track
our personal data, from smartphone location tracking to
motion sensors with inbuilt video cameras filming your
movements.

45 Millions of us are giving away our private data without even
realizing it, despite many of us valuing privacy more than
ever. This has an impact on children as well as adults. There
is a growing industry of "smart toys" equipped with AI and **speech recognition** that
can interact with children, learn, and send data back to the manufacturers—potentially
50 violating the privacy rights of the child.

Three Ways Technology Can Protect Human Rights

1. Online learning and the right to education

More than 120 million children and adolescents around the world are out of school.
Technology is becoming a major asset in the pathway to ensuring a quality education
55 for all.

EdTech is disrupting education. Companies such as RoboTutor are creating open-
source apps that enable children with little or no access to schools to learn basic
reading, writing, and arithmetic. Chimple is using gamification and cognitive research
to develop open-source software to **autonomously** help children learn—in groups
60 or alone.

2. Big data and human rights

There is a now a vast amount of data available on environmental conditions,
migration, and conflict situations thanks to social media, crowd-sourced data, and
tracking devices on vehicles, mobile phones, and other sensors. Cloud computing and
65 big data analysis can use this data to analyze key trends and provide early warnings
for critical issues before they occur, aiding the prevention and **rapid response** to
humanitarian disasters.

freedom of opinion and expression (n.): the right to share your ideas

suppressing (v.): taking away the rights of people

speech recognition (n.) the ability of a computer to identify and respond to spoken language

rapid response (n.): describes individuals and teams trained to handle emergencies at short notice

3. Protecting human rights in the supply chain

Modern-day slavery still exists in the supply chains of many corporations. An estimated 70 30 million people are currently in forced labour in supply chains across multiple industries from electronics to fishing. Blockchain is an **authentication** mechanism that can enable **transparency** in supply chains from sourcing through to the customer purchase.

(681 words)

Hickin, R. (2017, December 11). How are today's biggest tech trends affecting our human rights? *World Economic Forum*. Retrieved from https://www.weforum.org/agenda/2017/12/how-are-today-s-biggest-tech-trends-affecting-human-rights/

After You Read

D. Indicate whether these statements are fact or opinion, according to the text. If you are not sure, read each statement in the context of its paragraph.

STATEMENTS	FACT	OPINION
LINE 6: The increasing use of AI and automation is disrupting the global jobs market and significantly impacting the right to fair and decent work.	☐	☐
LINE 18: Data is the key ingredient that makes machine learning possible.	☐	☐
LINE 26: In hiring practices, for example, algorithms mimic human decision-making, which can be based on bias.	☐	☐
LINE 30: More than 3 billion people now use the Internet, a 2.3 billion rise since 2000.	☐	☐

E. Review the numbers in the reading, and write notes about each one's significance.

NUMBERS	SIGNIFICANCE
85 percent (LINE 8)	
fifty times (LINE 32)	
34 billion (LINE 40)	
millions (LINE 45)	
more than 120 million (LINE 54)	
30 million (LINE 71)	

F. Indicate whether these statements are true or false, according to the text. Write the correct answers for those that are false.

STATEMENTS	TRUE	FALSE
❶ An increase in humans handling fewer interactions is likely to lead to greater unemployment.	☐	☐
❷ Since 2000, billions of people have lost access to the Internet.	☐	☐
❸ Governments generally reduce Internet access as a way to limit free speech.	☐	☐
❹ The Internet of Things poses considerable threats to areas that were once private.	☐	☐
❺ Smart toys are being used to give adults' information to manufacturers.	☐	☐
❻ The use of open-source apps gives more children a chance to learn.	☐	☐
❼ Analysis of data about environmental conditions has created critical problems.	☐	☐
❽ Blockchain is being used to increase slavery.	☐	☐

MyBookshelf > My eLab >
Exercises > Chapter 8 >
How Are Today's Biggest Tech Trends
Affecting Our Human Rights?

FOCUS ON GRAMMAR

Active and Passive Voice

In Reading 1, you saw examples of both the active and the passive voice. Use the active voice when the subject is doing the action. Use the passive voice when the subject is being acted upon or when you are not sure who is doing the action. Form the passive voice by changing the order and roles of the subject and object in a sentence. The subject becomes the object. Change the verb to the past tense and use a form of *to be*.

A. Compare these two sentences, and highlight the word that is the important factor in each: *vehicles* or *GPS*?

ACTIVE VOICE: GPS tracks vehicles.

PASSIVE VOICE: Vehicles are tracked by GPS.

In some sentences in the passive voice, the actor is unknown or unimportant.

PASSIVE VOICE: Vehicles are tracked.

B. Write three sentences about technology protecting human rights.

1️⃣ ACTIVE VOICE (education rights): _____

_____

2️⃣ PASSIVE VOICE WITH ACTOR (big data): _____

_____

3️⃣ PASSIVE VOICE WITH NO ACTOR (supply chain): _____

_____

C. Rewrite each sentence, either from the passive voice to the active voice or from the active voice to the passive voice. Add or delete words as necessary.

1️⃣ Gamification improves motivation.

_____

2️⃣ Data is collected by smart toys.

_____

3️⃣ Students use free software.

_____

4️⃣ The girl was taught by a robot.

_____

MyBookshelf > My eLab >
Exercises > Chapter 8 >
Grammar Review

5️⃣ The thief took their passwords.

_____

READING ②   **What Is Google's "Right to Be Forgotten"?**

Have you ever done something you regretted that you wish you—and others—could just forget? The answer is probably yes; most people have. However, what might once have been an embarrassment among family or friends is now more likely to become permanent if it is preserved online in a discussion or, worse, video. Should the ability to be forgotten online be a right?

VOCABULARY BUILD

In the following exercises, explore key words from Reading 2.

A. Choose the best word to complete each sentence. Key words are in bold.

1️⃣ By **bolstering** her passwords, she _____.

   a) quickly found hackers using her computer

   b) was able to keep her private files secure

   c) was targeted by many new advertisers

② It's usually an **inadequate** response to hacking _____.

    a) to just turn off your computer

    b) to install anti-virus software

    c) to get it checked by experts

③ When your rights are **infringed** upon, it means _____.

    a) they are outside of anyone's concern

    b) someone has disregarded your privacy

    c) few people have complete access to them

④ If a **legitimate** website requests your personal information, _____.

    a) it likely means that it's illegal

    b) there's no reason to give it to them

    c) you should understand why

⑤ Many people find pop-up advertisements **objectionable** _____.

    a) when they interfere with using your computer

    b) if the only object is to provide you information

    c) as long as it's something useful and interesting

B. Read each word in context and match it to its definition.

① We do not believe that individuals should have the right to have links to **accurate** and lawfully available information about them removed, simply because they do not like what is said.

    a) correct

    b) imperfect

② The applicant has the legal authority to act on the claimant's **behalf**.

    a) against the will of an individual

    b) in the interests of a person or group

③ You can demand information be destroyed if the data's erasure is necessary to comply with a legal **obligation**.

    a) awareness

    b) responsibility

④ All applications must verify that the links in question relate **specifically** to the applicant.

    a) in a precise way

    b) more internationally

⑤ Google faces the **unenviable** task of balancing its duty to comply with its users' "right to be forgotten."

    a) unintentional

    b) disagreeable

Before You Read

A. Paragraphs begin with a topic sentence. Review the first paragraph of Reading 2 and paraphrase it to create a simple topic sentence.

_____

_____

B. The third paragraph includes four types of personal online information that might be a problem. With a partner, think of one example of each, such as ones related to a crime.

INACCURATE: _____

_____

INADEQUATE: _____

_____

IRRELEVANT: _____

_____

EXCESSIVE: _____

_____

C. Like most persuasive writing, the following article is a mixture of opinions and facts. While you read, highlight the opinions.

What Is Google's "Right to Be Forgotten"?

Regulations **bolstering** citizens' privacy and digital rights have been given greater weight in recent years, with the European Court of Justice's (ECJ) ruling in 2014 around the "right to be forgotten" addressing the long shadows cast by information published in articles that can exist forever on the Internet.

5 It started when a Spanish citizen launched a complaint against a newspaper and Google in 2010 that an article about an action notice for his **repossessed** home had **infringed** his privacy, because it was out of date and no longer relevant. The case went to the ECJ, and the court subsequently ruled that search engines are controllers of personal data—meaning they are subject to Europe's data laws.

repossessed (adj.): taken back

10 Therefore, EU citizens were given the right to ask search engines to remove links to articles from search results if they contained personal information deemed inaccurate, **inadequate**, irrelevant, or excessive.

absolute right (n.): a right that is more important than all others

public interest (n.): something for the greater good

But the "right to be forgotten" is not an **absolute right** and must be balanced against other rights such as that of freedom of expression, the court said, with information
15 in the **public interest**, for instance, unlikely to be removed on request. Google, and any other search engine, must consider removing links to any information that is inaccurate, inadequate, irrelevant, or excessive, when a request is filed from an individual about their own search results.

Under GDPR [General Data Protection Regulation], then, an EU citizen has the right
20 to demand an organization erases their personal data if

consent (n.): permission

- the data is no longer relevant to the reason it was collected;
- the person withdraws their **consent** for their data to be used (and if the organization has no other legal basis for collecting it);
- the person objects to their data being collected for marketing purposes or where
25 their rights override **legitimate** interests in collecting data (for instance, where that is sensitive data concerning a child);
- the data was unlawfully processed;
- the data's erasure is necessary to comply with a legal **obligation**;
- the data belongs to a child and was exchanged for "information society
30 services."

Who Is Regulating the Right to Be Forgotten?

How Google handles complaints and requests to remove information from its search results will be looked over by a taskforce of European privacy **watchdogs**, referred to as Article 29.

watchdogs (n.): those who are responsible for protecting people's rights

35 Following the flood of requests received by Google, Professor Luciano Floridi, the person tasked with determining how Google can comply with the recent EU court ruling, said in 2014: "People would be screaming if a powerful company suddenly decided what information could be seen by what people, when, and where. That is the consequence of this decision. A private company now has to decide what is in the
40 public interest."

Google, currently responsible for almost 90 percent of web searches in Europe, faces the **unenviable** task of balancing its duty to comply with its users' "right to be forgotten" and preserving its reputation as the go-to source for online information and content.

Peter Barron, Google's director of communications for Europe, said, "The European
45 court of justice ruling was not something that we wanted, but it is now the law in Europe, and we are obliged to comply with that law. We are aiming to deal with it as responsibly as possible ... It's a very big process, it's a learning process, we are listening to the feedback, and we are working our way through that."

All applications must verify that the links in question relate **specifically** to the applicant
50 unless the applicant has the legal authority to act on the claimant's **behalf**, in which case this must be proven.

Is It about Privacy or Censorship?

The request form was launched by Google after the ruling received 12,000 entries from across Europe within twenty-four hours—at one point receiving up to twenty
55 requests a minute. This grew to 41,000 requests in the first four days.

There are concerns from many that the ability for users to request that information be removed from search results could result in the system being abused for **nefarious** purposes.

60 However, lawyers have assured those worried that politicians, celebrities, and criminals will probably not benefit from the ruling, as Google will have the right to reject applications that request removal of information deemed in the public interest.

It should also be noted that, while links to the **objectionable** information will be removed, the information will not actually be deleted from the web.

Following on from comments regarding the ruling, Baroness Prashar, chair of the Lords 65 Home Affairs EU Sub-Committee, said, "[We] do not believe that individuals should have the right to have links to **accurate** and lawfully available information about them removed, simply because they do not like what is said."

(772 words)

Afifi-Sabet, K., & Hopping, C. (2019, January 10). What is the "right to be forgotten"? *IT Pro.* Retrieved from http://www.itpro.co.uk/data-protection/22378/what-is-googles-right-to-be-forgotten

After You Read

D. Review these GDPR rules for the right to be forgotten, and rate them from most (1) to least (6) important.

_____ the data is no longer relevant to the reason it was collected

_____ the person withdraws their consent for their data to be used (and if the organization has no other legal basis for collecting it)

_____ the person objects to their data being collected for marketing purposes or where their rights override legitimate interests in collecting

_____ the data was unlawfully processed

_____ the data's erasure is necessary to comply with a legal obligation

_____ the data belongs to a child and was exchanged for "information society services"

E. Write short answers to the following questions.

1 What is the importance of a Spanish citizen's home being repossessed?

_____

_____

2 What concern was raised by Professor Luciano Floridi?

_____

_____

3 Why is Google particularly affected by the new law?

_____

_____

④ Why might it be important that only the affected person apply for the right to be forgotten?

_____

_____

_____

⑤ How are privacy and censorship different concerns in this ruling?

_____

_____

⑥ Why might politicians, celebrities, and criminals probably not benefit from the ruling?

_____

_____

MyBookshelf > My eLab >
Exercises > Chapter 8 >
What Is Google's "Right to
Be Forgotten"?

F. Reread the last paragraph of Reading 2. Think of an example of something embarrassing that a well-known person has said or done. Is it fair that the information is freely available online? Why or why not? Write your opinion on a separate page and discuss in a group.

FOCUS ON WRITING

Writing a Persuasive Essay

Essays organize your thoughts in a logical order. Often, an essay is used to construct an argument, leading the reader step-by-step from an opinion through evidence toward a conclusion that may call for action. Essays are not just used in academic settings. Speeches, newspaper articles, blogs, and other genres may also use the essay format.

A persuasive essay tries to convince the reader of a particular point of view. It has three sections: an introduction, body paragraphs, and a conclusion. Because an essay is formal writing, do not use contractions, and use the full forms of acronyms and initialisms followed by their abbreviations in parentheses.

A. Read the explanations of the sections of an essay, and write sentences to complete the body paragraphs. Note the rhetorical questions used throughout.

SECTIONS	EXPLANATION	EXAMPLE ESSAY
TITLE	Engage your readers by being informative and using language that makes them curious.	*Do You Deserve Privacy?*
INTRODUCTION	Give the reader a reason for caring about the information. Include a thesis statement that features three or more points that support your point of view. Each point will become a topic sentence, developed in its own paragraph. Note the rhetorical questions.	*When most people think about a loss of privacy, they consider the consequences in terms of financial loss or embarrassment. Celebrities, such as music and movie stars, often complain of both, sometimes in court. But celebrities are not entitled to the same degree of privacy because they boast about their wealth, expose family members to the press, and engage in behaviours designed to attract undue attention.*

SECTIONS	EXPLANATION	EXAMPLE ESSAY
PARAGRAPH 1	Develop the first—and usually strongest—point. There should be a smooth transition from the introduction to the first body paragraph. Each paragraph should provide evidence in the form of examples and explanations.	*You probably know about your favourite celebrity's wealth, homes, and expensive vehicles. This is often because celebrities willingly share that information.*
PARAGRAPH 2	Develop the second point, which is usually the second strongest.	*Is it fair for movie stars to have it both ways? They often complain about the press taking photos of their children, but include their children in "exclusive" paid photo shoots for glossy magazines.*
PARAGRAPH 3	Develop the third—and sometimes weakest—point.	*Some celebrities may enjoy quiet times at home, but many attract attention by taking outrageous and well-publicized holidays designed to increase the public's interest.*
CONCLUSION	Summarize the points and restate the thesis statement in a new way. You may include a call to action, asking the reader or others to make a change.	*When celebrities boast about their wealth, expose family members to the public, and engage in attention-seeking behaviours, they lose their right to privacy. Celebrities can only have privacy if they truly want it.*

B. Following certain steps can help you write a persuasive essay. Number these steps in the correct order.

_____ Share your draft with a partner. Ask your partner to proofread it and to give you feedback.

_____ Use key words from your thesis statement to search for support as well as ideas that contradict your point of view. You will need these to build your arguments.

_____ Review your draft. Read it out loud to make certain that it flows logically from point to point.

_____ While you write, check that you have clear transitions between sentences and paragraphs.

___*1*___ Use the question or topic you are trying to argue to write your thesis statement.

_____ When you have your notes, look for examples and explanations that support your point of view.

MyBookshelf > My eLab >
Exercises > Chapter 8 >
Focus on Writing

WARM-UP ASSIGNMENT

Write an Introductory Essay Paragraph

In 1842, when he was fourteen years old, an English boy, Henry Caitlin, was convicted of stealing the equivalent of twenty cents. He was charged with theft and sent to work as a prisoner in Australia for fourteen years. Although the punishment was according to the law, you would probably agree that he did not receive justice. *Laws* are a country's system of rules; *justice* refers to what is fair.

In the Final Assignment, you will write a persuasive essay. In this Warm-Up Assignment, you will choose the essay topic and write the title and introductory paragraph.

A. The assignment is to find a law, or a punishment, and persuade others that it is just or unjust. You may consider a law that does not go far enough, perhaps referring to an actual criminal case.

B. Use the library or the Internet to find and research laws and summaries of legal cases. You can research an old law or a current one, but you must develop a point of view about it that you can use to persuade people that it is just or unjust. You may consider laws from other countries.

C. Ask your teacher for approval of your choice of topic.

D. Organize your research notes using a mind map (see Chapter 4, page 95) or other visual aid.

E. Write the title of your essay. _____

F. Write the introduction on a separate page. In the introduction, give your thesis statement with the three points that you will use to persuade people. Review Focus on Writing (page 186), and refer to the Models Chapter (page 207) to see an example of a persuasive essay and to learn more about how to write one.

G. Proofread your introduction. Then, share it with a partner and ask for feedback.

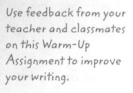

Use feedback from your teacher and classmates on this Warm-Up Assignment to improve your writing.

READING ③

Private Lives: We Need New Laws

In Missouri, USA, driving with a bear that's not in a cage is illegal. This old law likely came into place after one unusual event. Many other laws are created in attempts to keep up with new innovations in crime. The development of digital technologies has created enormous challenges for lawmakers around the area of individuals' rights to privacy. What types of personal information do you believe should be protected?

In the following exercises, explore key words from Reading 3.

A. Fill in the blanks with the correct word or phrase to complete the paragraph.

convicted	corruption	explicit	prosecuted	verifying

After police identify a crime such as _____, the alleged

criminals are then _____, where _____

evidence needs to be presented in front of a judge and sometimes a jury. After

_____ the evidence, the criminals are _____

and fined or sent to jail. Increasingly, the victims of the crime are consulted

about the judgments.

B. Match each key word to its definition

KEY WORDS		DEFINITIONS
❶ boundaries	_____	a) not suitable or appropriate for the circumstances
❷ compensation	_____	b) something that makes people feel upset
❸ inappropriate	_____	c) lines showing the limits of an area
❹ offensive	_____	d) limits on what can be done
❺ restrictions	_____	e) a payment of some kind to make up for a loss

C. VOCABULARY EXTENSION: Choose the word from task B that can be used to complete all of the following sentences.

❶ Everything he had to say was hateful and _____.

❷ Because he disliked being criticized, he tended to be on the _____.

❸ The general decided that the troops needed to go on the _____.

❹ There was an _____ odour coming from the broken-down fridge.

❺ The last-minute _____ tackle helped the football team win the game.

Before You Read

A. Persuasive writing mixes opinions and facts. Read the conclusion of Reading 3, and highlight opinions and underline facts. After, share your answers with a partner, and discuss how the opinions and facts complement each other.

> Arguments around personal responsibility, permission, and consequences may continue, but action to create laws, police them, and test them in the courts is necessary right now. And because digital information flows internationally, any solution needs to be international. In 1948, the United Nations created the Universal Declaration of Human Rights. It's time for a Universal Declaration of Digital Rights.

MyBookshelf > My eLab >
Exercises > Chapter 8 >
Vocabulary Review

B. Read the following four rhetorical questions from Reading 3. Consider your answer to each question, and then explain why the writer asked each rhetorical question. After, check your answers based on the context of the reading.

1 Is it fair that other users joining social media sites can create pseudonyms (false names) to post offensive messages, sharing racist and sexist content and bullying others?

ANSWER: _____

WHY IT WAS ASKED: _____

_____

2 Who gave businesses permission to track individuals?

ANSWER: _____

WHY IT WAS ASKED: _____

_____

3 But what would you do if you were sitting in your backyard and saw a camera-equipped drone hovering overhead?

ANSWER: _____

WHY IT WAS ASKED: _____

_____

4 It can be extremely difficult to catch a drone, let alone its owner, but what consequences do drone makers face?

ANSWER: _____

WHY IT WAS ASKED: _____

_____

C. While you read, look for examples of facts and opinions, and consider how they make the text more persuasive.

Private Lives: We Need New Laws

In 1931, notorious gangster Al Capone was **convicted** of income tax evasion. It was generally agreed that he was responsible for far worse crimes, including extensive **corruption** and countless murders, but he understood the law well enough to avoid being charged for those offenses (Bair, 2016). When new ways are found to get around existing laws, it takes time for lawmakers, police officials, and the courts to catch up. This is the case today with digital issues, and new laws are needed to outline the **boundaries** around personal responsibility, permission, and consequences.

Personal Responsibility

Everyone makes mistakes and does things they regret, but if they do these things online, the digital record of those misdeeds can last forever and be spread internationally. Many social media sites depend on rules around personal responsibility to protect themselves from being sued, but do little to protect their users. For example, although sites like Facebook have **restrictions** that require users to be age thirteen and above, younger children still routinely join, lying about the age question.

15 However, whether users are eleven or thirteen, they are still not adults and should not be expected to have a high degree of personal responsibility if they join **inappropriate** websites or post questionable content. Is it fair that other users joining social media sites can create **pseudonyms** to post **offensive** messages, sharing racist and sexist content and bullying others?

20 Laws should make the companies responsible for **verifying** the identities of all users, as is the case with countless other businesses and government agencies. Where personal responsibility boundaries are breached, both the social media organizations and the individuals involved should be **prosecuted**. At this time, the usual practice is simply to ban offenders after one or more complaints. No care or **compensation** is given to 25 victims.

Permission

The idea of permission has become difficult to measure in a world where every phone is also a video camera. Images and video files can be shared **effortlessly** with no regard to others' personal privacy. Moreover, so-called security cameras in businesses 30 and public streets not only capture endless images but can use facial recognition technologies to identify individuals and connect identities to other data. Who gave businesses permission to track individuals? The answer is *no one*.

Laws should restrict the collection, sharing, and use of others' images taken without 35 **explicit** permission. Enforcing such laws would be as easy. Makers of digital cameras could code information about the person or organization taking the image. Whoever takes an embarrassing image could be held 40 **criminally responsible** for any misuse.

Consequences

With every new technology, there are new opportunities for abuse of others' rights. Practical drones were first created in 1917 45 for use in war (Dormehl, 2018), and few laws governed their use. By the late 1990s, consumer drones began to be popular. Their threat to planes has meant that many airports have posted no-fly zones for drones, and cities have joined in on banning them for privacy reasons.

But what would you do if you were sitting in your back yard and saw a camera-equipped 50 drone hovering overhead? In 2015, Kentucky homeowner William Merideth's reaction was to use a shotgun to take one down; he was charged, but a judge **sided with** him and ordered his release (Thomasen, 2018).

It can be extremely difficult to catch a drone, let alone its owner, but what **consequences** do drone makers face? The individual flying the drone might be punished, but the 55 companies who built the technologies are not, even though they clearly assist in privacy crimes being more easily committed. Laws need to change to broaden the responsibility for crimes to include **enablers**, not just **perpetrators**.

Conclusion

Arguments around personal responsibility, permission, and consequences may continue,
60 but action to create laws, police them, and test them in the courts is necessary right
now. And because digital information flows internationally, any solution needs to be
international. In 1948, the United Nations created the Universal Declaration of Human
Rights. It's time for a Universal Declaration of Digital Rights.   (679 words)

References

Bair, D. (2016). *Al Capone: His life, legacy, and legend.* New York: Anchor Books.

Dormehl, L. (2018, September 11). The history of drones in 10 milestones. *Digital Trends.* Retrieved from https://www.digitaltrends.com/cool-tech/history-of-drones/

Thomasen, K. (2018, February 20). Personal drones, AI, and our privacy. *Policy Options.* Retrieved from http://policyoptions.irpp.org/magazines/february-2018/personal-drones-ai-and-our-privacy/

After You Read

D. Reading 3 sets out the writer's opinion of three areas where new laws are
necessary. Write the problems and examples as well as possible laws for
these areas.

AREAS OF CONCERN	PROBLEMS AND EXAMPLES	POSSIBLE LAWS
❶ PERSONAL RESPONSIBILITY		
❷ PERMISSION		
❸ CONSEQUENCES		

E. In Focus on Critical Thinking (page 174), you learned about testing a thesis by
imagining what facts would support the opposite point of view. Consider the
following three opinions from Reading 3, and write brief arguments for the
opposite point of view.

❶ Whoever takes an embarrassing image could be held criminally responsible
for any misuse.

_____

_____

❷ Laws need to change to broaden the responsibility for crimes to include
enablers, not just perpetrators.

_____

_____

③ It's time for a Universal Declaration of Digital Rights.

_____

_____

MyBookshelf > My eLab >
Exercises > Chapter 8 >
Private Lives: We Need New Laws

F. You have a lot of control over your online privacy, such as by reading the terms-of-use documents that accompany social media, not posting personal details online, and asking questions about how your information will be used each time it is requested. After working through this chapter, are you more likely to take better care around your personal information? Why or why not? Discuss your ideas in a group.

Academic
Survival Skill

Preparing for an Exam

After months of lectures and tutorials, you will usually face exams. It can be a stressful time, with last-minute cramming, practising new skills, and trying to understand and remember hundreds of details. But understanding, remembering, and applying what you learn should begin the first day of class, not just when you need to pass an exam.

A. Here are some tips on how to prepare for an exam. Discuss these with a partner. Talk about what you already do and what you might do in the future.

HOW TO PREPARE FOR AN EXAM	
FIND SPACE TO STUDY	Find a study space free of distractions, including from technology (e.g., your phone) and friends. Make sure you have the right tools and resources: books, notes, etc.
FIND TIME TO STUDY	Study after each class. Turn your notes into points to remember and questions to research.
PREDICT	Predict questions you might be asked based on the type of exam. Multiple-choice tests focus on many small details, while essay questions deal with understanding broad themes and evidence to support them. Write practice questions and answer them.
SHIFT INFORMATION	Shift information in your brain. Rewrite your notes in graphic organizers and summary paragraphs. Discuss with a study partner. Read your questions and answers out loud. Create flash cards to review while waiting in lines and on public transportation.
KNOW THE DETAILS OF YOUR EXAM	Imagine yourself at the exam, and think through all the steps that will get you there. Confirm the time, place, and type of exam (ask your teacher if you are unsure).
EXERCISE, EAT, AND SLEEP	Be physically and mentally fit. Get enough good food, water, exercise, and rest.
DURING THE EXAM	Don't panic. Scan the exam to understand the questions. Check the marks' weighting to see which sections are worth more than others and budget your time accordingly.
AFTER THE EXAM	Evaluate your study plan. If you didn't make the right decisions, revise your plan for the next time.

B. Think of an unsatisfactory exam experience you had in the past. Write what you could have done differently, and why. When you finish, discuss in a group.

_____

_____

_____

FINAL ASSIGNMENT
Write a Persuasive Essay

Use what you learned in this chapter to write a persuasive essay. Review Focus on Writing (page 186) and refer to the Models Chapter (page 207) to see an example of a persuasive essay and to learn more about how to write one.

A. Start with the title and introductory paragraph you wrote for Warm-Up Assignment. Review it to see what you can improve, based on feedback you received from other students and your teacher.

B. In the Warm-Up Assignment, you organized your research notes in a mind map or other chart. Review these notes and add to them if necessary. Use the notes to write your body paragraphs, providing examples and explanations. Try to use both the active and the passive voice (Focus on Grammar, page 180). Use transition words to ensure unity and coherence (see Chapter 6, Focus on Writing, page 130). Use what you learned in Focus on Critical Thinking (page 174) to organize your ideas persuasively.

C. Write your conclusion. Your conclusion should relate to and/or restate your thesis. Add a call to action—something that you want your readers to do based on the points you have raised in your essay. For example, you might encourage them to share the points with friends.

D. Proofread your essay. Then, share with a partner and ask for feedback.

E. Make corrections and write a final copy.

How confident
are you?

Think about what you learned in this chapter. Use the table to decide what you should review.

I LEARNED ...	I AM CONFIDENT	I NEED TO REVIEW
vocabulary related to privacy and the law;	☐	☐
to distinguish fact from opinion;	☐	☐
to identify and use persuasive techniques;	☐	☐
the correct use of the active and passive voice;	☐	☐
about the persuasive essay format;	☐	☐
tips on preparing for an exam;	☐	☐
how to write an introductory paragraph and a persuasive essay.	☐	☐

MODELS CHAPTER

This chapter provides models for the writing assignments found in *LEAP 2: Reading and Writing*. All are based on different aspects of the city. Using the city as a common topic lets you see how similar information can be organized for different writing assignments.

Before each model, **you will find**	• instructions that highlight the key characteristics of the writing assignment;	• if applicable, the plan that the writer used to prepare for the writing assignment.

MODEL 1 | **How to Write a Descriptive Paragraph**

The paragraph is the basis of many kinds of writing, including news articles and essays. A paragraph is a group of connected sentences on the same topic. It includes a topic sentence, supporting sentences, and a concluding sentence.

Instructions

• Write a topic sentence to suggest the reason you are writing, such as answering a question or solving a problem. The topic sentence explains your main idea but doesn't give detailed information.

• Add supporting sentences that expand on the idea or ideas of your topic sentence. A supporting sentence usually includes facts, examples, and explanations. There may be three or more supporting sentences in a paragraph. Sometimes more than one sentence is used to explain a single detail.

• Close with a concluding sentence that brings your ideas together. This sentence may restate the topic sentence in a different way or summarize the supporting sentences. Sometimes the concluding sentence is a transition to a new topic in the next paragraph.

• Choose a mind map as a graphic organizer when you are brainstorming ideas for a descriptive paragraph. If you are describing something over time, use a timeline. For the example topic (a description of Venice from the outside in), you could brainstorm on a copy of a map of Venice.

Example of a Descriptive Paragraph

Describe the city of Venice.

WRITER'S PLAN	
CHOOSE A WAY TO DESCRIBE IT	• work from the outside in, from the sea surrounding the city to the public squares at its centre
TOPIC SENTENCE	• introduce the city and stress that it differs from other cities • note it is worth exploring
SUPPORTING SENTENCE	• 118 islands separated by canals and connected by bridges • no cars so you walk or take boats
SUPPORTING SENTENCE	• daily markets offer fresh meats, fish, poultry, and fruits and vegetables for 270,000 locals
CONCLUDING SENTENCE	• public squares = heart of Venetian neighbourhoods • tourists (22 million) visit, but squares for Venetians

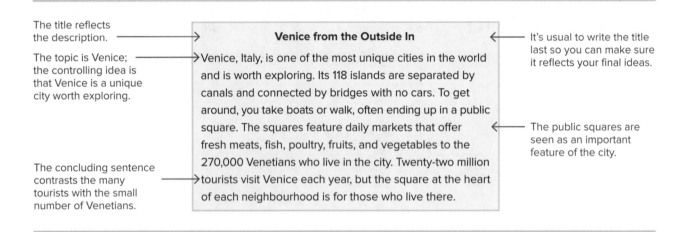

The title reflects the description.

The topic is Venice; the controlling idea is that Venice is a unique city worth exploring.

The concluding sentence contrasts the many tourists with the small number of Venetians.

Venice from the Outside In

Venice, Italy, is one of the most unique cities in the world and is worth exploring. Its 118 islands are separated by canals and connected by bridges with no cars. To get around, you take boats or walk, often ending up in a public square. The squares feature daily markets that offer fresh meats, fish, poultry, fruits, and vegetables to the 270,000 Venetians who live in the city. Twenty-two million tourists visit Venice each year, but the square at the heart of each neighbourhood is for those who live there.

It's usual to write the title last so you can make sure it reflects your final ideas.

The public squares are seen as an important feature of the city.

MODEL 2.1 How to Write a Cause and Effect Topic Sentence

When you write a thesis statement, it should help the reader understand your point of view and the points you will support it with, linking causes and effects.

Example of a Topic Sentence

Write a topic sentence about three things that will cause Venice problems.

STRATEGIES	EXAMPLES	
CHOOSE YOUR TOPIC	• changes to Venice, Italy	
CHOOSE A POINT OF VIEW ON YOUR TOPIC	• the changes are destroying the city	
THINK OF TEN POINTS THAT SUPPORT YOUR POINT OF VIEW Some points may be similar, but keep brainstorming without editing until you have many to choose from.	• bad for locals • cheap tourist souvenirs • frequent flooding • lack of jobs for locals • lack of toilet facilities	• locals renting apartments • restaurants overwhelmed • too many cruise boats • too many tourists • tourist crowds at religious sites

CONSIDER WHICH POINTS ARE MOST EFFECTIVE, BASED ON WHETHER THEY CAN BE SUPPORTED BY EXAMPLES AND EXPLANATIONS Rewrite them to make them clear.	• overwhelming numbers of tourists • loss of quality of life for traditional Venetians • the commercialization of traditional industries
WRITE A TOPIC SENTENCE THAT GIVES YOUR POINT OF VIEW AND MENTIONS THREE POINTS IN SUPPORT OF IT	The city's uniqueness is leading to Venice's destruction through overwhelming numbers of tourists, loss of quality of life for traditional Venetians, and the sale of cheap tourist goods.

MODEL 2.2 How to Write a Cause and Effect Paragraph

Cause and effect paragraphs may talk about things in the past, or may discuss past causes that will lead to effects in the future. A cause and effect paragraph includes a topic sentence, supporting sentences, and a concluding sentence. The concluding sentence often interprets the changes, commenting on them.

Instructions

- Write one or more background sentences that provide the writer's point of view.
- Write a topic sentence with three points to be developed in supporting sentences.
- Use one or more sentences to expand on each of the three points of the topic sentence.
- Close with a concluding sentence that brings your ideas together. This sentence may restate the thesis statement in a different way or summarize the supporting sentences. It may also restate the writer's point of view in a new way.
- Choose a table with columns and rows as a graphic organizer when you are brainstorming ideas for a cause and effect paragraph. In the first column, list the points; in the second column, list examples and explanations.

Example of a Cause and Effect Paragraph

Write an introductory paragraph and cause and effect paragraph about the future of Venice.

WRITER'S PLAN	
CHOOSE A POINT OF VIEW	• tourists may destroy Venice, Italy, one of the most unique cities in the world
INTRODUCE BACKGROUND	• explain why Venice is unique with three points
TOPIC SENTENCE	• explain three things that will cause Venice to change
SUPPORTING SENTENCE 1	• too many tourists • 22 million versus 270,000 locals
SUPPORTING SENTENCE 2	• loss of quality of life for traditional Venetians • crowded out from daily life
SUPPORTING SENTENCE 3	• loss of traditional arts and crafts • cheap imitations
CONCLUDING SENTENCE	• emphasize Venice's attractions will disappear • relate to rising sea levels to make it memorable

Venice Overwhelmed

The title sparks interest and also gives the writer's point of view: it's negative.

The first sentence gives background on the causes leading up to the present moment.

Venice, Italy, is one of the most unique cities in the world because of its historical significance, its 118 islands connected by bridges over canals, and its cultural charms. But Venice's uniqueness is leading to its destruction through overwhelming numbers of tourists, loss of quality of life for Venetians, and the sale of cheap tourist goods.

The thesis statement outlines three points that will be developed with examples and explanations.

Loss of quality of life is a primary effect.

Arriving by rail and boat, 22 million tourists visit Venice each year, vastly outnumbering the 270,000 locals and making it difficult for them to go about their daily business. This means a loss of quality of life for Venetians who increasingly move out of the city, renting their small apartments at rates that provide them with mansions elsewhere. The traditional arts and crafts of Venice, like Murano glassware, are increasingly supplanted by cheap imitations, depriving local craftspeople of incomes. The result will eventually be for Venice to become more like a theme park. Some worry about climate change making Venice disappear beneath rising sea levels, but Venice's attractions will probably first disappear beneath millions of tourists.

The numbers are examples; the explanation of their significance is how tourists interfere.

Moving out of the city is a secondary effect.

The cause and effect of the second point is implied; the increased worth of the homes as rentals encourages Venetians to leave.

The third point about the commercialization of Venice's traditional industries is followed by another sentence that gives the explanation of why it is a problem.

The conclusion summarizes the points as causing Venice to disappear.

The *climate change* comment makes the conclusion more memorable.

MODEL 3 **How to Write a Compare and Contrast Paragraph**

A compare and contrast paragraph shows similarities and differences. When you compare two or more items, you list similarities. When you contrast items, the focus is on differences.

Instructions

- Decide what you are explaining using points of comparison or contrast.
- Use one of the two methods of organization: the *point-by-point method* or the *block method*. The point-by-point method compares or contrasts each idea before moving on to the next. The block method talks about all the points of one of the things being compared or contrasted first and then repeats with the second idea being compared or contrasted.
- Comparison words include *similarly*, *likewise*, and *in the same way*.
- Contrast words include *although*, *however*, and *but*; *yet* and *on the other hand* highlight contrasts.
- Use a topic sentence, supporting sentences, and a conclusion. Note: The block method often requires two paragraphs.
- Use a Venn diagram as a graphic organizer for your compare and contrast paragraph notes.

Example of a Compare and Contrast Paragraph

Compare and contrast religious buildings in Cologne, Germany, and Kyoto, Japan.

WRITER'S PLAN	
INTRODUCTION	• religious buildings worldwide (comparison) • different materials: stone and wood (contrast) • different materials available in different places (contrast)
POINT-BY-POINT METHOD	• how long it takes to build a cathedral (Cologne Cathedral, 600 years) contrasted with a temple (Kiyomizu-dera, 2 years) • contrast roles of the craftsperson: stonemasons out of work after a job is done and don't pass down their skills; carpenters need to pass on their skills for repair and replacement work • conclusion: fire not a big threat to cathedrals, therefore stonemasons' skills unnecessary; fire a threat to temples, therefore carpenters' skills necessary
BLOCK METHOD	PARAGRAPH 1, CATHEDRAL: • time required to build a stone cathedral, up to 600 years • example Cologne Cathedral, Cologne, Germany • conclusion: stone masons' skills were not passed down after completion because they were not needed PARAGRAPH 2, TEMPLE: • time required to build a large wooden temple, 2 years • example Kiyomizu-dera, Kyoto, Japan • conclusion: carpenters' skills are passed down because repair and replacement are constant with wooden structures

POINT-BY-POINT METHOD

The title summarizes the three points. ———→

The topic sentence identifies the common factor (religious buildings) and a difference: stone versus wood.

Cathedrals, Temples, and Skills

→People have always built religious buildings from stone or wood. Building a stone cathedral was often a multi-generational undertaking, lasting as long as six hundred years, as in the case of the Cologne Cathedral. On the other hand, Kyoto's Kiyomizu-dera wooden temple was completed in just two years. Stonemasons who finished a cathedral would find few opportunities to use their skills. In contrast, wooden temples need constant upkeep as weathered, burnt, or insect-eaten portions are replaced. Stone walls may have preserved cathedrals from fire, but fire may have preserved the skills of Japanese carpenters.

←— Related points are set together for easy comparison.

The point-by-point format makes it easier to create a concluding sentence, in this case, contrasting the role of materials in preserving skills.

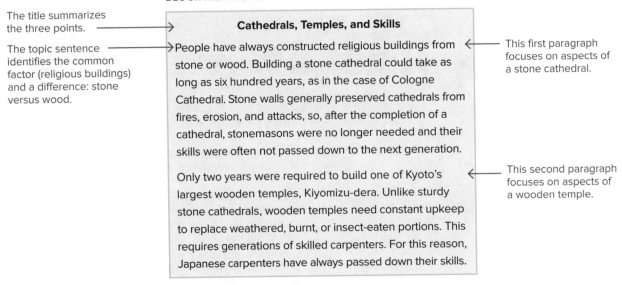

BLOCK METHOD

The title summarizes the three points.

The topic sentence identifies the common factor (religious buildings) and a difference: stone versus wood.

Cathedrals, Temples, and Skills

People have always constructed religious buildings from stone or wood. Building a stone cathedral could take as long as six hundred years, as in the case of Cologne Cathedral. Stone walls generally preserved cathedrals from fires, erosion, and attacks, so, after the completion of a cathedral, stonemasons were no longer needed and their skills were often not passed down to the next generation.

This first paragraph focuses on aspects of a stone cathedral.

Only two years were required to build one of Kyoto's largest wooden temples, Kiyomizu-dera. Unlike sturdy stone cathedrals, wooden temples need constant upkeep to replace weathered, burnt, or insect-eaten portions. This requires generations of skilled carpenters. For this reason, Japanese carpenters have always passed down their skills.

This second paragraph focuses on aspects of a wooden temple.

MODEL 4.1 How to Write a Short Definition

When you introduce a new term or concept in an assignment, you can include an informal definition or a formal definition.

Example of a Short Definition

Define a city.

Use one or more of these strategies to write a definition.

STRATEGY	EXAMPLE	EXPLANATION
synonym	A city is a **big town**.	Synonyms are usually informal definitions.
examples	A city, **like London or New York** ...	Examples should be clear enough that they are not confused.
words and phrases that signal a definition	A city can be **defined as** a large town.	Expressions include "that is to say" or "can be defined as" and "in other words."
a second sentence	A city is a big town. **A city can be several towns that have merged.**	The second sentence should repeat the key word to signal that it is a definition.
what it is not	A city **is not like** a town, which is unlikely to have all the professional services that the general public requires.	When defining something by what it is not, choose something close in meaning.
part of speech	A city (**noun**) is ...	This and the next two items are used in more formal definitions.
the class	A city (noun) is a **place** where a large number of people live and work.	A class defines the group the term belongs to.
an expression that separates the term from its class	A city (noun) is a place **where a large number of people live and work**, with a population in excess of fifty thousand people under a local political administrative unit.	Separating a term from others is called *disambiguation*.

How to Write a Definition Paragraph

A definition paragraph is an extended explanation of a term. It often combines several of the strategies in Model 4.1. Use a definition paragraph as a part of an essay where a common understanding of a key term is essential before further explanation can take place.

Instructions

- Write a topic sentence that gives a simple definition.
- Use supporting sentences to give additional information.
- Do not write a concluding sentence; it is seldom necessary in a definition paragraph unless the point of supplying the definition is to transition to another paragraph.
- Use a mind map as a graphic organizer when you are brainstorming ideas for a definition paragraph.

Example of a Definition Paragraph

What is a city?

WRITER'S PLAN	
TOPIC SENTENCE WITH A SIMPLE DEFINITION	• a city is a place • a large number of people live and work there
EXAMPLE WITH DETAILS	• Hong Kong began as a small village • grew into a major port because of its deep harbour
EXAMPLE WITH DETAILS	• surrounding farms have slowly been converted to land for homes and businesses
WHAT IT IS NOT	• no urban sprawl like Los Angeles • mountains and the ocean divide urban dwellers from those who live in rural villages

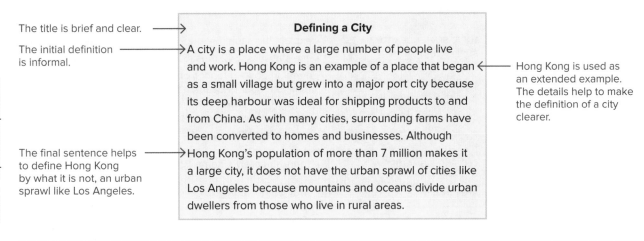

The title is brief and clear. ⟶

The initial definition is informal. ⟶

Defining a City

A city is a place where a large number of people live and work. Hong Kong is an example of a place that began as a small village but grew into a major port city because its deep harbour was ideal for shipping products to and from China. As with many cities, surrounding farms have been converted to homes and businesses. Although Hong Kong's population of more than 7 million makes it a large city, it does not have the urban sprawl of cities like Los Angeles because mountains and oceans divide urban dwellers from those who live in rural areas.

Hong Kong is used as an extended example. The details help to make the definition of a city clearer.

The final sentence helps to define Hong Kong by what it is not, an urban sprawl like Los Angeles.

MODEL 5 　How to Write a Formal Email

Unlike informal messages to friends and family, formal emails are written to share important information in academic, business, and other contexts.

Instructions

- Confirm the correct email address of the person you are writing to.
- Make sure your own email address is serious and clearly identifies you; avoid playful addresses.
- Explain your topic in the subject line; recipients may not read the email if they think the subject is unimportant.
- Use a paragraph format for the body of the message. Include a topic sentence that explains your reason for writing (e.g., a question, request, or message of thanks).
- Add supporting sentences with brief facts, examples, and explanations.
- Write a concluding sentence. If your email is a request, include a clear statement of what you would like to happen as a result of the message. The term for this is *a call to action*.
- End with a closing—a farewell word or phrase followed by your name. Formal emails most often close with *Yours sincerely*.
- Signatures are not required on emails. If appropriate, include your name and title or role.
- Explain any attachment. In letters, the term *encl.* (enclosure) is used, but emails more commonly use the word *attached*.
- Use a mind map as a graphic organizer when you write notes for an email.

Example of a Formal Email

Write a formal request to modify a building site.

WRITER'S PLAN	
TO	• the mayor (the person most likely to be able to help with the problem)
SUBJECT LINE	• Reopen Caliban Road Paths
TOPIC SENTENCE WITH SUPPORTING IDEAS	• explain the situation: the site is currently used as a path • use statistics: 642 trips (514 pedestrians; 128 cyclists) • mention consequences of closing the path: an additional 11 minutes per pedestrian trip
CONCLUDING SENTENCE	• emphasize the mayor's concern and role in the issue • make a specific request
CLOSING/SIGNATURE	• Yours sincerely + name + title
ATTACHMENT	• copy of the survey

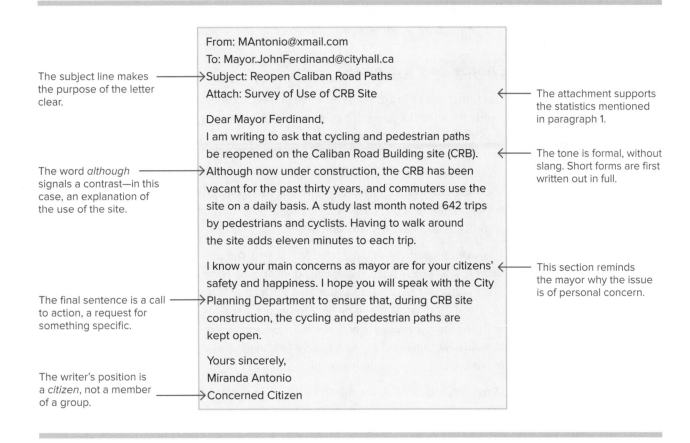

The subject line makes the purpose of the letter clear.

The word *although* signals a contrast—in this case, an explanation of the use of the site.

The final sentence is a call to action, a request for something specific.

The writer's position is a *citizen*, not a member of a group.

From: MAntonio@xmail.com
To: Mayor.JohnFerdinand@cityhall.ca
Subject: Reopen Caliban Road Paths
Attach: Survey of Use of CRB Site

Dear Mayor Ferdinand,
I am writing to ask that cycling and pedestrian paths be reopened on the Caliban Road Building site (CRB). Although now under construction, the CRB has been vacant for the past thirty years, and commuters use the site on a daily basis. A study last month noted 642 trips by pedestrians and cyclists. Having to walk around the site adds eleven minutes to each trip.

I know your main concerns as mayor are for your citizens' safety and happiness. I hope you will speak with the City Planning Department to ensure that, during CRB site construction, the cycling and pedestrian paths are kept open.

Yours sincerely,
Miranda Antonio
Concerned Citizen

The attachment supports the statistics mentioned in paragraph 1.

The tone is formal, without slang. Short forms are first written out in full.

This section reminds the mayor why the issue is of personal concern.

MODEL 6 How to Write a Summary

A summary gathers the key points of a longer article, book, or lecture. Summaries are used in paragraphs or essays or for study. Attribute the source material with the names of the authors, the date, and publication details. This helps you find the source material later and reference it in an essay or presentation.

Instructions

• Skim the source text to get a general understanding. Then read in detail, asking yourself *who*, *what*, *when*, *where*, *why*, and *how* questions. Highlight key points.

• Write a topic sentence that explains what the summary is about. Include the author's or authors' name(s) as well as the title and the source of the text.

• For each paragraph, write one or two sentences that summarize the main idea. Filter the information by asking yourself what is worth knowing. Ignore unimportant details.

• Write notes in your own words. However, don't add personal opinions; keep your summary factual.

• Review your summary to ensure you have unity and coherence.

• Use a mind map as a graphic organizer when you write notes for a summary paragraph.

Example of a Summary

Summarize the article titled "Utopias and Dystopias."

Utopias and Dystopias

The terms *utopia* and *dystopia* describe fantasy societies. Utopia comes from the Greek words for *no* and *place* and has primarily referred to a paradise. On the other hand, dystopia comes from the Greek words for *bad* and *place* and is a society that has broken down. The words can be defined as the best or the worst of what the world may become. For instance, in a utopian society, everyone is civilized, likely to be happy, and meaningfully employed in important roles, and enjoys full liberty. In a dystopian society, rights are diminished and people lead unhappy lives, are exploited in the workplace, and have few freedoms.

The word *utopia* was initially used in 1516 as the title of a novel by writer Thomas More (1478–1535), but it is a much older concept. For example, the Greek philosopher Plato (428–348 BCE) wrote about an advanced and perfect civilization on the island of Atlantis, indicating that it finally disappeared, sinking into the ocean. Subsequently, both the story of Atlantis and More's *Utopia* inspired Francis Bacon's (1561–1626) *New Atlantis*, published in 1627. Finally, Jonathan Swift's (1667–1745) *Gulliver's Travels*, published in 1726, featured a utopian society of highly refined talking horses.

More recently, in the twentieth century, popular novels and movies have been predominantly interested in dystopias—future societies where everything has gone wrong. These seem to fall into three categories. The most recent category concerns an unpredictable robot or artificial intelligence in armed conflict with people. The second category features a small group that starts off with an ideal society, but the civil structure breaks down and they begin to behave like primitive savages. The third dystopian category is where the leaders—or the bulk of society—have created arbitrary rules that only benefit themselves.

Why do dystopian novels and movies like the twenty-first century's *The Hunger Games* have such an impact for the current generation? One answer is found not just in the fiction, but also in ourselves. Writers and other artists have the habit of superimposing popular fears onto our entertainment. Now that we are a society that relies on computers, we may be secretly afraid of what would happen if they either failed or rebelled.

We are familiar with the principles of natural selection among plants and animals, and fear a paradigm shift enabling robots to become our masters. Similarly, we are amazed at the power of nuclear fusion even though we do not understand the mechanics of it, but contemplate the negative outcome of nuclear weapons being controlled by a crazed physicist—or a machine—and the unliveable world that might result.

But a crucial difference between being overwhelmed by exposure to bad news in the media—as opposed to being temporarily frightened by a novel or scary movie—is that fiction usually offers a solution. For example, dystopian novels often include the potential for a dynamic individual rising to defeat the evil forces in a dystopian society, making use of the thematic device of a single small person overcoming overwhelming odds. In contrast to the problems of real life, this structure gives us comfort: even if bad things are inevitable, there will always be someone brave enough and smart enough to rescue us.

Despite advances in technology, we may never create a true utopia, but, as a result of searching for it, we at least explore what is important, ensuring the chance to improve our daily lives.

(575 words)

Beatty, K. (2019). Utopias and dystopias. In K. Beatty, *LEAP 2 Reading and Writing* (pp. 204–05). Montreal: Pearson.

WRITER'S PLAN	
TOPIC SENTENCE	• the author's or authors' name(s) and the date • the main point: defining utopias and dystopias
SUPPORTING POINTS	• historical writing about utopias • modern views of dystopias • three types of dystopias
CONCLUSION	• understanding utopias and dystopias can help us defend society against dystopian trends and encourage trends that will lead toward utopias • actually achieving a utopia may be impossible
REFERENCE	• include the reference in APA format

The title makes it clear that this is a summary. →

The mention of the author and date is important to properly attribute the information.

Specific examples are cut: "several writers" include More, Plato, Bacon, and Swift.

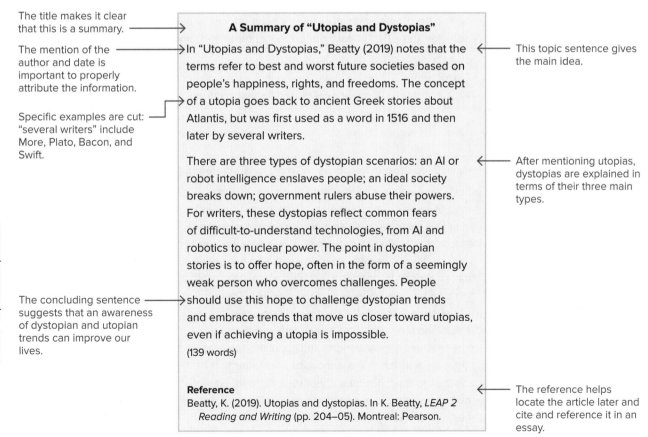

A Summary of "Utopias and Dystopias"

In "Utopias and Dystopias," Beatty (2019) notes that the terms refer to best and worst future societies based on people's happiness, rights, and freedoms. The concept of a utopia goes back to ancient Greek stories about Atlantis, but was first used as a word in 1516 and then later by several writers.

There are three types of dystopian scenarios: an AI or robot intelligence enslaves people; an ideal society breaks down; government rulers abuse their powers. For writers, these dystopias reflect common fears of difficult-to-understand technologies, from AI and robotics to nuclear power. The point in dystopian stories is to offer hope, often in the form of a seemingly weak person who overcomes challenges. People should use this hope to challenge dystopian trends and embrace trends that move us closer toward utopias, even if achieving a utopia is impossible.

(139 words)

Reference
Beatty, K. (2019). Utopias and dystopias. In K. Beatty, *LEAP 2 Reading and Writing* (pp. 204–05). Montreal: Pearson.

This topic sentence gives the main idea.

After mentioning utopias, dystopias are explained in terms of their three main types.

The concluding sentence suggests that an awareness of dystopian and utopian trends can improve our lives.

The reference helps locate the article later and cite and reference it in an essay.

How to Write a Process Paragraph

A process paragraph explains how something is done or how something happens—for example, how to find a bus station or how buses make commuting more efficient.

Instructions

- Review the question to understand what process—or part of a process—is being asked about.
- Choose a topic that you understand well and include it in your title.
- Consider your audience. Decide how much background information you will need to give.
- Write a topic sentence to explain what will be covered and why.
- Explain technical terms at the beginning of the paragraph or as part of the step where they appear.
- Write the steps in the correct order. Use transition words to signal the order of steps—for example, *first, begin by, before, next, then, as soon as, finally,* and *last.*
- Use a flow chart as a graphic organizer when you write notes for a process paragraph.

Example of a Process Paragraph

How do cities grow in response to transportation needs?

WRITER'S PLAN	
TOPIC SENTENCE	• write generally about how cities form
SUPPORTING SENTENCES	• outline the process with an example of one city on the banks of a river • note how the arrival of each group creates new needs and develops the city
CONCLUDING SENTENCE	Note: Process paragraphs don't need a concluding sentence, but you can add a benefit or extra point. • explain that, even if the original reason for the city disappears, the city continues to grow

"How" signals a process. ———→ **How Cities Grow in Response to Transportation Needs** ←——— The title is adapted from the question.

The topic sentence makes a statement with examples. ——→ Cities form at breaks in transportation, such as at the edge of a desert, lake, mountain range, ocean, or river. Imagine a group of travellers who once stopped at the edge of a river. First, to get across, they created business ←——— The second sentence sets up a general example that develops throughout the paragraph. for a small ferry operator. Next, as people on both sides of the river needed the ferry, shipping companies, hotels, and banks appeared. In turn, as the number of people

The term *permanent homes* is defined by its opposite, *shacks and tents.* ——→ who ran businesses grew, permanent homes replaced shacks and tents, attracting carpenters, plumbers, and other builders. Finally, the growing population wanted better services for health, education, and entertainment and built schools, hospitals, theatres, and parks. Cities

The concluding sentence offers an observation. ——→ grow in response to transportation needs, but even when the original reason for a city disappears—such as a bridge replacing a ferry—most cities continue to grow.

How to Write a Persuasive Essay

An essay is organized in three sections: an introduction, body paragraphs, and a conclusion. There are usually three or more body paragraphs. A persuasive essay aims to convince readers of an idea—or set of ideas—and possibly to take action.

Instructions

- Choose a topic and a point of view on that topic; this usually involves being for or against something.
- The introduction states the topic of the essay and the writer's point of view. Introduce ideas in a way that attracts the reader's interest. Write a thesis statement, a sentence that summarizes your point of view in the essay and includes three or more points.
- Use the body paragraphs to explain each point. Each paragraph begins with a topic sentence, related to one of the points in the thesis statement. Offer evidence in the form of examples and explanations.
- Avoid contractions; keep your essays formal by using the full forms of abbreviated terms followed by the initial letters in parentheses.
- Add a conclusion that summarizes the points and restates the thesis statement in a new way. Some essays include a suggestion for something to happen, such as the reader to take an action.
- Use a mind map or another type of chart such as a graphic organizer to plan your persuasive essay.

Example of a Persuasive Essay

Personal cars should be banned from city centres.

WRITER'S PLAN	
CHOOSE A TITLE	• choose a title about banning cars in city centres that will attract the reader's attention
THESIS STATEMENT	• explain that personal cars in city centres cause many problems • three points: personal cars waste space; people with cars make poor housing choices; increased congestion means worse emergency services
SUPPORTING PARAGRAPH	• city centres need a lot of space to accommodate cars, including roads, parking, and gas stations
SUPPORTING PARAGRAPH	• people without cars choose to live close to their work and the services they need
SUPPORTING PARAGRAPH	• reducing congestion can allow faster access for emergency services such as police, fire, and ambulances
CONCLUSION	• city centres don't need cars and should find ways to discourage them

City Centres Are for Walking

The title gives a point of view.

The first sentence sparks interest among readers.

Imagine a city centre without personal cars. It is easy to do if you visit older European cities where calm and delightful narrow winding streets are reserved for pedestrians and cyclists. Personal cars are a relatively recent innovation in the history of cities, and while taxis and delivery vehicles will remain necessary, personal cars must be eliminated. In city centres, personal cars cause many problems including wasted space, poor housing choices, and problems for emergency services.

The thesis statement focuses on three points, each of which is developed in its own paragraph.

The second paragraph develops the first point of the thesis statement.

As city centres become denser with ever-higher office and apartment blocks, there is a need for a large amount of space to accommodate cars. Taylor (2018) points to the example of Los Angeles, "which has more than 1000 hectares of surface car parking" (para. 2). In the surrounding county of Los Angeles, 14 percent of the land is set aside for parking. Although underground parking can absorb a small portion of a building's needs, wide roads, curb-side parking, parking lots, and gas stations all mean that there is a squeeze on space that would otherwise be available for more pleasant urban activity spaces and parks.

The paragraph supports the ideas with a reference and examples.

The last sentence suggests an alternative use of space.

The third paragraph develops the thesis statement's second point.

Of course, many people who live in city centres decide to live without cars. Why not? They are already close to their work and the services they need from groceries to entertainment to schools for their children. But busy city centre streets are often seen as unsafe. Keesmaat (2018) notes that, over a two-year period, ninety-three Toronto pedestrians and cyclists were killed as the result of being struck by cars. Such statistics make young families consider leaving city centres for life in the suburbs. With these escaping families go any hopes for building neighbourhoods of mixed demographics.

The paragraph builds an argument by focusing on a particular group of city centre dwellers: young families.

The last sentence shows the consequence of unsafe city centres.

The fourth paragraph develops the second point of the thesis statement.

One of the greatest annoyances of personal cars in city centres is the relentless traffic jams. For example, Tanner (2018) notes, "Of those who participated in regional trip-diary surveys, 89 percent said high traffic volumes made them feel frustrated and 61 percent said congestion cost them money in transportation and lost wages or productivity every week" (para. 6). She goes on to explain that the idea of introducing tolls to reduce traffic tends to be politically unpopular. But reducing congestion by eliminating most personal cars would allow for faster access for police, fire, and ambulance services. It would make for safer city centres and also encourage the growth of more efficient mass transit systems.

Include opinions if they are supported by facts.

Citing research on the topic adds weight to the argument.

The last sentence shows a benefit of fewer personal cars.

The conclusion briefly restates the thesis and offers solutions.

Personal cars in city centres will continue to be a problem unless local governments find a mix of incentives and disincentives that make people relinquish them. Incentives might include free public transportation for those without cars, and disincentives might include raising parking fees and taxes on car purchases. The next time you're in a city centre in your own car or someone else's, consider whether it would make more sense to get out and walk.

The last sentence is a call to action; it's often a good idea to ask the reader to think or do something.

Including properly formatted references supports the persuasive essay's arguments.

References

Keesmaat, J. (2018, June 14). We designed Canada's cities for cars, not people – and the people are dying. *The Guardian*. Retrieved from https://www.theguardian.com/commentisfree/2018/jun/14/canada-toronto-cycling-pedestrian-deaths-cars

Tanner, A. (2018, June 1). Study suggesting road tolls to reduce Vancouver traffic congestion appears headed to the dustbin. *The Globe and Mail*. Retrieved from https://www.theglobeandmail.com/canada/british-columbia/article-study-suggesting-road-tolls-to-reduce-vancouver-traffic-congestion/

Taylor, E. (2018, January 28). The elephant in the planning scheme: how cities still work around the dominance of parking space. *The Conversation*. Retrieved from http://theconversation.com/the-elephant-in-the-planning-scheme-how-cities-still-work-around-the-dominance-of-parking-space-87098

PHOTO CREDITS

ALAMY

p. 102 top: © Doug Blane/City of Milton Keynes.

GETTY IMAGES

pp. viii, 28–29, 51: © gremlin; pp. viii, 76–77, 97: © BROOK PIFER; pp. viii, 98–99, 121: © RyanJLane; pp. iv (left), ix, 122 (left), 123, 145: © James Brey.

RAWPIXEL IMAGES

pp. viii, 52–53, 75: © rawpixel.

SHUTTERSTOCK

pp. viii, 2–3, 27: © waewkid; p. 4 (left): © Oleksiy Mark; p. 5: © Gorb Andrii; p. 22: © KeyStock; p. 24: © joshya; p. 31: © Ivano de Santis; p. 33: © Jacob Lund; p. 36: © vhpicstock; p. 43: © g-stockstudio; p. 53: © tele52; p. 55: © j.chizhe; pp. iv, 56 top: © majson; pp. iv, 56 (middle): © yomogi1; p. 58: © BlurryMe; p. 59: © Ursula Ferrara; p. 66: © pedalist; p. 68: © Africa Studio; pp. iv, 79: © Dean Drobot; p. 81: © Gergely Zsolnai; p. 82: © IR Stone; p. 87: © Olga Danylenko; p. 88: © Eugenio Marongiu; p. 89: © alphaspirit; p. 91: © gualtiero boffi; p. 94: © pryzmat; p. 99: © Keith Bell; p. 101: © GaudiLab; p. 102 bottom: © TunedIn by Westend61; p. 104: © Yakov Oskanov; p. 105: © BWlad74l; pp. iv, 106: © Supavadee butradee; p. 108: © ALPA PROD; p. 109: © franz12; p. 110: © Everett Historical; p. 112: © Everett Historical; p. 115: © Sergey Nivens; p. 117: © ESB Professional; p. 118 (left): © Blulz60; p. 118 (middle left): © higyou; p. 118 (middle right): © Lightspring; p. 118 (right): © james Steidl; p. 125: © Rattana.R; p. 126: © Syda Productions; p. 128: © Zapp2Photo; p. 129: © Scharfsinn; p. 132 top: © Montri Nipitvittaya; p. 132 bottom: © Supamotion; p. 134: © Gorodenkoff; p. 135: © Romaset; p. 136: © Aila Images; p. 138: © Franck Boston; p. 142: © Syda Productions; p. 143: © kaczor58; pp. v, 146–47, 169 bottom: © Lia Koltyrina; p. 148 (3): © John T Takai; p. 148 (4): © Neyro; p. 155: © Solis Images; p. 156: © Lightspring; p. 158: © Oleg Golovnev; p. 159: © Monkey Business Images; p. 160: © sakkarin sapu; p. 163: © Pressmaster; p. 165: © sirtravelalot; p. 173: © Mohamed Hakem; p. 174: © lexaarts; p. 176: © FeelGoodLuck; p. 177: © metamorworks; p. 178: © metamorworks; p. 181: © one photo; p. 183: © Tero Vesalainen; p. 184: © Photographee.eu; pp. v top, 188 top: © THPStock; pp. v bottom, 188 bottom: © MihaiDancaescu; p. 190: © Mangostar; p. 191: © Goldution; pp. v top, 194 top: © arek_malang.

THINKSTOCK

p. 4 (middle left): © marcoscisetti; p. 4 (middle right): © Mega_Pixel; p. 4 (right): © Ridofranz; p. 7: © IPGGutenbergUKLtd; p. 9: © Monkey Business Images; p. 13: © Robert Churchill; p. 14: © martinbalo; p. 15: © shironosov; p. 18: © IPGGutenbergUKLtd; p. 20: © Jacob Wackerhausen; p. 26: © simonkr; p. 30: © Monkey Business Images; p. 34: © Vladislav Ociacia; p. 38: © julos; p. 39: © zhu difeng; p. 40: © Balefire9; p. 46: © muratsenel; p. 48: © Mike_Kiev; p. 49: © Jacob Wackerhausen; p. 50: © JinHui1988; p. 63: © 36clicks; p. 64: © capdesign; p. 65: © in8finity; p. 67: © Ingram Publishing; p. 70: © VeselovaElena; p. 71: © poco_bw; p. 72: © Denis Raev; p. 73: © Alexander Raths; p. 75: © Goran Bogicevic; p. 85: © Highwaystarz-Photography; p. 86: © Chepko Danil; p. 93: © mtr; p. 96: © Monkey Business Images; p. 120: © puchan; p. 121: © LuminaStock; p. 130: © Dragana Jokmanovic; p. 144 top: © ildogesto; p. 144 bottom: © 4774344sean; p. 148 (1): © DivVector; p. 148 (2): © totallyPic.com; p. 149 (1): © kotoffei; p. 149 (2): © Azaze11o; p. 151: © gpointstudio; p. 152 top: © Goodshoot; p. 152 bottom: © vectorarts; p. 153: © SZE FEI WONG; p. 169 top: © simonkr.

UNSPLASH

pp. v bottom, ix, 170–71, 194 bottom: © Jerry Kiesewetter.

TEXT CREDITS

CHAPTER 1

pp. 8–10: "Looking for Money" by N. M. Scarborough. (2014). From *Essentials of entrepreneurship and small business management* (7th ed., pp. 474–476). Reprinted and Electronically reproduced by permission of Pearson Education, Inc., New York, NY. pp. 14–16: "Youth Entrepreneurs" by A. Hasham. (2012, March 2). *Toronto Star.* © Toronto Star Newspapers Limited. All rights reserved. Used by permission and protected by the Copyright Laws of the United States. The printing, copying, redistribution, or retransmission of this Content without express written permission is prohibited.

CHAPTER 2

p. 32: "Apple iPhone sales correlates with people who died by falling down the stairs" by T. Vigen. (2018) *Spurious Correlations.* http://tylervigen.com/spurious-correlations. pp. 34–45: "Will Robots Bring about the End of Work" by T. Walsh. (2017, October 1). *The Guardian.* pp. 40–41: "Half of all Jobs Today Will Disappear by 2030" by E. Sherman. (2013, September 25). From "Half of all jobs today will disappear by 2030 and other scary predictions." *AOL Jobs.* © Eric Sherman.

CHAPTER 3

pp. 58–60: "This Is How Important Sleep Is for Your Mental Health" by D. Smith & L. Lyall. (2018, May 17). *World Economic Forum.* pp. 63–65: "Body Energy: Spending It and Storing It" by J. B. Reece, et al. *Campbell biology* (Canadian Edition, pp. 103, 564–565). Toronto, ON: Pearson. Reprinted with permission by Pearson Canada Inc.

CHAPTER 4

pp. 81–82: "Eleven Ways to Walk Away Stress" by W. W. Bumgardner. (2018, June 17). *Verywellfit.* Verywellfit.com. pp. 87–88: "Taking Care of Stress" by Canadian Mental Health Association. (2014). From Benefits of good mental health. Canadian Mental Health Association—Calgary.

CHAPTER 5

pp. 110–11: "The Quirky Secrets of the World's Greatest Innovators" by J. Surowiecki. (2018, April 9). *strategy+business, 91.* Adapted and reprinted with permission from "The Quirky Secrets of the World's Greatest Innovators." © 2018 PwC. All rights reserved. PwC refers to the PwC network and/or one or more of its member firms, each of which is a separate legal entity. Please see www.pwc.com/structure for further details. No reproduction is permitted in whole or in part without written permission of PwC. "strategy+business" is a trademark of PwC. pp. 116–18: "Anyone Can Be an Innovator" by University of California – San Diego. (2018, April 19). From Anyone can be an innovator, research finds: Students given incentives to innovate are just as skilled as the self-motivated. *ScienceDaily.* University of California School of Global Policy.

CHAPTER 6

pp. 127–29: "Guide to Augmented Reality" by Onvert. (2014). Harmony/Onvert. pp. 134–35: "How Can Augmented Reality Be Used for Social Good?" by B. Matthews. (2018). *Montfort.*

CHAPTER 7

p. 147: "Territory size is proportional to the population" by Worldmapper. (2018). From "Tertiary Education." *World Mapper.* Worldmapper.org. pp. 152–54: "To Adapt MOOCs, or Not? That Is No Longer the Question" by S. M. North, R. Richardson, & M. M. North. (2014). *Universal Journal of Educational Research, 2*(1), 69–72. Horizon Research Publishing Co., Ltd. pp. 158–60: "The SOLE of a Student" by S. Mitra. (2013, February 28). From The Sole of a student: TED winner Sugata Mitra's blog. *NDTV.*

CHAPTER 8

pp. 177–79: "How Are Today's Biggest Tech Trends Affecting Our Human Rights?" by R. Hickin. (2017, December 11). *World Economic Forum.* pp. 183–85: "What Is Google's 'Right to Be Forgotten'?" by K. Afifi-Sabet. (2018, June 7). *ITPro.* IT Pro/Dennis Publishing Limited 2018.

NOTES

NOTES

NOTES

NOTES

NOTES